E. M Church

Chapters in an adventurous life Sir Richard Church in Italy and Greece

With a Portrait

E. M Church

Chapters in an adventurous life Sir Richard Church in Italy and Greece
With a Portrait

ISBN/EAN: 9783337002589

Printed in Europe, USA, Canada, Australia, Japan

Cover: Foto ©ninafisch / pixelio.de

More available books at **www.hansebooks.com**

Chapters in an Adventurous Life

SIR RICHARD CHURCH

IN

ITALY AND GREECE

BY

E. M. CHURCH

WITH A PORTRAIT

WILLIAM BLACKWOOD AND SONS
EDINBURGH AND LONDON
MDCCCXCV

NOTE.

THE Editor begs to acknowledge his obligations for the kind permission to reprint those chapters in this volume which originally appeared in 'Blackwood's Magazine' and 'The Monthly Packet.'

CONTENTS.

CHAPTER I.

EARLY SERVICES.

Escape from Quakerdom—Egypt—Malta—First expedition to Calabria—Commandant of Capri—Attacked by the French—A daring feat—The Ionian Islands . . 1

CHAPTER II.

THE NEAPOLITAN SECRET SOCIETIES.

Visit to Vienna—Count Nugent—At the Congress of Vienna—The Buonaparte tablet—The Carbonari and the Calderari—Commission as general to destroy the secret societies 21

CHAPTER III.

A BAND OF BRIGANDS.

Cerignola—News of the Vardarelli—Interview with the chief—A levee—Reviewing the brigands—Fate of the Vardarelli 30

CHAPTER IV.

THE DECISI.

The diploma and qualifications—Secret signs—Francesco Perrone—Murder of Dell' Aglio—Accidental capture of Perrone 56

CHAPTER V.

THE VENGEANCE OF THE SOCIETIES.

Punishing a malcontent—The widow's vow—Biding her time—Arrival of General Church—Justice at last . 74

CHAPTER VI.

CIRO ANNICHIARICO, FOUNDER OF THE DECISI.

Ciro's history—His "justification"—Trying General Ottavio's horses—A sudden disappearance—An unexpected reappearance 88

CHAPTER VII.

THE MASSACRE OF MARTANO.

The old feudal castle—Surprised by Ciro—Slaughter of the inmates—Murder of the princess—The one survivor . 99

CHAPTER VIII.

THE ADVENTURES OF CIRO.

His activity—General Church's plans—Banquet at Lecce—A brigand wedding—Arrival of the troops—Ciro in straits—Escape in disguise—The General at San Marzano—Capture of Ciro 108

CHAPTER IX.

CAPTURE AND EXECUTION OF CIRO.

His defence in Scaserba—A parley—Surrender—March to Francavilla—Trial and execution—Rejoicings of the people 135

CHAPTER X.

THE CHIEFS OF THE DECISI.

General Church's militia—Talk with Colonel Schmerber—Martina—A warning—Lecce—An envoy from Ciro—Arrest of the Council of the Decisi—Their execution—Scene with Don Felice 143

CHAPTER XI.

CIRO AND THE VARDARELLI.

Castel del Monte—*Rencontre* with Vardarelli—Sending out a spy—Meeting between Ciro and Don Gaetano—The spy's narrative 177

CHAPTER XII.

A DEADLY FEUD.

Nardelli and De Bernardis—The fate of Don Blasi—De Bernardis's bargain with Ciro—Murder of Nardelli—De Bernardis's concealment—Betrayed by his greed—Capture—A devout brigand 194

CHAPTER XIII.

A DAY AMONG THE *MASSERIE.*

The masked ball—The Masseria dell' Duca—A novel battering-ram—Sullen peasants—Boehmer's discovery—The Piè di Monti—A brief repose—De Feo's disguise—News of the brigands 222

CHAPTER XIV.

THE MAN OF THE SEVENTEEN MURDERS.

General Church's progresses—Notice by Sir John Rennie—A night in a *masseria*—Capture of Occhio Lupo—Execution of the last captain of the Decisi 251

CHAPTER XV.

THE PACIFICATION OF APULIA.

Government ingratitude—Don Luigi Gentili—A complaint to the king—The General's firmness—General Church and the tailor 268

CHAPTER XVI.

REVOLUTION IN SICILY.

General Church appointed to command of troops in Sicily—Outbreak in Palermo—Open rebellion of military—Imminent danger of the General—His imprisonment—Petitions for his liberation 287

CHAPTER XVII.

Some notes and personal reminiscences by his nephew, Canon C. M. Church, give the sequel of the life of General Church in Greece from 1827 to 1873 . . 305

CHAPTER XVIII.

LAST DAYS.

Sir Edmund Lyons—Letters from Lord Palmerston and Mr Gladstone—The succession to the Greek throne—Cession of the Ionian Islands—Destruction of the Senate—Finlay's 'History'—The end 343

GENERAL SIR RICHARD CHURCH.

CHAPTER I.

EARLY SERVICES.

ESCAPE FROM QUAKERDOM—EGYPT—MALTA—FIRST EXPEDITION TO CALABRIA—COMMANDANT OF CAPRI—ATTACKED BY THE FRENCH—A DARING FEAT—THE IONIAN ISLANDS.

MATTHEW CHURCH, a merchant of the city of Cork, and member of the Society of Friends, sent his second son, Richard, to school. But school and Quakerdom were not to the lad's taste, and before he was sixteen he ran away, and took the king's shilling. It must have been a blow to his parents, but they seem to have made the best of it, for his father purchased for him a commission in the 13th (Somersetshire) Light Infantry, and his home letters show that there was never any breach between him and his family. But though his relations forgave him, the "Connection" did not, for we find that he was "disowned" by them in 1800, in which year he was gazetted Ensign.

His first service was in Egypt, and in February 1801 he writes to his mother :—

We are about two or three days from Alexandria, where the French have their chief army, and where we expect the greatest resistance. . . . We have here *Le Tigre* and Sir Sidney Smith; he is to command a battalion of marines and seamen and act on shore: with him there must be success. . . .

He goes on :—

Shocking idea!. Five paras, a coin of this country worth only a halfpenny, is the inducement held out to these wretches, the Turks, for the head of a Frenchman, —and wonderfully well it succeeds; but it matters not whether French or English, so they have an opportunity of murdering him—his head goes to the Grand Vizier, and the assassin receives his paras. The Greeks, who are slaves to the Turks, and are Christians, are as opposite a people as possible—a brave, honest, open, generous people, continually making us presents of fruit. If they make any money by trade, when it pleases the Turk he takes it from him, and if he murmurs, death is his redresser. Oh, how I hate the Turks!

This expression of feeling in the boy of sixteen is curious, when we remember how he fought for the freedom of Greece years after, and spent all he had in the service of his adopted country. That he never repented the sacrifice, is shown in a letter written to his sister-in-law more than forty years later, in which he says :—

A man who, like myself, has sacrificed everything for a cause, and thereby totally ruined himself, must be excused if he falls off from communication with even his nearest relatives. Yet I must say, that except as it relates to you and my nephews, I do not regret having sacrificed everything in the world to the cause which I embraced, and to whose triumph I hope I contributed.

And he adds :—

Were it to be done again, I should again embark in the same difficulties and dangers.

But to return. In the letter to his mother already quoted he adds :—

We, the army, certainly go through more than any people in fatigue, hardship, dreadful living, and storms; living on salt pork towed three days astern of the ship, and still so full of salt you cut it with the greatest difficulty; foul water, maggoty biscuits: such living is common to us, and happened no less than four times riding at anchor, twice before enemy's towns—Vigo and Cadiz—and twice in Tetuan Bay. I felt that I never knew the real sweets of home; and how many dangers, hardships, and fatigues would I now go through, and smile at, for the happiness of a return home to my dear parents, sisters, and brothers!

The boy's longing for home was not to be gratified yet. He took part in the battle of

Aboukir Bay in 1801 (where he used to say that a big, good-natured sergeant encouraged his slight, boyish officer with, "Don't be afraid, sir, you'll soon get used to it!" as Richard showed a tendency to duck his head as the balls whistled by); and he was at the capture of Rosetta and the siege of Alexandria, which fell in August of that same year. But the time did come, and doubtless the truant was welcomed with pride and delight, even by the grave Friends who had shaken their heads at his very un-Quaker-like and reprehensible beginning.

In April 1805 our young hero, who had exchanged into the 39th Regiment, sailed with an expedition of 7000 men under command of Sir James Gibson-Craig to Malta. They were to keep the Court of Naples out of the arms of the French, and, in company with a large force of Russians, to protect Naples itself from invasion. The Bourbon King and Queen of Naples do not seem to have been in the least anxious for an English alliance, and under such circumstances the plan was sure to fail. An account of the Court intrigues and military operations is to be found in Sir Henry Bunbury's Recollections.[1] We will only go into so much of

---

[1] Sir H. Bunbury's Passages on the Great War.

the matter as concerns Richard Church. He was all his life a reader, and his voluminous note-books show that he thought as well as read. As the expedition was delayed at Gibraltar on its way to Malta, he made the most of his time, "in reading the few books I have, amusing myself with fortification as usual, occasionally taking a row about the fleet, bathing. Ossian, Ariosto, and Plutarch's Lives are my chief authors, and one constantly relieves the other."

In July they reached Malta. In September he was made adjutant of the Light battalion, then being formed under Colonel Kempt. He writes home :—

We consist of 890 select men from all the British regiments on the island, and placed under the command of Colonel Kempt, a very excellent officer, who was military secretary to Sir R. Abercromby in Egypt, and in all his campaigns elsewhere. I am placed on the staff as adjutant to the Light Infantry battalion. Believe me, that I am sensible that there are many officers whose abilities make them more fit for the situation. There were no less than fifteen applications made by different officers, and all strongly recommended by their commanding officers, and I am really astonished that I succeeded in obtaining what I so little deserved or expected. It is of all others the most advantageous situation an officer of my rank could obtain.

He adds :—

We sail to-day [November 8], supposed for Naples;

and it is believed we shall proceed 200 or 300 miles in
Italy without having any affair with the French. A
great many regiments who served in Egypt are with
us, and if we meet 'the invincible army of Italy,' I
hope Grenadiers and Light Infantry of the British will
be able to give a good account of them. The last
cannon from the fleet has fired.

They embarked at Castellamare, November
20, and then took place a grand review before
the King of Naples, and volleys were fired in
honour of the battle of Trafalgar. But in
December of that year Austerlitz had been
fought, the Bourbons had fled to Sicily, and
Joseph Buonaparte was set on the throne of
Naples. The English fleet sailed to Messina,
and the young adjutant had plenty to do, his
knowledge of Italian making him especially
serviceable in intercourse with the people.

He was at the battle of Maida, and Sir
Charles Stuart writes of him to the Horse
Guards:—

His zeal and attachment to the duties of his profession were conspicuous in a series of services that
occurred within my own observation. I hardly know
a more promising young man, or professionally a more
deserving one. I gave him to Kempt as brigade-major,
and he always fully appreciated him.

At this time Calabria was infested by banditti, and the weak Sicilian Government tried

to play them off against the French—a scheme in which Sir Sidney Smith took part.

There were many secret societies in the kingdom of the Two Sicilies, and as one of their rules was to protect their members, all who were "in distress, and every one that was in debt, and every one that was discontented," not to mention every one who was fleeing from justice, joined some such society. Ferdinand, then, thought he was doing a very politic thing in encouraging them, promising amnesty for the past, and redress of grievances, as soon as ever he should return to his kingdom in Naples, without making much inquiry as to what the real state of affairs was, and on which side the grievance lay. Calabria was certainly in a miserable state; the inhabitants fled to the mountains to escape the French barbarities, and found the brigands their best protectors. Some one was wanted to see what was going on, and to find out what really was the state of the French armies in Calabria. It was just the post which suited Richard Church's dash and daring, and he volunteered to go. His colonel, the Hon. Lowry Cole, hesitated at first, but then consented, though he declared he had no peace of mind till the young man was safe back again. Accompanied by only twelve Neapolitan cavalry, Richard Church rode to Nicastro. He says:—

I found Nicastro in a most dreadful state of confusion and dismay, from a threatened massacre and pillage by the *masse* [bands of brigands]. Half an hour previous to my arrival two of the inhabitants had been murdered in the streets; and the syndic, governor, and many others had been repeatedly fired at. . . . During the day parties continued to arrive, until they amounted to about 1500. . . . Towards evening they attacked the house of Don Giuseppe Nicotera, with the avowed intention of massacring the whole family and pillaging the house. I am happy to state, before they had found any of the family or carried away anything of consequence I arrived at the house, and from the steady conduct of the detachment of cavalry, and by making use of threats and persuasions, I succeeded in forcing them out of the house, and immediately ordered their chiefs out of the town to take post towards Scigliane, with which order the greater part complied: a number still remained, and I thought it necessary to patrol the whole of the night.

Sir Henry Bunbury says of these *masse:*—

They are ready enough to rob and ravage and murder; they will massacre the stragglers, or even cut off small outposts of the enemy. Sometimes they will defend themselves pretty obstinately in a strong mountain village, but they never have shown courage when attacked by regular troops, nor perseverance in keeping together and sustaining a warfare in their mountains. . . .

And again:—

The captains of the *masse* seized the moment of confusion to set off in all directions to plunder the towns and villages, confident in their numbers and in the arms lavished on them by the British admiral. . . . These were the people whom Queen Caroline cherished as the props of her crown, and whom Sir Sidney Smith was proud to reckon under his command.

Richard Church returned in safety, and was thanked for his service and his report by Generals Stuart and Fox. He says in a home letter :—

I feel more real pleasure at having been the instrument in the salvation of these hundreds [of women and children] than in having assisted in the destruction of the thousands of our enemies at Maida.

Soon after this he was promoted to the rank of Captain in the Corsican Rangers, and for two years—from October 1806 to September 1808—was in command of Ana Capri, the upper town which looks down over Lower Capri : the island had been taken by Sir Sidney Smith, and was held by the English against the French. Richard writes to his sister soon after his arrival :—

How fast the scene changes! A twelvemonth has not yet passed, and I have written you from Malta, from various parts of Italy, from Sicily, from Calabria, from Sicily again, from Capri. . . . I have served an unsuccessful campaign allied with the Russians against the French in Italy, and been on a most glorious expedition against the same enemy in Calabria. I have been under arms three times to be reviewed by two crowned heads—twice for the King of Naples, and once for the King of Sardinia. I have witnessed an earthquake; scarcely been, even for a week, out of sight of Mount Etna, Vesuvius, or Stromboli. I formed a party with the army selected to besiege Scylla, and was at the taking of it; and had the good fortune to be actually shipwrecked at Charybdis! . . . I have been mixed up alternately with Russian and Neapolitan troops, Calabrese, Sicilian, and French. . . . I have served in the various capacities of lieutenant, adjutant, brigade-major, and captain, and have had no less than four different commanding officers in that space of time. To conclude this history, I am now, through the great favour of my present commanding officer, Colonel Lowe, duly installed captain-commandant of Ana Capri.

He thus describes the island and the outlook :—

From Capri you have the most beautiful view imaginable of Naples and Vesuvius, as well as of Baiæ, Pozzuoli, the Elysian Fields, Portici, the Palace of La Favorita, and all the towns in the Bay of Naples towards Castellamare. . . . You have a fine view of the Apennines and the highlands in the Neapolitan territory for many miles. From the back of the island you command a prospect of the Gulf of Salerno and the various towns on its shores. So much for the views; now for the island itself. It is about three and a half miles in length, and perhaps its greatest breadth is not above two. It is divided in two parts, Capri and Ana Capri, and has three towns, or rather villages, several convents and a bishop, and several remarkable ruins of palaces, &c., built by Tiberius when that wretch made it his residence. The whole island is a perfect garden, is covered with vines, figs, &c. Capri is the chief town and port, and has a castle; it is the seat of Government and the headquarters of the regiment, and has about 3000 inhabitants. The roads are hilly, narrow, and for the most part in steps. Ana Capri is about two-thirds of the island, and once up, a level terrace abounding in fruit, wine, and oil: it has no place of anchorage for shipping, but several creeks and small bays where an enemy may attempt a landing. The only road from Capri here is up a rock, cut into 600 perpendicular steps. . . . Fancy me leading a high-spirited Arabian horse up these steps! which I have done, and he is the only horse in the island. . . .

I am sole governor here, civil and military. My military force consists of two companies, besides an officer's detachment of forty men, making my regular troops about 200, and two four-pounders. Besides these I have about sixty militia, and some few of the King of Naples' gamekeepers. I am at the advanced post, the first to be attacked when King Giuseppe [Buonaparte] shall be that way inclined. I am totally independent of the commanding officer, except what relates to the regiment, and communicate with him by telegraph and night signals. The population consists of about 900 people, not one of whom can go down to Capri without my passport. There is here a convent of nuns, and a college for ecclesiastical education. I am on great terms with the *abbadessa*, a most respectable old lady, who was obliged to fly from Naples by the French, and is much attached to the English. We correspond almost daily, and as often as possible I make her a present of fish, fresh butter, hams, and anything else I can pick up!

In April 17, 1807, his letter to his brother shows that the life is becoming monotonous:—

I have now been nearly seven months commandant

[he says], I am nearly tired of it. . . . On March 1 a division of 2000 or 3000 French under General Merlin embarked from Baiæ, and were half-way across, when a tempest arose which obliged them to put back. . . . We have worked night and day to increase our strength. . . . I have plenty to do, as Colonel Lowe has made me chief engineer and inspector of the coast, and I have the whole of the fortifications of Ana Capri to design and complete with my own resources, according to my own ideas. . . . By offering rewards for the balls fired by the British ships into the island when the place was taken, and which were to be found in vineyards, I have recruited as far as 500 extra rounds; . . . since then we have received from Messina a large supply of ammunition and provisions.

"Capri is much changed for the worse since the days of Augustus and Tiberius," he writes to his sister in the following year. "It is *not* a delightful residence." And in another letter :—

This is a rascally island. I have arrested some priests detected in correspondence with the French. This is a nuisance, for we are now obliged to fortify against the inhabitants on shore as well as the enemy at sea.

Now came the time when "the quiet and unpopular Joseph Buonaparte" gave place in the kingdom of Naples to "the fiery and impetuous Joachim Murat," who on the 6th September 1808 made his entry into Naples, and his first idea was to make himself master of Capri. No wonder, when one remembers that he could see it, with the British flag flying, any day from his palace windows! So he quietly armed his vessels, while he sent an Engineer officer in a fishing-boat to hang about Capri, and see what would be the easiest place for landing.

Unfortunately, by way of strengthening the garrison of Capri, a Maltese regiment was sent there, under command of Major Hammill; "swelling its number," says Sir H. Bunbury, "but by no means improving its quality. The Corsicans . . . were, on the whole, a brave and well-instructed body of men, led by intelligent officers. But the Maltese were of inferior caste: a few of their officers, indeed, were British, and their commander, Major Hammill, was a gallant soldier. . . . But, in truth, Capri was fancied to be so strong . . . that it mattered little what description of soldiers were to make a show along the cliffs, or fire from behind rocks upon the landing-place." Richard Church was therefore relieved by Major Hammill, and with his Corsicans joined Colonel Lowe at Capri.

On the night of 3d October the French expedition sailed, and in the morning Colonel Lowe found his island menaced by the enemy on every side. "And where," asks Sir H. Bunbury, "was his Britannic Majesty's frigate the Ambuscade? Instead of dashing on the enemy or hanging on their skirts, . . . Captain D'Urban sailed away for Ponza, to apprise the Neapolitan squadron on that station, and any English ships he might meet, of the attack upon Capri, and call them to the rescue." The enemy cannonaded the landing-place at Capri, while a company of *voltigeurs*, unobserved by the Maltese, crept up quietly among the rocks, and had taken possession of Ana Capri before the dismayed Maltese knew what they were about. Major Hammill was killed, and his men fled with all speed. Three companies of the Corsican Rangers under Captain Church had been sent to help the Maltese, but when the French scaled the cliffs these companies were watching the paths below. Two of them effected their retreat, unperceived by the enemy. Captain Church, with the third, found that his company was cut off from the others and his retreat intercepted. What was to be done?

He, with his little force, remained quiet till eight o'clock in the evening, hoping that the enemy would re-embark, and leave them free to descend the rocky stairs and rejoin their friends at Capri below. But just then the moon rose, and under her calm clear light the enemy were to be seen forming into columns, and advancing across the plain, with beat of drum and fire of musketry. "Finding all hopes of defending the post I occupied entirely dissipated," he says in his report, "I threw the gun I had with me into the sea, and commenced my retreat by the left, marching through the vineyards and narrow roads leading from Dama Conta to the Capo di Monte, the only retreat I had left, all others being occupied by the enemy." But, to his amazement, they had not gone a quarter of a mile when they were met by a challenge. They had marched straight upon a large body of French troops! Richard Church's ready wits did not desert him: reflecting that the dark uniforms of his Corsicans would be a protection, he answered readily in French that they were French troops pushing on to rejoin their comrades below; and as Murat had a regiment of Corsican sharpshooters, they were allowed to pass without difficulty. But the red uniforms of some Maltese who were following them discovered the trick, and brought down a volley upon the adventurous captain and his men, doing no harm, however, for the Corsicans knew the country, and speedily dispersed among the sheltering rocks.

But to descend the rocky stairs to Capri was

manifestly impossible, and yet to Capri they were bound to go. There was nothing for it but to climb down the face of the rock which divides Ana Capri from Capri; and this they did, scrambling along a goat-track through the darkness, clinging to bush here, to crag there: not daring to speak even in whispers; feeling sometimes that all was up with them if a pebble, dislodged from its place, bounded echoing down the cliff; and at last finding themselves safely at the bottom, with the loss of only one poor fellow whose foot slipped, and who was killed by falling from the rocks into the valley below.

This daring feat received its due meed of praise from the colonel and commandant, Hudson Lowe. "Captain Church's exertions," he reports, "were peculiarly conspicuous. The orderly retreat of this detachment, through parties of the enemy and down precipices heretofore deemed impracticable, forms the highest eulogium on the officer who guided it. They had been twenty hours under arms and in constant movement."

The garrison of Lower Capri held out against the French for a fortnight, but then was obliged to capitulate and withdraw to Sicily. Richard Church was wounded in the head by the last shot fired by the enemy, but was soon well enough to ride across the island to Messina, where he became assistant-quartermaster-general under Colonel Bunbury.

We will now pass over a year, and come to Richard Church's life in the Ionian Isles, a time which he always looked back upon with keen pleasure. English troops, among whom were the Corsican Rangers, sailed in September 1808 from Sicily under sealed orders, and attacked Zante, then occupied by the French, who, being taken by surprise, capitulated: Cefalonia, Ithaca, and Cerigo followed. Richard Church led the landing at Zante, and drew up the terms of surrender. He also commanded at Ithaca, and "made the French commander surrender unconditionally." Sir H. Bunbury says: "Besides the advantage of ports and supplies for the English squadron in those seas, we found warm friends in the islanders, a people hating the French, and earnestly desirous to assist us in driving them out." For five years Richard Church's life was spent in active service in those beautiful islands. "It was work that was in every way suited to his special capacity; it tended more than any other experience to confirm the high opinion which he had, from the very first contact, formed of the Greeks, and which moulded the whole course of his later life.

B

His genius lay in the command and discipline of native regiments; he seemed to possess a potent charm which gave him ascendancy over rough and untutored ragamuffins, whom none but he could convert into something like orderly troops. Hardly had he arrived on the shores of Greece than he began to prepare for the levy of native regiments." He began "a series of inquiries into the condition and resources of the Ionian Islands and the adjacent mainland, and to report the results, illustrated by plans and maps of Corfu, Zante, Santa Maura, &c., to General Coffin at Messina. . . . In 1810-11, he was hard at work raising a force of 900 men," called the Duke of York's Greek Light Infantry, and under his command they assaulted and took the fortress of Santa Maura; "but in the moment of victory Church's sabre was smashed by grape, and his left arm at the same instant shattered by a bullet. For two months he was seriously ill; . . . but in the summer of 1811 was allowed to go on leave, . . . and with two companions he rode through Northern Greece, Thessaly, and Macedonia, visiting Delphi, Chæroneia, Thermopylæ, Pharsalia, Philippi, and other homes of classical associations; at Constantinople he found a hospitable welcome at the Embassy, and began a lifelong friendship with Stratford Canning, the twenty-four-year-old minister at the Porte [Church himself was about twenty-six], while a row up the Bosphorus to the murmuring rocks of Jason, and an excursion to Smyrna and Magnesia, completed a tour replete with intense interest to Church's romantic imagination." [1]

He returned to the Ionian Islands, and is able to write in November 1811 :—

> I am now full and approved major in his Majesty's service, and commanding a regiment originally raised, organised, and disciplined by myself.

He adds :—

> To you, mother, I do not boast; but I have now, thank God, . . . converted these men from the most lawless of mankind, not only into good soldiers, but also into praiseworthy members of civilised society. These men, who once knew no law but the sword, are now the admiration of the inhabitants for their correct, quiet, and obedient conduct. . . . Should Government wish for men, I will answer from my character alone in this country to raise 6000 or 8000 men in as many months.

General Oswald encouraged him to form a second regiment, to be placed under his orders as lieut.-colonel, and he eagerly set about it. In June 1813 a despatch from Lord Palmerston gave him the necessary permission, and there was no difficulty in finding volunteers to fill

[1] Sir Richard Church. By Stanley Lane-Poole.

the ranks. It is striking to find the names of many of the leaders in the Greek War of Independence among the recruits of Zante. But in 1814, peace came and put an end to military operations. The Greek regiments were disbanded, the men went home, the young colonel's occupation was at an end, and a good deal of money spent in recruiting was lost. However, he was thanked and praised and congratulated by the commander-in-chief and others in authority.

CHAPTER II.

THE NEAPOLITAN SECRET SOCIETIES.

VISIT TO VIENNA—COUNT NUGENT—AT THE CONGRESS OF VIENNA—THE BUONAPARTE TABLET—THE CARBONARI AND THE CALDERARI—COMMISSION AS GENERAL TO DESTROY THE SECRET SOCIETIES.

THE Peninsular War was over; but the monotonous course of ordinary military service was by no means to Richard Church's mind. And, as it happened, a more adventurous course opened before him, under his friend and fellow-countryman, Count Nugent. During his leave of absence in 1813, he writes from Vienna to Colonel Bunbury:—

Lord Castlereagh . . . has given me a commission equally flattering as agreeable. He has directed me to proceed to join General Nugent, with whom I am at present here. We leave to-day for Agram, and the corps under his command is destined to open the communication with the Adriatic, &c.

His brother, John Dearman Church, in a

letter in 1813 to the lady who became his wife, playfully defending his country, says :—

John Bull without Paddy would do badly. It is the sons of Paddy that have driven Buonaparte to the Pyrenees! You find those clever fellows in all parts of the world: another Paddy is driving the French from the south of Italy, General Nugent, with whom is *another Paddy*, my brother Dick. By last accounts he was at Fiume, acting with the Austrian army under General Nugent against Beauharnais.

Richard Church felt a warm and enthusiastic friendship for his brilliant, dashing countryman, which was kept up through life; but his remarks on the Austrian army are the reverse of complimentary. "My proceedings will depend on having a command that is *not* subject to any Austrian general, General Nugent excepted," he says. However, the Austrians under Nugent did brilliantly, drove the enemy from before Carlstadt, occupied Fiume, and opened communications with the British fleet in the Adriatic.

After the disbanding of his Greek regiment, Richard was summoned to the Congress at Vienna, November 1814, to make his report on the Ionian Islands. Next came the news of Buonaparte's escape from Elba in the following spring, and at Nugent's special request Richard Church went with him as British Military

Resident with the division of the Austrian army which was to act against Murat.

His reports from headquarters to Lord Stewart at Vienna have been preserved, and form a connected narrative of a short, little-known campaign, in which Murat's army was driven from Mantua to Naples. . . . Step by step the Austrians and Tuscans, in a series of small engagements, pressed "King Joachim" southward, while Nugent and Church, marching with their customary rapidity 100 miles in three days, occupied Rome and prepared for the advance upon Naples. The usurper's army was gradually melting away; 400,000 had dwindled to 10,000, and when Nugent with but a tenth of their number forced battle on the Neapolitans at Miguano near San Germano, hardly 700 escaped to announce the destruction of "the Army of the Interior." The remnant capitulated at Capua; Murat took to flight, and the imperial army escorted Prince Leopold of Sicily into Naples. . . . Church's conduct received the unqualified approbation of the general commanding the forces in Sicily, and the thanks of the king; he was decorated with the Order of the Fleur-de-Lys, and created major-general by his restored Neapolitan majesty, Ferdinand IV.[1]

Next we hear of Richard in Provence, still with Nugent, helping to put down Buonaparte's adherents; and here happened an incident which is perhaps worth relating. There is a square copper tablet, preserved in the family, which he always prized, and which lies

---

[1] Sir Richard Church. By Stanley Lane-Poole.

before me now. Upon it is engraved these words :—

> "NAPOLÉON TRAHI S'ÉLOIGNA DU TRÔNE ET SE RETIRA À L'ÎLE D'ELBE. RAPPELÉ PAR LES VŒUX DE LA NATION, C'EST ICI QU'IL DÉBARQUA LE 1ER MARS 1815. LE 87EME REGIMENT LUI ÉRIGEA CE MONUMENT."

Richard Church tells its history in despatches to Lord Burghersh from Nice, July 1815. "I have the honour to inform your lordship that I arrived at this place in the Undaunted, frigate, Captain Smith, on the night of the 19th inst., having come on before General Nugent and the convoy with troops on board from Naples and Genoa, in order to make some necessary dispositions in the place." He tells how, pending Count Nugent's arrival, he requisitioned 1200 men from the governor, and how, on the Count's arrival, he, with Captain Smith, sailed to Antibes, and demanded permission of the governor there to land and occupy the town. But when "Captain Smith and myself went on shore, we were received with every mark of hostility, and it was evident that the white flag which floated on the walls was but a shield under which the garrison hoped to shelter themselves from an attack by the Allies, it having been hoisted but one day previous to our arrival."

The troops were landed, without resistance, on the shore close by the monument erected to commemorate Napoleon's landing at Elba, and took possession of the town and the heights round it, and there waited till Count Nugent and the rest of the troops arrived, when they sat down to besiege the garrison in the fort, which before long submitted. But here is the story of the copper tablet, in a despatch dated before that submission :—

Although perhaps it may not be a subject of importance sufficient to insert in an official report [modestly says the young officer], I have much pleasure in informing your lordship that the monument erected by the garrison of Antibes at St Juan, where Buonaparte landed on his return from Elba, . . . has been destroyed by my orders by the loyal inhabitants of the place. Underneath it we found a box containing a *procès verbal* of the commemoration of the event, signed by all the officers of the 87th and 106th, devoting themselves to Napoleon's cause. . . . In the same box were various gold coins, stars, and crosses, and Eagles of the Legion of Honour, and a brass plate [copper] bearing the inscription, a copy of which I enclose. The same regiment forms at present the garrison of Antibes. . . . Two of the field officers are now at their headquarters, protesting their having been always faithful to the king, not knowing that the *procès verbal* . . . is now in our hands.

After Murat's flight and execution the Bourbons returned to the throne of Naples, "having learnt nothing and forgotten nothing." Colletta says, "The old kings had governed by prestige, the new by force. Prestige had vanished. . . . The people were not sorry for Murat's fall, but were suspicious of his successor." Perhaps Ferdinand meant what he said, when he so readily promised amnesty for all past offences, reform of taxes, &c.; but he had to feed and pay the Austrian troops who had set him on his throne again; he had heaps of private debts always accumulating in that corrupt and luxurious Court. He was the laziest, most self-indulgent of men, always shutting his eyes to difficulties and shirking disagreeables. Therefore he took up first one party, then another, and broke faith with any one if it suited him at the moment. When he was in exile he encouraged the secret societies, as we have seen, hoping to use them as a tool against the French. So they were exultant at his return to the throne, but soon found that they were thrown over.

Of these secret societies the first and oldest was the Carbonari or charcoal-burners, to which the others seem to have been at times affiliated. The Filadelfi, Patrioti Europei, and some other societies, aimed at nothing less than a universal republic; but the Carbonari professed constitutional principles. Some of them were excellent and honest men, only anxious for such reform as might be for the welfare of their country, and by no means glad that their ranks should become a refuge for the criminal and discontented. In 1813 their number had increased beyond all bounds, and the leaders determined to reform the society. The members who remained kept the name of Carbonari; those who were expelled took that of Calderari. There was great hatred between the two bodies, and the disorders in the kingdom were worse than ever.

Then Prince Canosa, Minister of Police, thought to mend matters by helping on the division in their ranks; so he put himself at the head of a reformed secret society, also called Calderari. General Church says:—

Canosa thought to make a counterpoise against the Carbonari. By his principles man was reduced to abject slavery and ignorance; he was obliged by his oath to be faithful, passive, and subservient, whether for right or wrong—the people were made for the king, and the king by divine right could and ought to do whatever he pleased with the people. Prerogative was everything, and by virtue of this same divine right all men were considered as blades of grass, bound to kiss the earth and never again to rise—if it pleased the king to put his foot upon their necks! [cries the sturdy soldier who loved all his life to fight for the oppressed people]. But [he adds] the good sense of the country revolted against the absurd doctrine of Canosa and his Calderari, and the king himself, with great good sense, set his face against this society and prohibited it.

And well it was he did so, for instead of the other secret societies being in any way checked by this new method, there simply grew up a crop of spies and informers, and the magistrates found that they had one more mysterious foe to fight against, and gave up in despair all attempts to keep order and punish offences—for any such attempt brought upon them threatening letters. As has been said, every malefactor belonged to some secret society, and every society was bound to protect its members against every other authority and under all circumstances. This was doubtless the case more or less in all parts of the country, but more especially in the provinces of Apulia, which so swarmed with brigands that travellers dared not thread the passes, trade was at an end, and the fields lay uncultivated.

Count Nugent was at Naples, in command of the Austrian troops, and his influence must have decided Richard Church to take service there too; for Lord Exmouth writes advising him to stick to Naples, "under Nugent's wing," and his old colonel, Hudson Lowe, writes mentioning the consent of the Horse Guards to Church's Neapolitan appointment. We find him, then, accepting a commission as general from King Ferdinand to put down and destroy the secret societies with which the province of Apulia was infested. He was invested with the *alter ego*, which gave him full power to try, condemn, and execute all such offenders, without any form of trial.

Not that General Church (as he was now called) ever used this power to its fullest extent: he mentions again and again that he never put to death even the worst of brigands without a fair trial. He has left behind him several MS. books relating to this period of his life, written in an old-fashioned slanting hand, and containing a curious mingling of his own adventures, with descriptions of scenery, dissertations on the history of the province in ancient and modern times, accounts of heroes of various nations and periods, especially his favourite Manfred, explanations of military law, and descriptions of the different men with whom he came in contact. Out of this mass we shall gather enough to show what manner of man this was, and what was the material he had to work upon.

CHAPTER III.

A BAND OF BRIGANDS.

CERIGNOLA—NEWS OF THE VARDARELLI—INTERVIEW WITH THE CHIEF—A LEVEE—REVIEWING THE BRIGANDS—FATE OF THE VARDARELLI.

WELL, then, let us picture our General on his way from Otranto to Naples, travelling with post-horses, but in his own carriage, accompanied only by his servant Raphael and his aide-de-camp, Captain Quandel—a young Swiss in the service of the King of Naples, a brave, cheery, ready-witted fellow. It was ten o'clock at night when they alighted at an old palace on the skirts of the town of Cerignola and were hospitably received by the *padrone*, an old Don Girolamo, who ushered them across a large courtyard, shut in by huge rusty gates, to his house. The General tells us that from the front door a flight of broad stone steps led to the first-floor landing, from which opened a suite of immense rooms, adorned with old armour and family portraits, and lighted by several high, narrow, iron-barred windows. They were evidently expected, for a fire blazed in the huge grate, and several wax tapers shed their cheerful radiance on the dark old walls—a pleasant sight to travellers on a chilly stormy night!—while the old *padrone*, excusing himself for the non-appearance of supper, left them, promising to hasten preparations and return immediately.

"How is your appetite, Quandel?" asked the General, as he warmed his hands at the cheerful blaze. "Supper will be ready soon, I trust——but what's the matter?" for the young aide-de-camp, who had been seeing to the unpacking of the carriage, wore a perplexed and troubled aspect, as, shutting the door carefully behind him, he approached his chief.

"*Mon Général*," said the young man, "it's all very fine to talk about supper. I doubt if we shall have much time for supper! We are likely to get visitors whom we don't want. In fact, the Vardarelli are in the neighbourhood."

"The rascals!" exclaimed the General. "My good fellow, where did you pick up that piece of information?"

Thereupon Quandel told how, when he paid the postilions—giving them, as was the General's fashion, a liberal *buona mano*—he had overheard one mutter to the other something about the Vardarelli, and the pity it would be if so free-handed a gentleman should fall into their hands; whereupon the quick-witted young officer called the men back, and said: "Look here, my friends, I've made a mistake in the dark, I find; I gave you only 10 carlini, and the General bade me give you 20. Here, take them, and drink his Excellency's health. You may be sure he will give you a good character, and when we come back safe, you may look for just such another *buona mano*."

The postilions looked at each other, hesitated, peered round in the darkness to be sure there were no listeners, then, as they took the money and thanked the gentleman, one of them whispered: "I heard at the last station that Don Gaetano Vardarelli and his band were hereabouts. It would be a pity the General should come across them—he is truly a *galant' uomo*, and we should be sorry if he fell into their clutches. Take the warning, signore, and good night. The saints protect you;" and they mounted and rode away.

Here was a pleasant predicament for the travellers! It is true that they were armed, but their force consisted only of their two selves and one servant, and they were in a lonely, defenceless house, and could expect no assistance from the poor old proprietor. The

General twisted his moustache and said, "What are we to do?"

The aide-de-camp shrugged his shoulders, but had no suggestion to offer. "We are but three, General," said he, rather ruefully, "and we have but three pair of pistols. All the doors of this confounded old house are rotten; and as to the staircase, why, it's as wide as the staircase at the king's palace—no hope of defending that!"

Just then the door was pushed open, and old Don Girolamo entered, cheerful and garrulous, ushering in, with many complimentary phrases, the *sindaco*, or chief magistrate, of the neighbouring town of Cerignola. There followed the usual exchange of amenities and introductions, after which the *sindaco* requested to have a few words in private with his Excellency, and the other two gentlemen withdrew. As soon as they had left the room, the poor magistrate threw up his hands with a gesture of despair, and gasped out, "*Eccellenza*, we are lost, we are lost! we are all dead men! The Vardarelli are in the town—over a hundred of them, in Cerignola! And there are no troops; all the troops are hunting for the brigands somewhere else. O *Signore Generale*, what are we to do?"

It was lucky for our General that he had had

some slight warning of this unpleasant state of affairs. It enabled him to suppress all signs of dismay or surprise, and to answer cheerfully, "How kind of you to come and tell me this, *signore sindaco!* I am so anxious to see these Vardarelli, and I did not feel absolutely sure where they were to be found. Gaetano and his band are not such bad fellows after all, and by no means unpopular in this neighbourhood, eh, *signore sindaco?*" and he looked the magistrate in the face with a meaning air.

The fact was, that though General Church was quite unacquainted with his visitor, he knew full well that as the brigands were supreme throughout the country, people were forced to make a league with them, and to pay them tribute to ensure their own safety; and he felt not the slightest doubt that the worthy *sindaco* had taken care, for his own sake, to be on the best of terms with the powerful chief of the Vardarelli. It was an ugly business, and he must get out of it as he best could; so, taking a sudden determination to try what audacity would do, our General calmly desired the astonished *sindaco* to go straight back to Cerignola and desire the brigand chief to present himself and his band to the English General, who greatly desired the honour of their acquaintance.

The poor magistrate remonstrated piteously, declaring that he was lost, that he was a dead man, that he should infallibly be murdered by those rascals. In vain: he was met by a short, stern, "Do what I command you, *signore sindaco*, and do it without delay. This will not be your first interview with Don Gaetano Vardarelli, I'll be bound!"

"It is true, your Excellency," answered the poor man, "that I have spoken to him—only for a moment!—only just——"

"That will do," was the curt reply.

"Here, Quandel!" and in five minutes' time an order was written by the aide-de-camp, and signed by the General, desiring Don Gaetano Vardarelli to come immediately, and present himself and his whole troop to General Church. The order was handed to the *sindaco* with the remark, "As you have paid one visit to these gentlemen on your own account, you can have no objection to paying them another on mine. You can tell the chief that I have come here with the friendliest feelings towards him—in fact, my coming here at all proves it. Don't delay a moment in delivering this order and message."

The *sindaco* made his bow, and a very low bow it was, and departed.

"Now, Quandel," said General Church, when

he and his aide-de-camp were left alone, "we have no time to lose. We have to see if this tragedy can be turned into a comedy! I will tell you exactly what to do; and if we are lucky in our first deal, we may win the game. Tell Raphael to stand at the head of the stairs, and do you take your stand in the ante-room, next the supper-room." (The supper-room was the centre room of a suite of three, of which the one where they were conversing was the third, and the ante-room the first.) "Tell Raphael to treat those rascals civilly, but to keep them on the landing while he summons you. Then you must keep them in the ante-room while you announce their coming to me. Be good-humoured, but don't allow any familiarity. Let the chief understand that we feel the most perfect confidence in him, and are quite delighted to see him. When you come to me tap gently, and don't be in a hurry to tap again if I should not answer you immediately. Of all things don't seem hurried or flustered—that would ruin us—and bring the chief only to me. Let the others wait outside. Don't ask any one to sit down, or sit down yourself; don't let anything on the supper-table be touched—a glass of wine might lead to quarrelling, and a dispute would be fatal to us. Keep up an air of official dignity, and if you find the scoundrels more than you can manage, retreat in good order upon me, and leave me to manage matters. We have our swords and pistols, and if the worst comes to the worst, we will sell our lives dearly. After all, these fellows are in straits I fancy, and they may not be sorry to come to terms."

Having finished his harangue, the General looked at the aide-de-camp, and the aide-de-camp looked at the General, and then—the comicality of the whole situation, the foolishness of having thus put their heads into a trap, was really too much for them! They burst out laughing, a regular fit of laughter, much to the delight of Don Girolamo, who at that moment opened wide the door, cheerily announcing, "It is late, your Excellency, and the macaroni and fried fish are ready; and capers—we are famous for capers here; and mushrooms—your Excellency knows we are famous for mushrooms. *A tavola, a tavola!*" and he seized the General by the hand to lead him into the next room, where the supper-table was laid with many kinds of fish, fruit, and poultry, besides macaroni and the famous mushrooms and capers.

But alas for the hungry travellers! Just when the old *padrone* had warned them that his wine was a *little* strong and fiery—just when he had tucked his white napkin under his chin, and was brandishing a huge silver spoon wherewith to help the macaroni—the tramp of horses was heard in the courtyard below. Don Girolamo turned pale and dropped the spoon. "We are lost!" he gasped. "I am a dead man! Excuse me, General. God preserve your Excellency! I must conceal myself;" and in the twinkling of an eye he had disappeared into some secure lurking-place.

In another moment the *sindaco* entered to announce that he had done the General's bidding; but the worthy man could not be persuaded to do more than just enter the room, announce the fact, wish his Excellency "*felice notte*," and so depart, glad, doubtless, to be well out of the scrape.

It was now drawing towards midnight, and a horrible night it was, with thunder and lightning and torrents of rain. The old *padrone* and his servant were nowhere to be seen, so General Church, Captain Quandel, and Raphael took up their appointed positions, and waited the coming of their visitors. Soon they appeared, some remaining outside on horseback to guard the gates, while the others, fifty or sixty in number, headed by their chief, entered the great door, and, firelock in hand, ascended the wide staircase. On the landing they were met by

Raphael, who succeeded in keeping a brave front to the foe, though, poor fellow, he was secretly in the greatest trepidation.

General Church observes that talking was much more in Raphael's line than fighting, but that he had absolute faith in his master's good luck, and on this occasion he seems to have taken his courage by both hands, and played his part of the comedy extremely well.

With the utmost politeness he barred Don Gaetano's way as he was ascending to the landing, and requested the *signore capitano* to remain there one moment while his arrival was announced to his Excellency the General. Don Gaetano, with equal politeness, assented, only saying, "You will understand, Signore Cameriere, that, with all possible respect for his Excellency, prudence requires us to keep our eyes open;" and he sent some of his men up-stairs to reconnoitre the upper storey, while others took up their station on the landing. A wild-looking, picturesque set of fellows they were, dressed in velveteen jerkins much adorned with braid and buttons, with steeple-crowned hats, and belts stuck full of pistols and daggers; also, every one had a sabre at his side, and carried in his hand firelock or carbine or rifle.

General Church heard afterwards that the brigands were thoroughly puzzled and astonished by his bold move, that they were somewhat inclined to try and come to terms with the Government, and that after holding a council of war, they determined to accept his invitation, but to come armed and in full force, in case of treachery. But to go on with our story.

Captain Quandel, at Raphael's summons, came forth to receive the brigand chief, saying, "Enter, Don Gaetano, but be good enough to remain here, in the ante-room, while I inform his Excellency of your arrival."

"And my officers, signore?"

"With pleasure, Don Gaetano." So four tall fellows accompanied their chief, and remained with him in the ante-room, while Quandel crossed the supper-room and knocked gently at the General's door.

Receiving no reply, after a pause he knocked again.

"Who is there?"

"*C'est moi, Excellence.*"

"Who is it?"—repeated impatiently.

"*C'est moi, Excellence*—Quandel."

"Oh, Quandel!—come in," and he went in, closing the door behind him.

A few rapid sentences sufficed to tell that the brigands were there, that they had taken possession of the whole house, that they were armed to the teeth, but that their behaviour was good-humoured and respectful; and having received directions from General Church, Quandel returned and proposed to introduce Don Gaetano, who at first demurred to going alone, but finally said, "Let us go, *signore capitano*. The General is a *galant' uomo*. I trust in his honour;" and they went in together.

It must have been a curious scene! The huge lofty chamber, with its wax candles flashing back dim reflections from the old armour hanging on the walls, or half-lighting up some portrait of grim warrior or stately dame dead long ago; the great open fireplace, where burning logs blazed and spluttered; and the two figures who surveyed one another curiously: the Englishman, slight, spare, erect, with sharp features, and keen dark-blue eyes shaded by thick black brows; he was dressed in uniform, his sword by his side, and a pair of good English pistols loaded, within reach of his hand, as he stood by the tall mantel-shelf: and the brigand chief, a splendid figure, in his picturesque costume and handsome arms, holding in one hand his high plumed hat, in the other his loaded carbine.

He stepped briskly forward with a little flourish. "Here I am, your Excellency. I am Don Gaetano, the famous chief of the Vardarelli, at your Excellency's orders."

The General returned the salutation with equal courtesy. "I am delighted to make your acquaintance, Don Gaetano. I have heard of you as a brave and humane man, and I wish much to do you a good turn, if you will only alter your way of fighting. What shall I say about you to the King?"

The brigand drew up his tall figure with a haughty air. "Your Excellency is really too good. I have nothing to ask for. I don't know whom your Excellency calls the king. Am not I King of Apulia? Have not I beaten three royal generals? The flocks of Apulia are mine, the people own my sway, I can help myself to the travellers' purses if I choose, all the nobles and gentry of the province hold me in awe. Your Excellency must know that Ferdinand can do nothing against me;" and he brought the butt-end of his carbine down on the floor with a force that threatened damage to the old planks.

But he had to do with a man who was not to be daunted by bluster, and the General, after surveying his formidable guest, quietly replied, "Signore Capitano dei Vardarelli, I don't care a fig what you are or what you are not. I know this, that you were soundly thrashed by Estorio, and by Sannito, and by Corre too. Have you then forgotten Altamonte? Have you forgotten Minerrimo and Castel di Monte?"

"*Per Santo Diavolo!*" cried the chief, "your Excellency speaks truth. But it was a different thing with the *gendarmerie*, and—I may speak frankly, since your Excellency is an Englishman—we *were* forced to take to our heels on those occasions. For the accursed wine of the country is strong, very strong, and my fellows had taken too much of it, and our heads belonged rather to our heels than to our hearts! I would not say so much to any one but your Excellency," he added confidentially, "but if it were not for myself, my brothers, my nephew, and some fifteen more of my followers —well, all the rest of the band are good for nothing;" and he snapped his fingers in the air. "But," he added, "it is time to say *Addio;* it is late, and we have far to go."

General Church did not feel that he had made much way with his guest; besides, his curiosity was not yet satisfied, so he did not take the hint. "Come, Don Gaetano," he said, "tell me something of your own history and mode of living."

"It is a long story, *Signore Generale*," answered the brigand—"too long to be told fasting; besides, your Excellency's patience would be tired out. It is enough to say that I was once a soldier, and that injustice drove me to this life. After all, it is a fine life—to gallop over the plains, and breathe the fresh air of the mountains."

"Have you shed much blood, Don Gaetano?"

"By the Madonna! no, your Excellency. Little, very little."

"If so, why not make your peace with the Government?"

"Well, *Signore Generale*, there are difficulties—and this is a good trade, after all. One lives like a king, the great people fear us, the poor look up to us, the women adore us. We get plenty of money, and spend it freely. It's no bad thing to be accountable to nobody, and above all law!" cried Don Gaetano.

General Church's keen eyes rested with a certain pleasure on the dashing figure before him, but he answered with grave emphasis, "As you please, Don Gaetano. If you like your trade, stick to it. I am to understand, then, that you do *not* wish me to say anything for you at Naples?"

"Why, as to that——" the chief hesitated and looked askance—"I don't quite say that, your Excellency. I have spoken to you frankly, and I don't mind saying that you may tell

Ferdinand that I should not object to serve him —only I must keep the command over Apulia; and if I engage to serve him, I will live and die worthy of my name. But I could not come in for the sake of a pardon merely. Your Excellency knows that I have my enemies, and I must take care of myself. I must also always go armed because of the *vendetta.*"

"Take care, my friend," answered the General; "you will get yourself into a scrape one of these days."

"Bah!" was the answer. "I don't care a fig for all the king's generals put together."

"Ah, but, my friend," said the General, laughing, "*I* may have to hunt you down myself!"

"Rather any one else, General," with a frank smile, "for I have such a respect for your Excellency, I should be so truly sorry to fire upon you. But if such should be my fate, it would be a great honour for me, truly a great honour!"

"Come, Don Gaetano," said the General, who had really taken a liking for the bold brigand, "I advise you to submit. Are you an outlaw?"

"Holy Madonna, yes! I feel your Excellency's kindness, but it's of no use."

"Well, as you will. But I promise you one

thing—a fair trial; and when I catch you, you shall not be—hanged!"

"I understand your Excellency. I shall at least die a soldier's death. I am content."

"Keep out of my way, Don Gaetano, my friend, I beg, or else make your submission," cried the General; "for it would be a real grief to me to have to carry the law into force against you—and I couldn't help it, you know. I have no choice. So divert yourself in other parts of the kingdom, and don't meddle with my province, if you please! My soldiers are excellent horsemen and marksmen, as you know, and when once they put the left foot into the stirrup, there'll be no child's play! Now, will you be good enough to parade your squadron for my inspection?"

"How, your Excellency? At this time of night? In this tempest?"

"Why not?" was the tranquil reply. "They are all here, I believe, and I want to see what kind of fellows they are."

"But your Excellency will be wet to the skin!"

"We are neither made of salt nor of sugar, Don Gaetano, so what matters that?"

"At your commands then, General; but give me leave first to introduce my officers."

He put his fingers to his mouth and whistled,

upon which a tall brigand strode hastily into the room, followed closely by Captain Quandel, who was alarmed at the shrill whistle, and did not know that the brigand chief had a different call of this kind for each of his brothers.

"I perceive," drily remarked General Church to his aide-de-camp, "that this tall gentleman has not learnt that it is customary to wait to be announced."

He spoke in French, but Don Gaetano understood him, and was profuse in his apologies for this breach of etiquette before he presented "My brother, Don Girolamo;" and after his departure, "My brother, Don Geronimo;" and then came the favourite, "My *dear* brother, Don Giovanni."

Handsome fellows they were, and well equipped, especially the last, who received a few extra compliments from the General, in consideration of his being the chief's best beloved brother. Then a fourth whistle brought in the most perfect young dandy and coxcomb imaginable, wearing, in addition to the brigand's velveteen jerkin, a shirt-collar and frill, which had the quaintest effect. His left hand, too, was gloved, and his right sparkled with valuable rings. "This is my nephew," quoth Don Gaetano, with evident gratification and complacency, as the handsome lad made his bow.

"He calls himself twenty, but his mother cuts him short of that by a couple of years. What care I, when he is equally ready to lead the dance with a pretty girl, or exchange shots with Ferdinand's *gendarmerie?*"

"He looks truly a splendid young cavalier," said the General with a smile; and with a few kind phrases, and "*Grazie, molte grazie,*" from the youth, he too departed.

Now, our General's spirits rose higher than they had done at the beginning of this curious scene. Evidently things were going well, and he and his guest were on the most friendly terms. So far, so good. Still, the danger was not over: a trifle might raise the brigand's suspicions that they were being tricked; and that, he well knew, would mean death to him and Quandel. However, there was no choice but to play the game out, win or lose!

So he sent for torches, and, while Raphael was seeking for some, requested Don Gaetano to summon his men, and then came out on the landing, accompanied by one of the chief's brothers. Some fifteen stout fellows, two of them the trumpeters of the band, pulled off their high-crowned hats, and greeted him with shouts of "*Evviva! Evviva!*" crowding round him rather more closely than was pleasant, and evidently wishing to attract his notice. He gave them a few good-humoured words as they all descended the stair together and crossed the courtyard to the gates, outside of which the men were being mustered, and ranged in line on horseback, on the wide road, all facing the gateway. Don Gaetano stood beside the General and proudly surveyed his troop : the smoky red glare of the torches cast fitful gleams on the wild faces and arms and accoutrements; the lightning flashed, the thunder pealed, the rain fell in torrents. Behind stood Quandel, Raphael, and the trembling old major-domo, holding the torches and sheltering them from the storm as well as they could. A weird, strange, picturesque scene — more pleasant, one would think, in remembrance than in reality. We may be very sure that the General never forgot that midnight parade!

Now Don Gaetano's favourite mare was led up, a beautiful creature, black as jet, fleet as the wind, having carried her master safe from the pursuers many and many a time, and he patted her affectionately, and beamed with delight at the General's warmly expressed admiration; and when he said in French to Quandel, "What a beautiful mare, and worthy of so handsome a cavalier!" and Quandel answered, "Faith, General, it is a thousand pities he is not one of us!" the brigand chief evidently heard, for he smiled and bowed low as he sprang into the saddle, and gave the signal to his men. They passed before General Church slowly, in single file, the trumpeters leading, and as they passed, a single brigand left his place in the rank, dismounted, dropped on one knee, respectfully kissed the General's hand, and then, without a word, remounted, and fell into rank again; and soon after another repeated the same manœuvre. When all had passed—a hundred in all, including the officers—Don Gaetano rode up to General Church, alighted, took off his hat, and thus addressed him—

"*Eccellenza*, a little affair requires my presence at a distance, and I must now take my leave; but at any hour after daylight an escort shall be at your Excellency's orders on the road to Ordona, to conduct you safely within sight of the post-house, where you will probably find some of Ferdinand's soldiers. Also, I may assure your Excellency that you may pass through this valley in perfect safety for some days to come." He smiled, as one who knew that the safety of travellers through that valley depended upon the Vardarelli being engaged elsewhere.

"Thanks, Don Gaetano, a thousand thanks," was the reply; then in a lower tone, "Pity you should not alter your line of life; but I shall have a good word to say of you at Naples, depend upon that."

"Your Excellency speaks well—and who knows? Perhaps yes—perhaps no! If the conditions please me—but Ferdinand must remember that Apulia is mine!"

"One moment," said the General: "who were those two men who dismounted and saluted me?"

"Austrian deserters—Tyrolese by birth. Does your Excellency desire an escort?"

"No, no, Don Gaetano. There may be troops" (meaningly) "nearer than you think, and I should be sorry to get your fine fellows into a scrape."

"A thousand thanks for your Excellency's consideration. Now I have thirty miles to ride before daybreak, and I shall want all my force. Allow me again to recommend myself to your Excellency's consideration and to kiss your hand." He kissed the General's hand, his brothers and nephew followed his example, and then with "*Addio, addio, Eccellentissimo Signore Generale!* May your Excellency live in prosperity a thousand years! *Addio, addio!*" he mounted and disappeared at a rapid pace, followed by all his band.

There was a pause, while the General and

his aide-de-camp stood looking along the road which their strange visitors had taken. The last echoes of their horse-hoofs died away, the torches spluttered and burnt low, the storm continued as violent as ever, and the General turned to re-enter the house; and as he entered the door he turned to his young companion and said, "Let us thank God, Quandel, that the play is over and we are safe, and there's no further occasion to stand out in the rain! Let us go up-stairs and finish that macaroni."

The first thing was to unearth poor old Signore Girolamo, and that took some ten minutes of searching and shouting. At last, however, he crept out of a cellar, rushed into General Church's arms and embraced him, heaping blessings on the Madonna, who had preserved them all, and then they all joyfully proceeded to the supper-room. One would think the viands must have been perfectly cold by this time, but the hungry General does not mention this fact, and dwells on the excellence of the food, and the wine, and the old *padrone's* stories of old times — of the Saracens, and Manfred, and the cruel Charles, and the fate of the young Conradin. Then the old gentleman insisted on drinking to the memory of Gonzalo di Cordova, the great captain who defeated the French on the plain of Cerignola, not far from this very *palazzo*, and of various other worthies, winding up with a bumper to the health of the present king; after which, the good wine having done its work, he fell back in his arm-chair, and in two minutes was fast asleep.

"Now, my dear Quandel," said the General, "go to the post-house and get horses as quickly as possible."

"Now, General? to-night?" The young man looked decidedly rueful at the prospect of leaving these comfortable quarters.

"Yes, now, immediately. I don't distrust Gaetano himself, but as to those rascals of his, they are as likely as not to quarrel with him for letting us slip through their fingers, and insist on coming back to look us up. We should be fools to risk it. The coast is clear now, for they will feel sure of our being in bed till daybreak. Go, order the horses; tell Raphael not to light the carriage-lamps, and take care there is no cracking of postilions' whips or lighting of cigars."

So Quandel went, while the General helped to carry the *padrone* up to bed, slipped a gratuity into the old major-domo's hand, left messages of thanks and compliments to his sleeping host; and in a quarter of an hour the carriage was ready, and off the travellers started.

"Now, Quandel," said the General, when they were on their way, "we had better arrange that one of us should sleep while the other watches." But *one* was sound asleep already, and the General, after contemplating the young aide-de-camp's sleeping form with an indulgent smile, took the watching upon himself, and they rolled swiftly and silently along the road which led towards Naples.

Of these Vardarelli, General Church says: "They harassed the provinces, fought the troops, robbed right and left, but seldom if ever committed murder in cold blood." After a while they made up their minds to submit to the Government, and make terms of peace. An unpublished letter, dated March 18, 1818, says:—

A year and a half ago there was in this valley of Bovino a desperate chieftain, Gaetano Vardarelli. . . . He fought against the king with such success that the Government entered into a convention, agreeing to pay him a certain monthly sum, Vardarelli engaging on his part to protect the valley of Bovino. . . . Subsequently the Vardarelli refused to act according to the orders of the Government. General Church was sent for. . . . He said, "I give no opinion as to what *has* been done; but if Vardarelli does not keep to his convention, *make him!*" The fellow, when he found General Church was sent against him, thought proper to obey. . . .

Vardarelli's sister was one of his troop, and fought as a man, but was wounded in an affair with the king's troops. Not being able to carry her away, he killed her, to prevent her falling into the hands of the soldiers.

There is something about Gaetano Vardarelli which gives one an interest in him, and one cannot help feeling sorry when one hears the end of his history, which shall be given in General Church's own words :—

Don Gaetano, his brother, and most of his band, lost their lives in the village of Urruri, in the Abruzzi, where on a former occasion they had committed excesses which were not forgotten by the inhabitants. They had returned there with confidence, as they had been pardoned, and were now in the service of the Government. But the inhabitants, calling to mind their former bad conduct, laid an ambuscade for them, and one morning, as they mounted their horses and blew their trumpets, they were surprised by a discharge of musketry from all the windows by which they were surrounded, and Don Gaetano and most of his band thus lost their lives.

Truly, poor Don Gaetano had cause for his fears of the *vendetta* overtaking him, even if he held his pardon from the Government!

As to the rest of the band, they met with a more dreadful fate a few years later, being *smoked* to death in a cellar in which they had taken refuge, after a fight with some of the Government troops. But with this General Church had nothing to do.

CHAPTER IV.

THE DECISI.

THE DIPLOMA AND QUALIFICATIONS—SECRET SIGNS—FRANCESCO PERRONE—MURDER OF DELL' AGLIO—ACCIDENTAL CAPTURE OF PERRONE.

THE Vardarelli chieftain and his band may have carried with them a certain glamour of romance, which reminds one of Robin Hood and his merry men; though, as "a person who had suffered by their misdeeds justly observed, it was very easy to give 100 ducats to the poor, out of the thousands stolen from the rich!" But there were other bands which had not even this glamour about them, and who deserved nothing but to be hunted down like savage and treacherous beasts of prey.

There were many secret societies, as has been said before. Among them all there was none so dreadful as that of the Decisi, founded by Ciro Annichiarico.

There lies before me a sheet of paper, yellow

with age, inscribed with characters and flourishes somewhat faded, but clear and legible enough, which is the diploma or commission of a member of the secret society of the Decisi —" Decided ruffians " General Church translates their title.

The diploma bears in each of the upper corners a death's-head rudely drawn in pen and ink, and in each of the lower corners two marrow-bones crossed and tied together by ribbons of red, yellow, and light blue. It is bordered by lines of these same colours—red yellow, light blue,—and in each corner, above the death's-head or below the marrow-bones, is a word, "Tristezza—Morte—Terrore—Lutto." Near the upper right-hand corner, within a double circle, bearing a wreath of leaves, are two axes and the fasces, with the cap of Liberty stuck upon the top; a skull below, and the characters D L A Δ, of which I can find no explanation. Near the lower right-hand corner is a corresponding circle, with round balls representing thunderbolts, and zigzag lines representing lightning striking a royal, an imperial, and a papal crown; the legend is "*S. D. del Tuonante Giove*"—that is, *Società Deciso del Tuonante Giove.*" This was the seal of the society. The diploma belongs to Gaetano Caffieri, registrar of the dead, which signifies that his special duty was to keep a list of all the victims murdered by the society. It was taken, with other papers, at Grottaglia, as we shall hear presently. It is headed by the following initials: L D D T G S A F G C I T D U G S E D, which stand for "*La Decisione del Tuonante Giove Spera a fare Guerra contro i Tiranni dell' umane Genere. Salute e Decisione.*" These letters and most of the other initials are written in blood, and the rest of the paper sets forth that Gaetano Caffieri is a Fratello Deciso, and invites all philanthropic societies to help him at need, as he has determined to obtain liberty or death. It is signed by Pietro Gargara, grand-master, by Vito de Serio (we shall hear of him again too, by-and-by), and by Gaetano Caffieri himself. There are four dots beneath the signature of Pietro Gargaro, which indicate his power of passing sentence of death. When the *Decisione* wrote to any one to extort money, or to issue any other command, if these four dots were added, he understood that death would follow disobedience; if the dots were not added, some milder punishment, such as burning his house or laying waste his fields, would ensue.

There were various preliminaries to be gone through before a man could become a *fratello* of the Decisi. He must first be able to prove that he had committed two murders with his own hand, in cold blood, and he must present a petition for the honour of being admitted into the body. The next step was as follows:—

The Fratelli Decisi being assembled together and the petition read, the grand-master No. 1 was to sound the trumpet and say, "Attend, O Fratelli Decisi, put yourselves in order, with your arms prepared, for the *fazione morta*" (the sentinel, who let no one pass without his diploma) "has notified that a pagan presents this petition. He stands without, desiring to enter: if it be your will to admit him, well; if not, speak." If there was no reply, the grand-master blew the trumpet again, and the candidate was brought in blindfold. Then followed severe questioning, threats, and bodily tortures, to see what metal he was made of; and if he still stoutly declared that he was determined to belong to the order, a last attempt to shake his resolution was tried. The grand-master cried out with a loud voice, "So you are determined to be a member of our society! Seize him, comrades, and tear him to pieces; let no vestige of his body be found: he is a scoundrelly republican, an enemy to the king. Tremble, O man, who hast had the boldness to declare thy sentiments in our presence! But this is not enough. In a few hours thou shalt see thy family destroyed, and thy possessions laid waste, and all thy relations shall be infamously put to death!"

If the petitioner still did not flinch from these threats, the grand-master went on: "The pagan braves it out. Draw up in order, comrades; be ready at the sound of the *squillo*." The candidate was then placed in the centre, the *fratelli* gathered round him, the bandage was taken off his eyes. On all sides he saw dark faces, carbines pointed towards him, a finger laid on every trigger, the grand-master standing ready to sound the fatal blast.

This was the last trial. If he stood this, he was accepted as a worthy member of the band of ruffians, and the diploma, with its ghastly emblems and characters written in blood, was drawn up and signed and handed to him.

Here is a translation of a petition which was found at Grottaglia among other papers belonging to the Decisi :—

I, Francesco Perrone, of the city of Taranto, submit myself in everything and for everything that the society of the Decisi may desire, and as far as my strength will allow of my exact performance. I hope, therefore, from your goodness, that I may enter and share in your sacred mysteries of the said society, with the peace and satisfaction of all the members composing it; so that I

may give proof of my sincere sentiments, and overthrow the enemies of humanity, the King and the Pope.
Salute e Decisione!
I, Francesco Perrone, desire as above.

The number of the Decisi being small, they easily recognised each other. Besides, they had special signs, made by different motions of the fingers—the *parola di necessità*, the *signo di salute*, and others. This was the *signo di salute:* The right hand was laid on the breast, with the thumb bent underneath; then the hand was raised to the hat, with the thumb under the brim, the hat was taken off and replaced, and the hand brought down to a level with the thigh.

If you wished to discover whether a man was a *fratello* or *pagano*, you accosted him thus:—

Q. "From what country are you?"
A. "From the world."
Q. "Have you brothers?"
A. "I have two."
Q. "How old are they?"
A. "A century."

At times an unfortunate victim who had in some way offended against the regulations of the society was dragged, bound and blindfolded, before their court of judgment, called

La Decisione. Then a trumpet, called the *squillo*, was blown four times. At the first blast the assassins unsheathed their poniards; at the second they aimed them towards the victim; at the third they drew close round him; at the fourth they all, beginning with the director of funeral ceremonies, plunged them into his body.

But death was not always inflicted thus, with a certain decorous solemnity, and to the sound of the trumpet, after sentence pronounced in the *Decisione*. Often, very often, it was in revenge for some quarrel, or it was the work of a hired assassin, or some individual plunderer, who sheltered himself under the dreaded name of the Fratelli Decisi. Sometimes tortures were inflicted or murder committed out of mere wanton cruelty. At one time it was necessary for the Government to make a law that any one in the dress of *Policinello* found with arms about him should be summarily put to death, because these brigands were in the habit of using this grotesque disguise to enable them to mingle with the country-folk at market or merry-making as welcome and unsuspected guests; then all of a sudden the laughter was turned to shrieks of terror, and the *Policinelli* would rush from the scene, leaving some of the guests wounded or dying.

The General tells a gruesome story of how one winter night there came a knocking at the door of a farmhouse, where a merry party were celebrating the wedding feast of the farmer's only daughter, and how the door opened, and the long nose and gay cap of *Policinello* peeped in, and was greeted with shouts of welcome and clapping of hands. They danced, they sang, they drank, they screamed with laughter at his witty sallies and grotesque contortions. Then all of a sudden the scene was changed. Unnoticed by the merry throng, other masked figures had silently entered the room and mingled with the guests. Another moment and the men were seized, bound, dragged into one room—the women dragged into another, bound, slashed with stilettoes, treated with every indignity,—the bride and bridegroom, and her old father, killed. Finally, the wretches decamped, after drinking all the wine that remained, and carrying off all the valuables they could lay their hands upon. Fortunately this happened while General Church was in power, and he relates with much satisfaction that within a week the whole band of miscreants were seized and "made to grin after another fashion." They had laid aside their masks to carouse with greater comfort, and this made identification easy!

Let us go back to the petition presented by Francesco Perrone, and see in what manner his diploma—which, by the way, he only kept for some six months—was gained.

There was a certain old Signore dell' Aglio, a gentleman of Francavilla, whose life had for many years been a burden to him, because of the threats and exactions of the brigands. Again and again had he received letters, and had had to buy his life for such or such a sum of money. Still, he paid the money when it was demanded, with some grumbling no doubt, but with the feeling that while he paid he was under protection, and could walk the streets of the little town, or visit his vineyard, or stop to chat with a friend, in tolerable safety—at least as long as it was daylight. But at length he grew tired of these perpetual exactions, and determined to keep his life safe by shutting himself up altogether—and for four years he kept to this resolution, never stirring outside his own house, where he lived with his old sister, her maid, and his man-servant. Friends came to visit the old gentleman, doubtless all the gossip of the little town was faithfully retailed by the old servants; but summer or winter, rain or shine, he was not to be persuaded to put his foot outside his door.

Then there came reports of a new secret

society, more terrible, more bloodthirsty, more mysterious than any of the old ones had been. Its chief and founder, the Abbate Ciro Annichiarico, was said to be more than mortal. Strange stories were told of his sudden appearances and disappearances: he had been seen here, and in a miraculously short space of time he was heard of miles away; some one had ventured to speak against him in a company of friends, and had never been seen alive again. It was said that though he was chief of the new society of the Decisi, all the other and older bodies owed him some kind of allegiance, and that his spies were everywhere.

When the Signore dell' Aglio heard of these things his heart failed within him. He had new and stronger bolts and bars put to all his doors and windows; and he commanded that as soon as the rim of the sun touched the blue waters of the bay, every shutter should be put up, every window barred, every door locked and bolted fast; no one was to go out or come in from sunset to sunrise in the Casa dell' Aglio. His dearest friend might travel twenty miles to see him, but if he reached that house after sunset no tugging at the ponderous knocker, no clanging at the rusty bell, would be of the least avail. Perhaps if he went on long enough a voice, shrill or surly, as it happened to belong to the signor's man or the signora's maid, might bid him begone and not keep honest folks out of their beds after nightfall; or in the latter case there might be a little colloquy.

"*Perdonate, signore—ma—impossibile!*"

"But, my good woman, you know *me*! *Il Signore* ——, your master's old friend!"

"*Perdonate, signore—è impossibile.*"

"But I have come far—and the twilight has scarce commenced."

"*Mille perdone, signore — ma.*" And no amount of pleading, or reasoning, or remonstrance would get beyond that "*è impossibile!*"

The old gentleman, sitting in his arm-chair up-stairs, enjoyed these conferences hugely. A shrill tone would catch his ear, and he would rub his hands, and say with a chuckle, "Truly it is grievous to lead so lonely a life, and to refuse my kind friends; but what would you have? Who was it, Marta?" or "Giacomo? Ah, how I should have enjoyed a chat! But, *pazienza*—'tis safer as we are!"

Never but once did the Signore dell' Aglio depart from the rule which he had laid down —never but once, and that once cost him his life!

We have seen that Francesco Perrone was anxious to become a Fratello Deciso. Now he was a notorious ruffian, who had been concerned in many a murderous fray, but he had not yet managed to find opportunity of committing two murders in cold blood, with his own unaided hand. So he cast about for victims, and why he fixed upon poor old Dell' Aglio it is impossible to say. He certainly can have had no feeling of enmity towards him, for the two men were absolutely unacquainted with each other. One would almost say he was actuated by the spirit of the chase, and determined to hunt down so difficult a prey as poor old Dell' Aglio. " Indeed these wretches seem to have murdered *de gaieté de cœur*," says General Church.

For three whole months he haunted about the Casa dell' Aglio, but the *padrone* never set foot out of doors, and a perfect stranger like Perrone had not a chance of getting in. So he changed his tactics, and leaving Francavilla, he travelled to Naples, where dwelt a brother of Dell' Aglio's to whom he was fondly attached. When there, Perrone contrived somehow to scrape acquaintance with this brother, to visit at his house, and to obtain specimens of his handwriting.

Some of these Decisi were men of good education, and lived in the towns, apparently leading lives of peaceful citizens, or following honest trades, and Perrone was soon able to copy the handwriting of his new acquaintance, at least perfectly enough to deceive an old man, half-blind, like Signore dell' Aglio.

One day there came a letter to Francavilla, purporting to come from Signore dell' Aglio's brother at Naples, to say that he was seriously ill, quite unable to travel, and that having some very important matters to communicate—matters which he could not venture to trust to the ordinary post—he would send a trusted messenger with a confidential letter to be delivered into his brother's own hands. Furthermore, he begged his dear brother, our Signore dell' Aglio, to write to the enclosed address at Barletta, fixing the time and place where he would see this messenger in private.

The poor old gentleman fell into the trap. How could the most wily fox have suspected there *was* a trap? One is astonished at the amount of trouble, the ingenuity, the time spent in fashioning such a snare!

So one November evening, just a little after sunset—it was some way to Barletta, and a stranger, not knowing the rules of the house, might be excused from being a little late—Perrone knocked at the great door, and with a thrill of triumph heard the great bolts drawn back and the key turned to admit him. The old man-servant was not there, but the signora's old maid let him in, and bade him follow her up-stairs, first taking good care that the door was fast bolted and barred behind them. Upstairs sat old Dell' Aglio and his sister, each in a large arm-chair on either side of the cheery wood-fire. A third chair was placed between them for the guest, and a table with refreshments drawn up near the hearth. All looked cosy and homely—a pleasant sight on a November evening, when a drizzling rain beat against the windows, and no moonlight lay fair over the sleeping sea.

The old gentleman and his sister turned to greet their guest, with a pleasant sense of novelty in seeing a stranger from the world without, and some one who could give them news of their brother, and who brought with him a letter which would explain the former mysterious message. After a little friendly talk, the old signore asked for his brother's letter, and the stranger rising, delivered him a sealed packet, which Signore dell' Aglio took, putting on his spectacles, and bending over the light to read it better. But in a moment he lifted his grey head with a perplexed expression. "Signore," he said, "there is some mistake. This is not my letter," and he held up the enclosure. It was a blank sheet of paper!

"A mistake? Ay, truly, so it seems. But if the letter is not meant for you, *this* is," and in a moment the assassin's right hand had plunged a stiletto into the heart of the old gentleman, while his left hand stabbed the old lady in like manner. Then taking a light, he made his way down-stairs, opened the door, and left the house to pen the petition which we have already heard of, proudly conscious that by these two lucky strokes he had rendered himself eligible at once for admission into the brotherhood of the Decisi.

There followed the usual *procès verbal*, and Perrone was suspected of being the author of the crime, but the terror inspired by the Decisi caused the matter to be hushed up at the time. Then when General Church came on the scene Perrone disappeared.

The General marched about, here and there, going from village to village, making inquiries, hearing complaints. On one occasion, when an old man had been murdered with circumstances of especial barbarity, and the only person who could know anything of the crime, his only son, solemnly swore that he was quite unable to identify the murderers, the General took the course of sending the young man to prison, and bringing him before the Military Tribunal on a charge of having murdered his own father. People cried out at this, for the two were known to have been devoted to each other, and the young man was both pitied and liked; but the General knew what he was about. The youth begged to be allowed to confess to a priest, and having done so, returned to the court and told all the horrible story clearly and firmly, explaining that in the midst of fearful tortures, the father had bound the son by an oath never to reveal the names of the murderers,—this being the only way to save the young man's life. But since the priest had absolved him from this, he was ready to speak freely. But this is by the way.

One uncommonly fine morning in March 1818, the year following that of Dell' Aglio's murder, General Church and a small body of troops were marching from Francavilla to Ostuni. They were not marching along the highroad, for the General much preferred crosscuts and forest roads when he was on the look-out for this kind of game; and now, after a wild bit of pathway, they came to a walled field, with a gate at each end of it through which they had to pass. They were in excellent spirits, as gay as the lark which rose up just at their feet, and soared, singing, up into the clear air. The men were in front, the General rode behind, chatting with several gentlemen of the province who had volunteered to be of his company.

They were crossing the field, and had nearly reached the second gate, when somebody noticed a man who suddenly jumped over the wall at a little distance, and stood as if irresolute whether to advance or retreat. Of course to turn and fly would argue guilt, but to walk on was to run the gantlet of the whole column of soldiery, on the look-out for brigands. Nevertheless the second course seemed the safer of the two, so he slouched his hat and moved on, saluting as he passed by, lifting his hand to his hat, but not daring to remove it, lest there should be any one there who should recognise him. Neither did he venture to quicken his pace, but walked on steadily with a would-be careless air, and actually succeeded in reaching the last file of soldiers without detection. He had touched his hat to the General, and was just beginning to quicken his pace, breathing more freely, no doubt, as the danger seemed so nearly over, when the very last man of the file, and, as it happened, the only man who had ever seen Perrone, a sergeant of militia, cried out excitedly, "*È Perrone! quello che ammazzò il vecchio Dell' Aglio!*" (It is Perrone, who killed old Dell' Aglio.) On hearing the cry, Perrone started at a run. But it was too late. A sign, a word from the General, and a couple of mounted *gendarmes* were in pursuit, and it was but the work of a minute or two ere the wretch was securely bound, and marching off to Ostuni, where he was well known, so that there was no difficulty in identifying him.

A few days later he was hanged before the door of the Casa dell' Aglio.

CHAPTER V.

THE VENGEANCE OF THE SOCIETIES.

PUNISHING A MALCONTENT—THE WIDOW'S VOW—BIDING HER TIME—ARRIVAL OF GENERAL CHURCH—JUSTICE AT LAST.

THE betrayal of secrets of any of the societies was punishable with death.

General Church tells a story which illustrates the inevitableness of this rule.

One day, just about the time when he first took command of Apulia, some quarrel took place among a company of brigands—whether of the Decisi or of some other society does not appear—about the division of some plunder, and one of the leading members of the band considered himself unfairly used. However, he was so entirely in the minority that he had no chance of making good his claim, and he turned away in high dudgeon, fingering his stiletto, and muttering something of being tired of this life, and that more might be got elsewhere, and he knew what he knew, and could speak if he chose, and there were those who would be glad to listen to him, and some had best beware. So he strode off, and went home, and having told his wife of all that had happened, and eaten a good supper, his wrath cooled and he went to bed, having forgotten the quarrel. But though he forgot, there were those who did not forget. At about midnight he was wakened by the peculiar call which was the well-known signal of the band. His ill-humour had passed away, and fancying that his comrades had come to summon him for some plundering expedition, he bade his wife open the door and admit them. There were two rooms in the cottage, both on the ground-floor, the one into which the outer door opened being the bedroom of the pair. The wife did as her lord and master commanded, and brought wine, which she set down in the inner room, the kitchen, and fetched a lamp, and raked together the embers on the hearth, and stood ready to serve the accustomed guests.

To her great surprise—for she was in all their secrets, and accustomed to hear their plans discussed beforehand, and to take charge of the spoil after they returned from the raid—they told her to go back to bed. They had something very special, very private to communicate to her husband, and did not desire her presence.

The woman obeyed, but feminine curiosity was not to be balked so easily.

Her bed stood against the wall which divided the sleeping-room from the kitchen, an old wall full of cracks. It was not difficult, by applying her eye to one of these cracks, to see, herself unseen, all that went on in the dimly lighted chamber beyond, and to hear all that was said among the band. And this was what she heard and saw. There was a preliminary drinking of wine from the great jar which stood on the table, and then she saw the rest of the brigands gather round her husband, and heard them reproach him with having threatened to betray those who were bound by the same oath as himself. It was but the colloquy of a minute. Before he could speak a word of answer or explanation, a dozen stilettoes were plunged into his body, and he fell dead without so much as uttering a groan.

The woman, trembling for her own life, had yet presence of mind to lie down in bed, turning her face to the wall, and her back to the door through which the brigands must pass in order to leave the house. She heard them steal through the kitchen on tiptoe, one after another, enter the sleeping-room and halt there, looking towards the bed where she lay. There was a small lamp burning in a corner of the room, which cast their shadows upon the wall against which the bed was placed; and the woman, as she lay with half-closed eyes, was thus able to take note of their movements and gestures as well as to hear their whispered words.

What moments those must have been to the poor creature, as she lay there in apparent sleep, breathing hard and regularly, yet with every faculty so agonisingly awake! knowing that those who had murdered her husband would not have the slightest scruple in murdering her also. How the horrible scene which she had just witnessed must have been printed on her brain, thrilling with fierce thoughts of vengeance against the assassins, yet forced to lie there, to keep still, to seem to sleep, because there was but a step betwixt her and death!

When they had nearly reached the door, she saw by the shadows on the wall that they made a halt, and then she watched a ghastly pantomime. One made a sign with his dagger that he would step forward and kill her; another shook his head, and signed that she slept; a third took his carbine from his shoulder, crept towards the bed and pointed it at her— and then indeed she thought that her last hour had come, but her courage did not fail, and she lay still and snored louder than before.

"*Che bella musica!*" whispered the brigand; and another added with a brutal laugh, "Let her alone. Her husband will come and wake her presently."

"Best kill her," whispered another; but the fellow with the carbine answered—

"Bah! she is not worth the trouble! Come away."

Then she heard from two or three, "Let us go. It is late," and then some one said, "Kill her or leave her, it matters not which; but be quick about it. 'Tis too great a risk staying on here."

"Let us go—we can settle her any time," was the final verdict, and they stalked silently out of the house.

Left alone, the poor woman breathed more freely, yet she dared not move, lest any of the ruffians should be lingering about, so she lay still through the weary hours of darkness. The last embers died out on the hearth, the lamp which she had set on the kitchen-table flickered and went out: perhaps that was better than peeping through the chink in the wall—which had a terrible fascination for her burning eyes —to watch the dark motionless heap on the floor which had been her living husband when the night fell.

A rough, brutal man, a tyrant to her, a

robber and a murderer, yet her "man," the lover of her youth; and as she lay there she clenched her hands, and lifted her hot tearless eyes in the darkness, and swore a solemn oath that she would have revenge on the murderers of her husband.

Even when in the early morning some workmen, passing by and calling in at the cottage, found the dead body, the wife maintained silence, or rather declared herself ignorant of what had happened. She had been asleep. Her husband had been murdered in the night, but when and by whom, how could she tell? He was always a peaceable man, but there were quarrels. She went her own way, and never troubled her head about the affairs of the men — and there were bad men abroad, doubtless. Alas! alas! she was a desolate widow—she could say no more; and the apron went up to the eyes, and the sturdy shoulders were shaken by sobs, and the magistrate who had questioned her, as in duty bound, had his own life to consider, and knew that ignorance was his best safety. So to the *procès verbal* was appended the usual verdict, "Murderers unknown."

But she was biding her time.

Life went on as usual in the little mountain village: the scanty patches of corn ripened;

the figs were gathered in; the goats were driven to their pasture and called home for the milking; the brown-faced children rolled in the dirt and quarrelled and played; the girls lingered by the well, and the lads knew at what hour they should find them there; there was the work and the play, the gossiping on doorsteps, and the preparing of polenta within doors; and as for the tragedy which had taken place two months ago, there was no more sign of it in the village life than there was sign of stirring in the village well ten minutes after its surface had been broken by the drawing up of the water which that sad, stern-faced widow carried home to her lonely cottage.

The neighbours pitied her, one and another would give a hand's turn to do her a service, all would have been glad to have been her confidential interviewers, and to have known something of what had happened on that dark night; but no one could ever get a word from her on that subject, even had they not feared to ask. But if her vengeance was slow, it was all the more sure. She had all the secrets of the band of brigands in her possession, and could afford to wait.

People were talking about this Englishman who was marching through the country. He was a marvellous man, this English General. You could not frighten him, and you could not bribe him, and he would listen to any one who cried for justice, however poor and uninfluential, and he would see that justice was done too. It was said that he had sworn to extirpate the robbers and murderers who infested the country. It was certain that he set about it in a very different manner from the other generals who from time to time had visited the province with this same avowed intention, and after failing to find the brigands, or having a skirmish or two with them, or even catching and putting into prison some minor ruffian, had gone back to Naples, leaving the poor country in much the same state as before. The woman listened to all that was said—said in whispers, and among friends at first, but by degrees more boldly, and in open day—and held her peace.

One day there was great excitement in the little village. The Englishman was coming into their neighbourhood. He was to be at the village of Berberano, not six miles away, that very night. All who could contrive to get so far, straightway determined that if they did not go all the way to Berberano itself, they would at any rate meet him and his *gendarmerie* on the way. But the widow went

F

stolidly about her daily work, only her great dark eyes gleamed in their hollow sockets, and the lines of her mouth were drawn into a greater expression of determination than ever. Towards the afternoon she put on her most decent clothing and left the village. Some one asked her where she was going, but she shook her head and answered nothing.

At the entrance of the village of Berberano that evening a crowd was gathered, with the *sindaco*, or chief magistrate, among them, all waiting to receive and welcome the English General. All the gentlemen of the neighbourhood were there, and the peasants of the place stood in groups, curious, somewhat distrustful —for had they not had such promises before? Besides, who could say whether any of the strangers who lounged about, apparently actuated only by a spirit of peaceful curiosity, might not be brigand spies, wearing concealed poniards beneath their garments? Even the children clung to their mothers, and looked, with bright eyes under dark brows, awestricken, for something mysterious, they knew not what.

It may be questioned whether the worthy *sindaco* even, with all his bustle of deferential welcome, was not looking forward in his heart to the next morning, when this perplexing, irrepressible, worrying stranger would ride away. Nevertheless, when the cavalcade of *gendarmerie* appeared, and behind them a small slight man, with sharp features, keen dark-blue eyes, and an air of energy and eagerness which somehow did not seem quite to suit the country, the *sindaco* hurried forward, with expressions of profoundest respect and joy, to welcome him.

General Church courteously dismounted from his horse to return the greeting, but hardly had he set foot on ground when a tall, gaunt-looking woman, decently though poorly dressed, rushed forward, making her way through the crowd with vigorous shoves and pushes, and throwing herself at his feet, cried loudly—" *Giustizia, giustizia, Eccellenza, giustizia!* " He raised her from the ground and bade her be calm. She should be heard, but she must not cry out in that manner. In vain ! all efforts to pacify her only resulted in louder cries of " *Giustizia, giustizia, Eccellenza, giustizia!* "

This would never do. The General's rule invariably was to hear every complaint himself, that he might judge in the first instance of what was the truth of the matter before sending it to the Military Tribunal. But, as he pathetically remarks, " To get at the truth two essentials were necessary—namely, time and place;" and in his opinion the public street and a crowd offered neither the one nor the other. Besides this, clamour would give alarm to the brigand spies, who were sure to be found in any assembly, and facilitate the escape of the criminals, whoever they might be. So he turned to the *sindaco,* and said in a voice loud enough for every one to hear—

"She is mad, poor creature! Send her about her business. Or stay——" and he handed his purse to an aide-de-camp, with a muttered word or two, and remounting, rode off to the house prepared for his quarters for the night, after an invitation to the *sindaco* to join him and his officers at dinner.

Of course the crowd followed in the wake of the cavalcade, and there only remained some two or three, among whom was the aide-de-camp, who, purse in hand, went up to the poor woman, and seemed to be trying to persuade her to go home, and to cease wringing her hands and rending the air with her frantic and despairing cries for justice.

After a while he succeeded in gaining her attention, and glancing round and seeing that they were now alone, he said in a low, meaning voice, laying his finger on his lips—a well-known sign of secrecy and intelligence, which she at once understood—" Don't be afraid. Come to " (mentioning a lonely, deserted house on the outskirts of the village) "at eight o'clock this evening, and you shall be heard. But keep quiet."

Then he rode after his comrades, and left her, poor thing, in the midst of her vehement but low-spoken thanks and assurances of comprehension.

Eight o'clock approached. General Church with some difficulty dismissed the worthy *sindaco* and some other guests of the neighbourhood, pleading fatigue, the writing yet to be done that night, the early start on the morrow.

It was a dark, moonless night as he stood at the door to wish them a courteous "*Felice notte*," which was as courteously returned. Soon after, some half-dozen cloaked figures stumbled along the lanes which led to the lonely house, speaking in low tones, and quite undistinguishable from any other belated travellers. Having reached their destination they pushed open the door, struck a light, and found their way to a room where, in a corner, sat the poor forlorn widow, patiently waiting the time she had looked forward to so long. The notary was there with his pen, ink, and paper, ready to take her deposition, and some of the officers as witnesses; and now, in an encouraging tone, she heard herself addressed by the stranger General, and bidden to tell her story without fear, for she should have the justice she claimed —it was her right. Sitting before them in that dark, lonely, bare hall, with just a table and a bench or two for furniture, and the autumn rain pattering outside, she told her story, with all the vivid turns of expression, and ejaculations and gesticulations, of her Southern race; and then she went on to a triumphant detail of all she knew of the secrets of the band in the days of former friendship. With gleaming eyes and exulting tones she told their names, and where they dwelt, and where they were most likely to be found. She knew all their haunts, the places where they deposited their plunder, any particulars about each one of them, all the atrocities they had committed (and they were, without exception, very much "wanted" by justice!), and their general habits and movements. One consequence of her information was, that after a time many persons recovered property which they had lost, and which was discovered packed away in various hidden receptacles. But this is by the way. What concerns us at present is, that the General was at once put on the scent of a band of notorious ruffians, and that they all met their deserts before another fortnight was over, some being killed in desperate fighting, some taken and hanged. "After all," he remarks, "the husband only got his just deserts, for he was as great a scoundrel as any of the lot, and his murder by his comrades only anticipated by a few months more or less the sentence of the law." As to the woman, she had something to answer for too, for she was tried and condemned as a receiver of stolen goods; but in consideration of the service which her information had rendered to justice, the General interceded for her, and the legal sentence of ten years' imprisonment was in her case commuted to two.

CHAPTER VI.

CIRO ANNICHIARICO, FOUNDER OF THE DECISI.

CIRO'S HISTORY — HIS "JUSTIFICATION" — TRYING GENERAL OTTAVIO'S HORSES—A SUDDEN DISAPPEARANCE—AN UNEXPECTED REAPPEARANCE.

LET us now give some account of the founder and chief of this terrible society of the Decisi.

Ciro Annichiarico was a priest, and sometimes exercised the functions of a priest in the midst of his blood-stained career. We hear of his celebrating Mass before starting on some wild expedition, and he complained of the Mission priests "that they did not preach the pure Gospel, but disseminated *illiberal* opinions among the peasants." At the same time he was cruel, sparing neither age nor sex; his life was openly immoral, and he boasted of his infidel opinions. When he lay under sentence of death, one of these same good Mission priests came to exhort him to repentance. "Let alone this prating," answered Don Ciro, with a sneer;

"we are of the same profession, don't let us make game of one another!"

As to his personal appearance, General Church says :—

He was a good horseman, and a capital shot; strong and vigorous as a tiger, and equally ferocious; his countenance was bad; he had large features, a very ordinary face, and never without a sinister expression, quite unlike the manly countenance of Don Gaetano Vardarelli. His eyes were small and of a reddish hue; his hair dark, thick, and bushy; he had shaggy eyebrows, and a short, rather turned-up nose.

The General adds :—

Ciro had friends and protectors in all the towns and villages of the province of Lecce, and had the effrontery at times to show himself in broad daylight apparently unaccompanied. He was a perfect Proteus in his disguises—as a woman, as a beggar, as a priest, as a friar, as an officer, as a *gendarme*. His usual dress was of velveteen, highly laced, with many rows of buttons, and belts in every direction, and he was always armed with pistols and stiletto, carbine or rifle. He always carried poison with him, in a small case, within a red pocket-book. He also always wore several silver chains, to one of which was attached the silver death's-head, the badge of the secret society, the Decisi, which he had founded, and of which he was the recognised head —that terrible society, whose first condition of admission into its ranks was that the candidate must have committed two murders with his own hand, and whose decrees and patents were written in blood. On his breast he wore rows of relics, crosses, images of saints, and amulets against the Evil Eye. His head-dress was a high-peaked drab-coloured hat, adorned with gold band, buckle, and tall black feather, and his fingers were covered with rings of great value.

Ciro Annichiarico was born of well-to-do parents, in Grottaglia, one of the little white towns which stud the green plain of Francavilla. He was early destined to the priesthood by his relations, who were quiet, respectable people, of the farming class mostly, though one of his uncles was a *canonico*, and "a man of learning, who never took any part in the crimes of his nephew." The first time we hear of Ciro he has stabbed a young girl of Grottaglia, betrothed to a fellow-townsman, Giuseppe Molotesi. Ciro, though already a priest, waylaid the poor girl, and on her scornful rejection of his addresses, murdered her, and afterwards murdered young Molotesi, his sister, and three brothers. This was in 1803.

The only member of the Molotesi family left alive was a little boy, who was hidden away by a faithful servant in his own desolate house, and who grew up there, barred and bolted in, never once, for fifteen years, venturing to stir outside the door.

The child grew to be a man. One day friends came to him, not as they were wont, with gentle tappings and passwords, before the fast-bolted door would open to admit them, but in broad daylight, exulting, saying that he was free, that the murderer of his family was dead, that he could come forth and breathe the fresh air of heaven. But the pale captive shrank back, fearing it was some snare laid for him, and refused to cross the threshold of his door. At last he was persuaded to creep out, trembling, dazzled by the sunlight, to go to the town-gate, and to look upon the ghastly head exposed there in an iron cage. There he stood, poor creature, half dazed at first, then breaking into wild tears and laughter, throwing himself on his knees to thank the Madonna and all the saints for his deliverance, then running off to the General's quarters to thank him too.

For the murder of the Molotesi, Ciro was condemned to fifteen years' imprisonment in chains; but in four years' time he had escaped, and betaken himself to the mountains, where he gathered round him a band of ruffians and outlaws, and became the terror of the neighbourhood. In a "Justification" which he sent to the Royal Commission appointed in 1817 to act against the brigands, the wolf thus complains of the hard measure dealt to him by the shepherds of the flock:—

The priest Ciro Annichiarico, of the town of Grottaglia, learns with surprise that the Commission . . .

demands the reason why Ciro Annichiarico resides out of his native country.

He proceeds to protest his innocence of the crimes laid against him, "feeling within me no tumult which reproaches me with having ever acted against reason, or offended against the sacred laws of virtue and honour;" and adds that in consequence of cruel persecutions, he had for years dwelt among the wild beasts, living by the compassion of peasants and shepherds, or on the wild fruits! But his conscience is at peace, though "the blame of every disturbance falls on him, and whenever robberies or murders are committed, it is put down to the *abate* Ciro Annichiarico!" He adds:—

When the glorious Bourbon dynasty returned and benignly determined to recall from exile those who had been banished from society, I presented myself to the authorities, and obtained leave to dwell at Bari under police supervision, and the most pleasant hopes arose within me of living at rest, in social order. I reflected on the obligations imposed upon me by my sacred profession, and determined to join the College of Mission Priests at Bari. I was on the point of doing this, when the thunderbolt burst upon me; I was secretly informed that my arrest was ordered, and I vanished, and betaking myself to my old haunts, recommenced a wretched and savage life.

Circumstances invited me to crime and vengeance: the feelings of nature and religion recalled me to duty.

I learnt with horror from the shepherds that brigands infested the mountains, and the account of their outrages made my heart bleed. I determined to help my fellow-creatures, and hoped one day to undeceive the Government about the calumnies heaped upon me. I came forth from my cavern, and took the road to Martina. . . . I can say with truth that the roads are now safe, that the traveller journeys without fear; the farmhouses stand open, the shepherd sings as he leads his flock to the pasture.

Let us turn to the real story of Ciro's life and ways.

He had escaped, as has been said, after four years' imprisonment, and had gone to the mountains. After a while, General Ottavio, a Corsican, was sent to put down brigandage, which had become troublesome, in Apulia; and he set about it by offering an amnesty and pension to Ciro if he would reside at Bari, forsaking his evil ways, and becoming a peaceful citizen. "It was a disgrace to the Government," says General Church, in his account of the affair; but General Ottavio was mightily pleased with his short and easy method of turning the wolf into the lamb, and at Francavilla a meeting took place, articles were signed, and Ciro became, indeed, the pet-lamb of the fold. But it did not last long. He tired of captivity, in spite of riding and dining with the general, who greatly delighted in his company; and the story of his escape recalls one of those old tales which were our childhood's delight.

One fine day General Ottavio and Ciro Annichiarico were strolling together, outside the walls of Bari, accompanied by some officers of the general's suite. Presently the general's horses were brought out for their usual exercise, and Ciro, who had been amusing the company with stories of wild adventures and hairbreadth escapes, interrupted himself to commend the horses, of which the general was vastly proud: among others there was a grey, which, saddled and bridled, was brought up by a groom for his master's morning ride. "Yes, 'tis a good horse—you shall try him, and give me your opinion of him," said the general. But Ciro modestly excused himself; he was growing stiff, he was out of practice. Yet, if his Excellency insisted,—and after much pressing, the *abate* obeyed, and mounted, rode a few paces, and would have dismounted, but at the general's repeated request took another turn, walked, trotted, galloped, and returned full of praises of the gallant grey. He had never ridden a better horse!

General Ottavio was pleased, but not satisfied. He must have Don Ciro's opinion upon a horse from Conversano; he must know if it would be safe to bet on the speed of the Conversano. The races would soon be coming off, and he knew no man whose judgment would be so good as the *abate's*. So Ciro obligingly consented to mount again, riding a little way, and returning to the gate where the general and his officers stood watching him. He was met with an indignant protest. "But this is nothing, nothing at all! You have grown lazy, Don Ciro; you must have a gallop out of him, or how can you give an opinion?" Don Ciro seemed strangely apathetic. Good living and comfortable quarters had taken the fire out of him apparently: still, to please his host, he consented and galloped off, taking a wider circuit, flashing along the white road which crossed the wide plain, lost to sight for the moment among the olive-woods, then returning at full speed, and declaring that it was an excellent horse, and fleet—though not perhaps quite so fleet as some among the general's stud. Yet a good horse, an excellent horse!

"Ah, you are thinking of my Andalusian. I am told he is five times as fleet as Conversano. What do you say?"

Don Ciro looked at the tall dark chestnut and shook his head. "No, no, your Excellency. Conversano would match that horse any day. But I will try him." So the Conversano was led back to his stable in the town, and the saddle and bridle were put upon the Andalusian. The general handed a whip to Ciro, saying, "*Andate, andate! presto, presto!*" and off he went, tearing along the road till he reached the turn to Brindisi. Some of the officers looked at one another significantly, but only for a few moments. Ciro reappeared, at full speed, and was soon among them again, loudly declaring that he preferred Conversano as a riding-horse a thousand times.

"Bah! bah!" answered General Ottavio, "any one can see that the Andalusian is the swifter of the two: you are prejudiced, *signore abate*, because the race of Conversano is the glory of Apulia. The chestnut is a little fat and lazy, that's all. You should have made more use of the whip!"

"Whip, your Excellency? There was no need of a whip! I rather needed a second pair of arms," said Don Ciro, wiping the perspiration from his brow. "The brute! *Madonna mia*, but he has nearly pulled my arms out of their sockets!" and he dismounted with apparent difficulty, rubbing the said arms, and muttering that the horse must be surely possessed by the devil, and that he should not be able to mount again for a month at least, at which his Excellency and the officers laughed uproariously.

So the Andalusian was led away, but General Ottavio was not satisfied. He was determined to have Don Ciro's opinion upon a thoroughbred English mare, of a bright bay colour, which he had just bought. "Come, Don Ciro," he said coaxingly, "what do you say to it? One turn more, just one little turn!"

"Impossible, your Excellency — really impossible: I am dead!"

"Come, *signore abate*, I must have you try the mare. Can it be the redoubtable Don Ciro Annichiarico, the first of horsemen, who refuses me?"

"Pardon me, your Excellency. I am not the man I was. In truth, you must excuse me."

"One more trial, my friend. Only one more! She has cost me 200 English guineas, hard cash, and I have set my heart on having your opinion."

Very reluctantly Don Ciro allowed himself to be persuaded, rubbing his aching arms, and after a short turn, begging to be allowed to dismount; but yielding to renewed entreaties, he took off his hat, bowed low, and saying, "At your Excellency's commands," was soon flying along the road, followed by the cheers of the spectators. Soon he had turned the corner of the road that led to Brindisi. Is it necessary to add that General Ottavio never saw his English mare again?

He did see Don Ciro once again, however, and it was on this wise. He was still in charge of the district, and was making an attempt to pursue some brigands. One day he was placidly walking in his garden alone when a man, armed at all points, sprang over the wall and confronted him. It was Ciro Annichiarico. "You and I have met before," he said; "you remember me, general? Pray don't be frightened. Your life is in my hands, but I will let you off this once for old acquaintance' sake. Only remember that I shall not be so lenient another time, and leave off hunting after me in this furious fashion! *Addio!* A thousand greetings. *Addio!*" and so saying he leapt back over the wall and disappeared, and we may be sure that General Ottavio took the hint!

CHAPTER VII.

THE MASSACRE OF MARTANO.

THE OLD FEUDAL CASTLE—SURPRISED BY CIRO—SLAUGHTER OF THE INMATES—MURDER OF THE PRINCESS—THE ONE SURVIVOR.

WHEN he was on his trial, Don Ciro was asked how many murders he had committed. "*Chi lo sa?*" he answered, coolly. "Sixty or seventy, perhaps!" One of these murders made a special impression on General Church. He not only relates the circumstances at length, but refers to it again and again. No wonder it *did* make an impression not to be effaced on the mind of the chivalrous, kindly Englishman!

The old féudal castle of Martano, he says, stands above the picturesque little town of the same name, and overlooks a magnificent view. There, across the blue waves, you see the opposite coast, and the Albanian mountains beyond, while nearer at hand stretch green plain, olive-woods, vineyards, as far as Otranto, fourteen miles away. This old castle belonged to the Princess of Martano, a beautiful orphan girl some twenty years of age, sole mistress of great wealth and fair estates, dwelling amongst her own people, in the home of her ancestors, adored by those around her, fair and innocent, happy and fearless,—why should she be otherwise?

Many suitors had she, but to none of them had she a word to say, laughingly declaring that the care of her own people, the company of her little cousin (an orphan boy of seven or eight years old), the kind guidance of her old chaplain and of her duenna — both distantly related to her and both devoted to her — filled up all her time and thoughts, and she wished for nothing more.

The houses of the town of Martano were scattered irregularly up and down, with very little in the way of a street, being mostly detached and surrounded by gardens. A steep road led up to the castle, which stood at some distance from the town, and apart from all other buildings.

One dark December night—it was in the year 1814—the inhabitants of the castle of Martano bade each other the usual *felice notte*, the old steward locked and barred the great gates according to custom (for though the moat was filled up and the ramparts had crumbled away, the walled courtyard and great portals remained), and all went peacefully to bed. The young princess had dismissed her maid and was preparing to go to rest, when there was a knock at the door of her apartment, and her duenna entered.

"You are not asleep, dear child? Well, so much the better; for you must dress yourself and come down to receive his Excellency the commandant of the province. The poor gentleman has been belated on his way to Otranto, and begs your hospitality. Will you come?"

"Surely yes, *cara mia*," the young girl answered. "Send Lucia to me, and I will follow you immediately."

"For," says General Church, "such is the hospitality of the nobles and gentry, and indeed of all the inhabitants of Apulia, that, arrive at their houses at what hour you will, you are sure of a welcome, and most likely the master of the house will himself come down to receive you." So, as a natural thing, the princess prepared to come down and receive her guest.

Alas! it was no belated traveller who knocked at the castle-gate that night; but Don Ciro, with a band of forty or fifty ruffians, giving the name of the commandant of the province, and excusing his late arrival by the darkness of the night, the inclemency of the weather, the disturbed state of the country, the distance to Otranto. He was readily admitted; the old steward, as he drew back the ponderous bolts, calling the sleepy servants to make haste and fetch light, and summon the princess. His orders were cheerfully obeyed; the serving-men hastened down the wide stone staircase, some bringing torches, some flinging logs on the smouldering hearth, some hurrying to fetch food and wine, all anxious to show respect to the commandant. No sooner had the gates been opened than a clatter of horse-hoofs was heard, and a band of armed men rode into the courtyard. Some remained on horseback to guard the castle-door, some dismounted and followed their leader as he pushed his way into the hall.

There was no possibility of resistance, no time to raise an alarm even: the old steward was stabbed as he stepped forward, hospitably anxious to greet the unexpected guests; the torches were seized from the hands of the servants with one hand, while the other dealt the death-blow; their bodies were flung into the courtyard, while the murderers rushed through the house, killing and plundering. The white-haired chaplain, the old lady, the servants—male and female,—none were spared. As for the fair young princess——

She was in her own room, chatting gaily with her maids, as she prepared to go downstairs and receive the commandant. The noise of footsteps on the stairs, a certain bustle and movement, attracted the attention of one of her attendants, and she went out into the passage to see what it was about. At the head of the stairs she was met by an armed man. Terrified, she gasped out, "What are your commands, signore?"

"Is that the princess's door?"

"Yes—what do you want?"

"Nothing."

There was a shriek, and the poor woman fell to the ground pierced by a dagger, while Don Ciro rushed past her and burst into the room where the princess stood, white and trembling, yet commanding herself bravely as became one of her birth and breeding, giving no way to tears or entreaties, and answering Ciro's curt salutation with gentle, youthful dignity. The colloquy was a short one.

"Princess, we know that you have a large sum of money in the house. Where is it?"

"In yonder iron chest."

"Where are the keys?"

"On the table by the chimney-piece."

"Where are your jewels?"

"In the small box on that table."

"Have you any others?"

"Not in the house."

"Very well. Allow me to examine them."

He unlocked and opened the chest, which contained 36,000 gold ducats, his eyes taking a red glow as he ran the coins through his greedy fingers; then he opened the jewel-box, and took out pearls and diamonds and rubies, sparkling rings and golden bracelets, which had adorned many a fair and noble dame of ages past; and then—it is horrible to relate, but it is true—crying fiercely, "Philosophers tell us that dead dogs can't bite," he stabbed both the princess and her maid with his poniard.

Meanwhile the rest of his band had finished their share in the bloody work, and fetching food and wine, and stirring the smouldering logs to a blaze, they feasted gaily in the hall stained with the blood of their victims, and quaffed huge draughts of wine to the health of "*la bella principessa.*"

After a time Don Ciro gave the word to depart, and after some disputing over the division of the spoil, they all rode away, setting fire to the furniture in the great hall, and carefully shutting the courtyard gates behind them, that casual passers-by might not suspect that anything was wrong within.

But there had been a witness of the foul deed, though they little guessed it.

The boy who has been mentioned, the hapless princess's little cousin and playfellow, had been awakened by the dying shriek of the attendant. His room opened within that of the princess, and he ran into her chamber for explanation and protection, just as Ciro himself burst open the door. The little fellow, in an agony of terror, crept under a table which was covered with a heavy cloth, deeply fringed with silk and gold, and there he lay, unperceived, a horror-stricken witness of the scene.

How long he lay there he could not tell, but at last he was roused from his stupor of terror by the choking smoke which began to pervade the apartment. With shaking limbs and chattering teeth, not daring to turn his eyes to the white heap which lay, so strangely still, upon the floor, the poor little fellow crept out of his hiding-place, and wandered from one silent room to another, too frightened to go down-stairs, until he reached a window which was sufficiently near the ground to enable him to drop down into the garden; then, stumbling through the darkness, he climbed a low wall, and found his way down steep and stony pathways to the house of the *sindaco* of Martano, just as the grey winter's dawn was beginning to rouse the inhabitants from their slumbers. Breathless and trembling, the child could only explain that something terrible had happened up there, at the castle; and the alarm being given, the townsfolk, headed by the *sindaco*, rushed to the castle-gates, which stood shut, and apparently just as usual.

But they yielded to a push, and flew apart, and then—ah, what a ghastly sight met the eyes of those who entered and passed into the great hall! There seemed nothing to be done save to bury the dead bodies and extinguish the fire. Every one knew whose that dark night's work had been. Every one had loved the fair young princess, and would have gladly seen her murderer brought to justice. The little boy was able to give a description of Don Ciro, and a full account of all that had taken place. Among the heaps of corpses on the floor, one man-servant and the woman who had first spoken to the *abate* still breathed, and being taken to the town and carefully tended, lived long enough to sign a deposition before the magistrates. But there the matter ended. Ciro Annichiarico had so surrounded himself with the reputation of a magician that the people dared not even curse him aloud, lest his familiar spirits should carry him a report of what was said!

CHAPTER VIII.

THE ADVENTURES OF CIRO.

HIS ACTIVITY — GENERAL CHURCH'S PLANS — BANQUET AT LECCE—A BRIGAND WEDDING—ARRIVAL OF THE TROOPS —CIRO IN STRAITS—ESCAPE IN DISGUISE—THE GENERAL AT SAN MARZANO—CAPTURE OF CIRO.

WE are told that "Ciro's activity was as astonishing as his artifice and intrepidity; and as he was always extremely well mounted, and found concealment and support everywhere, through fear or inclination, he succeeded in escaping from the soldiers repeatedly, even when confidential spies had discovered his place of concealment only a few hours before. This singular good fortune acquired for him the character of a magician, and he neglected nothing that could confirm this idea."

Ciro's ambition was to be the acknowledged head of all the secret societies in Apulia. In the month of December 1817 there were said to be 70,000 sectaries in the province of Lecce alone, and Ciro was attempting to gather all to a meeting, and to get them to make common cause against the king's troops; for he thought in this way they might get good terms with the Neapolitan Government. He was all the more eager to persuade other chiefs of banditti to join his party, because he knew there was very little hope of pardon for himself unless he could appear as the head of the great body of secret societies.

He had two meetings with Don Gaetano, the chief of the Vardarelli; but they did not come to terms, and finally he determined to go his own way, and take the field with his own band against the English General, who was now in command of Apulia.

Meanwhile General Church had been marching up and down the provinces, fixing his headquarters sometimes in one place, sometimes in another; sometimes welcomed, more often met with sullen apathy; keeping his men under strict discipline, and proclaiming peace and safety to all who would help him in establishing order and putting down murder, robbery, and lawlessness. Reports came in daily. Ciro had been seen here, heard of there. One officer of *gendarmerie* had talked to him for half an hour; another had heard at Ostuni that Ciro had slept in the adjoining house a day before.

Let us take a look at General Church as he sits in his room at Lecce studying the map of the province with his chief of the staff, Colonel Schmerber. They have stuck red pins into the loyal places, and black into those which are disaffected. The General has determined that the three towns of Grottaglia, Francavilla, and San Marzano shall be the centre towards which all his lines shall converge, so that his columns should all draw closer and closer till Ciro was fast caught, as in the middle of a net. This having been explained, the General throws himself back in his chair, rubbing his hands, and says, "Schmerber, my friend, Ciro is moving against us."

"Impossible, General. You are joking," was the reply.

"Not a bit of it: read for yourself," handing him a letter. "You see the black flag is hoisted. In fact, Don Ciro has been so considerate as to warn me that if I don't withdraw my men he must go to war with me in earnest, in which case one of us must die, and that one will not be Ciro Annichiarico!"

"Very good, General. We are quite ready for him."

"And, if you will believe it, Schmerber, the scoundrel offers me his friendship and protection if I will go away and let him alone!

He has published a manifesto, declaring that he is fighting for Liberty, especially reminding the *gendarmes* that they are mostly Carbonari, and therefore brethren."

"No fear of the *gendarmes*, General. They are devoted to you."

The General took up his map again. "Bentz and his battalion must march at once to Brindisi—that place is only kept in order by the garrison in the castle. Corsi to Gioja; Francia to Taranto; Bianchi to Ostuni. Fusco says Francavilla is all for Ciro, and our men are insulted in the streets. Well, I shall be there before long. Shall I tell you a piece of news, Schmerber? Vito del Serio is going to be married!"

"What the devil does that matter to us?"

"For once in your life, my friend, you are wrong. It matters so much, that if I cannot have the pleasure of assisting at the ceremony, I shall certainly send representatives. Oh, it will be a grand affair, I assure you. Read this."

The paper which General Church held out contained the news that Don Ciro was intending to make the marriage of one of his chief officers the pretext of a great gathering of the brigands throughout the country, and the signal of a general rising.

"This will be our opportunity, Schmerber, our crisis," cried the General. "Now, do you see? If we succeed here, the campaign is finished. Ciro has not done much against us as yet."

"He has tried one or two things," said Schmerber. "There was that dash on Brindisi, in hopes of freeing the galley-slaves, but the cavalry met him a mile outside the walls, and our gentleman had no mind to come to close quarters; so off he goes to Gallipoli, and as he met with the same reception there, he thought it best to retire and lie quiet for a while."

"We are not a day too soon or a day too late," exclaimed the General, pacing the room eagerly. "Send off the officers to their different posts. We could not have better news, Schmerber!"

That evening the General gave a farewell dinner to his friends at Lecce, preparatory to leaving the pleasant little town and taking the field against Don Ciro. There were loyal and complimentary toasts drunk, and then the General called upon his guests to drink to the downfall of Ciro Annichiarico, the curse of Apulia.

No one ventured to refuse; some heartily applauded; some agreed that it was well said, but, with shakings of the head and doubtful looks, asked how the thing was to be done? Ciro's name had been so long a terror to the land, the people dared not say a word: eighteen years' practice had made him perfect in the trade of an assassin. No one else was safe while he lived. But when General Church replied, "Well, gentlemen, have it your own way. Either act with me, heart and soul, or withdraw to your own houses, and keep out of it altogether. For my own part, I swear never to rest till I have destroyed the scoundrel Ciro Annichiarico and all his bloodhounds!" "I will ride with you!" cried one. "And I!" "And I!" "And I!" they said, catching the fire from each other; while a worthy lawyer—a great friend of the General's—declared with a laugh that though he was too fat to ride, and had a distinct dislike to the neighbourhood of musket-balls, he would put his unwieldy body into a carriage and go from place to place to exhort others to join in the good cause.

And now, let us turn to San Marzano and Vito del Serio.

A mountain village, straggling up and down amongst crags and walls, the houses jumbled among patches of olives, wherever there was a little bit of flat ground. At the top of all a castle, and below the village a belt of woods. Altogether a capital place for defence, and therefore a favourite haunt for banditti at all times; and the people, who were an Albanian colony of old time, were wild and rugged, and bore a bad character as favouring Don Ciro and his band.

The wedding-day had arrived, and the little town swarmed with guests armed to the teeth. The bride, a strapping *brigandessa*, did not depend on her splendid costume, bright eyes, and straight black brows entirely for her conquests apparently. She was also armed with carbine and stiletto, and her hands and arms looked as if she were as capable of using them as was the bridegroom himself. She was lodged in the castle, which belonged to a certain Marchese Bonelli, whose agent, in fear of his own life, surrendered the keys, and placed the good wine at the disposal of his uninvited guests. The farms and houses around had been requisitioned, and right royally the brigands feasted in the castle-hall, joined by most of the inhabitants, some from fear, some inspired by the eloquent harangues delivered, glass in hand, by Vito del Serio and his charming bride. As the day grew on, their courage grew too. The wine flowed freely, the people gathered round and swore fidelity to Ciro and the

Decisi with brimming glasses and ringing cheers. Then they swore to put down everything sacred on earth, and sealed the oath by rushing to the ramparts and discharging their muskets. And this was so delightful and inspiring that they shouted out decrees, ratifying each with a bumper and a volley. Death to the king!—to all kings and rulers!—to all Governments!—to the Pope!—to *il Generale Giorgio* (Church); and this was taken up and repeated with shouts of a "*Brindisi! Brindisi! Brindisi!*"[1] to the death of *il Generale Inglese!* and a fresh rush to the battlements, with shouts and firing of muskets, until, to relieve their excitement, the company called for a *tarantella*, the music struck up, and the dancing and drinking grew wilder and wilder, and the dancers were ready to defy the world!

Suddenly a bugle-call was heard in the direction of Francavilla. The dancing came to a sudden stop. Cheeks turned pale, eyes sought one another doubtfully. Vito del Serio ran to the top of the castle ramparts, and looked across the great green plain, dotted with white villages, and bounded by the Gulf of Taranto. He shaded his eyes from the low rays of the afternoon sun. "*Gli Albanesi!*" he cried

[1] A *Brindisi* means a bumper.

(General Church's Greek soldiers were called *Albanesi* by the people), " they are coming !— but they are few." And then, after a pause— " No, no; fear nothing—they are taking another road;" and he descended from his post of observation. The dancing began again, but not with the same spirit as before, though the talk was brave enough. " *Gli Albanesi* are out of sight," said the revellers. " They are afraid of us; they have run away. Ah, we shall hear no more of them !" But in a few minutes the sound of a drum beating a march was heard, and there was a rush to the walls.

" What is it ? What is it ? "

" Nothing, nothing; only some soldiers going to Taranto. *Buon viaggio, signori!* there they go !"

" Where, where ? "

" Over there. See—a small column; few, very few. They are marching towards the sea. Who's afraid ? "

No one, of course. Yet they ceased the attempt to resume dancing, and hung together in groups; and Don Ciro marshalled his men to their appointed posts—some to the flat roofs of the houses, some to the walls, some to the top of the castle. The inhabitants, too, were provided with arms and ammunition, and took their places as they were directed. There was a shot in the wood which lies about the feet of the little town; another, another; then half a dozen in quick succession. "To arms, friends and brothers!" cried Ciro Annichiarico and his officers. "They are coming! Courage, brothers, courage!" They *were* coming indeed; for at that moment the winter sunlight shone among the trees on the black-plumed helmets of the cavalry, slowly descending the opposite hill, and the shots in the wood told of a skirmish between the brigand outposts and the *gendarmerie*.

There was some sharp fighting, and the broken ground made it impossible for the cavalry to get to close quarters; but a body of infantry under Major Francia was just behind, and rushing on with fixed bayonets, they carried the place in spite of a galling fire. Many of the brigands fled, and were cut down by the Greeks and *gendarmes* who were posted in the wood outside San Marzano. Some hid in cellars, and were dragged forth and delivered up by their *quondam* friends. The bride and bridegroom were amongst these.

The soldiers were for taking summary vengeance on the villagers by burning the place to the ground, but this the officers would not allow; so the captive brigands were bound and marched off to Francavilla, where the General had now taken up his headquarters, and the inhabitants of the place showered curses upon them, and loudly protested their devoted friendship for the Government. As to firing on the troops, or in any way assisting Don Ciro, heaven forbid that they should do such a thing! But the old soldiers smiled grimly, and pointed to hands grimed with gunpowder, and mouths black from biting cartridges—evident tokens that the people had joined in the fight; and some forty stout fellows were marched up to the castle, there to remain prisoners till General Church's pleasure should be known. In San Marzano the troops captured 130 horses belonging to Ciro's followers, over 2000 firelocks, and several hundreds of pistols and stilettoes.

And what had become of Don Ciro?

He had escaped on his famous English mare, and no trace of him was to be found. But a few nights later a certain Don Giacomo di Montenegro was sitting over the fire, in his own home, in the outskirts of Brindisi, a cigar in his mouth, and a white nightcap on his head, peacefully ruminating, when he heard behind him the sound of stealthy footsteps, and turning his head, beheld a man, wrapped in a long cloak, approaching him on tiptoe. To his horror he recognised the chief of the Decisi. "Don

Ciro!" The cigar fell from the poor old gentleman's fingers.

"Yes, it is I, Ciro Annichiarico," was the reply—"I, and no other, and I have not time for compliments. You must help me to escape from my persecutors one way or another, or you will repent it. Hide me in your house, or find a vessel to put me across seas, I care not where — Tunis, Tripoli, Constantinople, — anywhere beyond the power of this infernal Englishman! Here are 200 ducats wherewith to charter a vessel, and I think you will hardly refuse Ciro Annichiarico."

A week earlier it would doubtless have been difficult to refuse such a request, but the taking of San Marzano, and the capture made at Grottaglia immediately after of ten of Ciro's chief officers, had put things in quite a new light. Ciro must have been astonished when the old gentleman rose, and, taking off the nightcap, faced the unbidden guest with a certain dignity and determination. "Don Ciro," he said, "I cannot protect you. I refuse your money, and despise your threats."

Ciro glared on him like a wild beast, trembling with rage at this unexpected check. "You refuse *me?* You despise *my* threats? Then look to yourself, for by——"

"Gently, signore, gently. I have no vessel

to place at your disposal, in the first place; and I could not hide you if I would, because my house is full of soldiers, and I am expecting the English General and his staff every moment. Just take the trouble to peep into the next room, and you will see the table prepared for supper. Hark, here they come!" Sure enough, the clatter of horse-hoofs was heard in the courtyard. "Fly!" cried Don Giacomo; "fly, or you are lost!"

"Where can I fly?" answered Don Ciro, bitterly. "Those confounded soldiers are everywhere."

"There, go in there." Don Giacomo pointed to a small door. "Bolt yourself in, and don't answer till you hear me say '*Il vento è buono*'"—and he dashed off to receive his guests. They proved to be some of the staff, and glad were they to find a roaring fire, and supper ready to be served up.

"But the General? where was he? Should the supper wait his arrival?"

"Oh no, by no means. He would arrive in an hour's time, and it would be a pity Don Giacomo's good things should be spoilt; and as to our General, he is related to those creatures who live on air!"

So the officers were shown to their rooms, and then sat down gaily to supper, and then

Don Giacomo was able to return to his prisoner, who opened the door at the given signal, asking eagerly, " Is all well ? "

" No, very ill," was the reply, " and the sooner you leave this house the better. Understand that I cannot protect you, and would not if I could."

" You say that to me! Take care!" And Ciro laid his hand on his dagger.

" Listen to me, *signore abate*. This Englishman has trusted me, and I will not betray his confidence. He was my friend once, years ago. No, it is no use putting your hand to your dagger. Of course you can kill me, but you can't get out of this house without my help. Look out of the window if you doubt it."

Don Ciro took three strides across the room, and looked down into the great courtyard. Armed and mounted sentinels guarded the gates, tall grenadiers paced the court or stood about in groups, officers and orderlies passed to and fro. All were armed, all alert—all on the watch for *him!* Ciro's hand was lifted, and then fell to his side with a gesture of despair. " Traitor!" he muttered through his set teeth.

" Not so, Don Ciro; I should be a traitor if I broke faith with the General."

" What is it about this Englishman that

makes you all run after him? You his friend —and why?"

"Well," answered the old gentleman, thoughtfully,—" well, we are old friends. I'll tell you the story. When Joachim Murat was King of Naples, an English frigate came and burned a French frigate here in our harbour, under our very noses!"

"That's true, for I saw it with my own eyes, and a gallant thing it was," interrupted Don Ciro.

"Well, I don't know that we liked the Englishmen the worse for doing it. The captain and a friend of his, an English colonel, lodged in my house for weeks. Fine fellows they were, and we became great friends. After a time the colonel went away on a mission to Zante for his Government, and while he was absent the captain and all his crew were drowned, by the upsetting of their boat in a sudden squall. All Brindisi lamented them, and when the colonel came back and learned the fate of his friends, he was like a man distracted; all the more so because, before he could find the bodies and have them honourably buried, an English frigate came and carried him away. He put a sum of money into my hands—not that I wanted money from him— begging me to do for his friends what he was prevented from doing himself, and we parted with many promises of undying friendship. I was glad to be able to let him know that the bodies of the captain and the sailors were found and buried with military honours, as he would have wished; and except for a letter of thanks, I heard no more of him. This was four years ago. When, some months since, I heard that the new General who had been sent to take charge of the province was an Englishman—the English are good people, thought I—I will go to Lecce, and pay my respects to this General, for my old friend's sake. So I went, and to my delight found that the General commanding was no other than my old friend himself!"

"You mean to deliver me up to him?"

"Not that either, signore. You shall get out of this house and out of Brindisi safe and sound for me. After that I wash my hands of you, and you must trust to your own devices, which have got you out of many a worse scrape ere this."

"You shall pay for this!" muttered the baffled villain under his breath.

But Don Giacomo heard him, and with a shrug of the shoulders and outward spreading of the palms, "Don't threaten, please," said he. "The house is full of soldiers, you know, and a word from me—but I am a peaceable man, and you are wise. Only, I don't choose to be insulted in my own house."

"Well, well, one must submit to fate," growled Don Ciro; "but in truth I am tired of this life."

"Truly you would do well to take to an honester one," answered Don Giacomo, sententiously. "Perhaps you might get a pardon as others have done."

"I get a pardon? No chance of that. This confounded General has sworn my destruction."

"How do you know that, Don Ciro?"

"He said it at Lecce, at his own dinner-table. It was reported to me by one who was there, word for word. Not that I care a fig about dying; but when I think of that man my blood freezes! Fifty plots have I laid against him, and all have failed. Oh, I have seen him! A little man, two inches shorter than I, and too young for a general. But he rides well, and he has an eye! I went to the theatre at Lecce on purpose to see him. I have tried to gain over his soldiers, but to no purpose. Even the *gendarmes*, half of whom are Carbonari, are my bitter foes now that this Englishman has come into Apulia. Did not they lead the attack at San Marzano? Carbonari, Calderari—the names go for nothing—

they all forget their differences to run after his pleasure! Did he not have the whole *Decisione* seized at Grottaglia, in their own council-chamber? Ay, and he got his information from Grottaglia itself, my own town. And now you, you yourself, Don Giacomo, are against me, and for him, the Englishman!"

"Come, Don Ciro; no use wasting time in words. Look here,"—and he flung a bundle on the ground,—"these clothes belong to my sister. Dress yourself in them, and put your own into this bag. I will be back directly."

He went to receive General Church, who was at that moment riding into the courtyard, and having seen him safe in the room prepared for him, returned accompanied by a little boy.

"Carlo, attend!" said Don Giacomo, putting his hand on the child's shoulder. "Look at me, and not at the signora, Carlo."

"*Si, signore,*" said the boy, stealing a wistful and wondering glance at the figure in female habiliments, the face muffled with veil and kerchief.

"Take the signora's bundle, *Carlo mio*—that is right—and conduct her to the shore, and set her across the harbour to the back of the castle. Do you understand?"

"*Si, si, signore.*"

"And when you have landed her, come back quick—and do just what the signora bids you."

"*Signore, si, si,*" cried the urchin, shouldering his bundle, in a hurry to be off.

"And mind you don't speak to any one, Carlo. *Addio, signora. Felice notte e buon viaggio;*" and Ciro and his little guide departed.

They passed through a long gallery purposely but dimly lighted, and were scarcely noticed by the officers who stood talking in groups; they descended the staircase and crossed the great hall unchallenged, though some curious glances and laughing remarks followed the passage of the muffled female and her little guide. Just as they reached the door, they nearly ran into a tall young captain of hussars just entering, and he exclaimed, "Holloa, my dear! don't be frightened. I've a mind to see what kind of a face is hidden under that hood;" but luckily for Don Ciro, Colonel Bentz was within earshot, and took up his young friend pretty sharply.

"You'll do nothing of the kind. What business is it of yours if the girl is handsome or plain? Any woman belonging to this house is to be treated with respect."

"All right, colonel," answered the young man, good-humouredly. "I was only joking."

"Some petitioner to the General—some *contrabbandista*," suggested another.

"Upon my word!" said another, "did you see her eyes? I caught a look, and thought such eyes only belonged to Ciro or the devil!"

"You young fool," answered Colonel Bentz, with a laugh, in which the rest joined, "you see Don Ciro everywhere. You must be precious afraid of him. Fancy looking for him in Don Giacomo's house!"

And while the discussion was going on, Ciro had slipped past, crossed the court, answered the challenge of the sentinels, and in due time had been rowed across the harbour, and deposited at the foot of the castle. The little boy returned to Don Giacomo, and reported that the *signora donna* had shaken her fist and poured forth "*mille maledizioni*" as she sprang ashore, and added shrewdly, "For my part, signore, I don't believe that the *signora donna* is a *signora donna* at all."

Then Don Giacomo went up-stairs to the General's room and told him the whole story, winding up with, "And now — I can only throw myself on your Excellency's friendship for Giacomo di Montenegro."

General Church had listened without a word of interruption. Now he looked up, and there was a comical twinkle in his eye. "Do you think I am angry with you, old friend, for letting the scoundrel go? Not a bit of it! How could you give him up, when you had passed your word? If you had been capable of such a thing you would be no friend of mine."

Happy Don Giacomo! Before General Church knew what was coming, his hand was seized and repeatedly kissed.

"Well, well," said the General, "pray let's say no more about it. It would be awkward for us both if the story got abroad."

"I am well aware of that so far as I am concerned. But, your Excellency, I have still a favour to ask—for the honour of my house."

"I guess your meaning, my friend. How long will it take to get twenty miles from Brindisi?"

"Four or five hours."

"Then don't let us say another word about Don Ciro till daybreak. That will give the fellow rope enough, I think!"

One cannot help fancying that it must have been with a certain shamefacedness that the quixotic General told the story next morning to his trusty chief of the staff, who drily remarked in reply, that by this time Ciro was probably off to the mountains. To which

General Church retorted that Ciro was certainly gone to his own town of Grottaglia, which he would think all the safer because of the General's foray lately made there.

So now, some days were spent in riding about the country from place to place, wherever any trace of the chief of assassins was to be heard of. In the saddle at daybreak, with no refreshment but a cup of coffee and a biscuit, off to this village or that *masseria*, visiting outposts, questioning peasants, and back after thirty or forty miles' ride to Francavilla to dine, and then snatch a couple of hours' sleep on a sofa, booted and spurred, and wrapped in his long cloak. Once as he rode with his troops, accompanied by some gentlemen of the province, along a deep-cut lane leading to Grottaglia, Ciro himself was hidden among the bushes above him: so close was he that by stooping he could have touched the General's plume! and he was raising his carbine to fire, when the sudden appearance of some soldiers in the high field where the brigands were concealed forced them to mount and dash away for dear life. Meanwhile General Church rode through the lane below, chatting cheerfully, and unaware of the nearness of his foe. Grottaglia was reached, and the soldiers passed through silent and deserted streets. Not a woman looked forth from her window to see the troops ride by; if a man appeared, he averted his face and hurried by without look or greeting. But just as they rode through the gates of the rebellious little town, a venerable-looking white-bearded old monk met them. Throwing back his hood, he gazed earnestly on the martial array, then raising his hands, he solemnly invoked a blessing from heaven on the leader and his men.

"Thanks, many thanks, good father," said General Church, saluting the old monk respectfully. "Thanks all the more because yours is the only salutation I have met with since I entered the city of Grottaglia."

Soon after this General Church appeared before San Marzano. Out came the people to meet him, the *sindaco*, the clergy in their robes, the women carrying olive-branches. There was an ovation of welcome to the deliverer, and protestations of joy at the defeat of the brigands, and of hope for Ciro's overthrow — to all which the General answered never a word, but sat like a statue, surrounded by his officers, apparently absorbed in his own contemplations. The *sindaco* implored him to enter the city, where a feast was prepared for him. Still no reply. The women (and this was the trying part of the business, says the General pathetically, for many were handsome and graceful, and of respectable families!) knelt before him with waving of olive-branches and frantic cries of "*Misericordia! Pieta!*" Still he hardened his heart, requested the fair dames and damsels to rise, and, turning to the *sindaco*, said that he would not enter San Marzano in peaceful wise till it had made up for its late bad behaviour. As to the priests, who came forward in their turn, he would have nothing to say to them. It was their duty to teach the people obedience to the law, peace, and charity; whereas the conduct of San Marzano showed that the people had been very ill taught indeed. "I will never enter your town," he said, "till you have wiped away the disgrace of having fought against the king's troops. I give you five days wherein to find Don Ciro, or put me in the way of finding him. If you do not do this, San Marzano shall be burnt to the ground. You may send away your women and children, but not a man of you will leave this place without a permit from me or one of my officers, on pain of being sent for trial to the Military Commission at Francavilla." And he rode away.

Three days later, General Church reached Ostuni after a forty miles' ride, and having made arrangements for the following day, dismissed Colonel Schmerber and the aides-de-camp for a few hours of much-needed rest. But there was to be no sleep for them that night. The General had just wrapped his military cloak around him, when far away, through the silence of the winter night, only broken by the "*Qui vive?*" of the sentinel at the gate, he heard the ringing of horses' feet. He threw open the window. Surely that was in the direction of Francavilla? Truly the rider rode fast, and came nearer and nearer; now he stopped at the gate of Ostuni, for that was the sentinel's challenge. Then came the clattering hoofs, full gallop, along the narrow little paved street: he drew rein at the courtyard of the General's quarters, and again there was the "*Qui vive?*" the password, the unbarring of the great gates, the entrance within the court, the parley at the castle-door. How long it seemed while the huge key was turning in the rusty lock, and the bars being pushed back, to let the messenger in! The General hurried from his room, and nearly fell into the arms of Colonel Schmerber, who rushed breathless up-stairs.

"A courier, General—a courier from Francavilla! We've got him, General, we've got him; the devil has abandoned him at last!"

Close at his heels, covered with mud from head to foot, came the courier. "God fights for your Excellency, and Ciro is fast in the net. Francia, Bianchi, Guarini, Corsi, send their congratulations. They salute your Excellency. Here is the despatch."

"Fusco, you shall choose the best horse that you can find for this!" and as he spoke, the General broke the seals of the despatch, and read as follows:—

"*Eccellenza*,—Don Ciro is in the tower of Scaserba, closely surrounded. He can't escape. He has killed and wounded several of our men. The troops are enthusiastic, the militia behave well. The volunteers were the first to discover him. He defends himself desperately. Your arrival will finish the business, if it is not finished before. The troops of Francia, Corsi, Bianchi, surround Scaserba, while the guns threaten Grottaglia; but even that town is for us now. The road is too bad to bring the guns here.

"Guarini."

"*Montez, montez, messieurs!*" cried the General, all fatigue forgotten. "For you, Fusco, eat, drink, sleep, and then join me at Scaserba."

"Heaven forbid, your Excellency! I need nothing but a fresh horse;" and in a few minutes they were riding full speed through the sleeping town, leaving for the master of the house the following note, written by the General on a scrap of paper: "The *abate* is in the net. Pray God for a happy ending to our enterprise."

On they dashed, through grey olive-woods and leafless vineyards, under the rocky heights of Cisternita, past the fortified *masserie* that are scattered round the Monte di Martina, drawing rein for the first time as the day was breaking, at the top of a ridge, whence they saw stretching below them the wide plain, dotted with white towns and towers, and among them the tower of Scaserba. Not a word had been spoken since they left Ostuni, and Schmerber broke the silence by saying, "This time, General, we have him fast!"

"We shall see, *mon cher*," was the answer; "seeing is believing! Spur on! Forward, gentlemen!"

On, on, across the plain, till they neared the tower. Peaceful it lay, in the misty sunshine of the February morning; no sound or sight of war broke the stillness. They accosted some peasants, and heard that the siege was over, and Ciro a prisoner. As they reached Grottaglia the news was confirmed by seeing that the camp outside the city, with its two cannon set to overawe the place, had been taken away. So they were late for the finish, after all!

CHAPTER IX.

CAPTURE AND EXECUTION OF CIRO.

HIS DEFENCE IN SCASERBA—A PARLEY—SURRENDER—MARCH TO FRANCAVILLA—TRIAL AND EXECUTION—REJOICINGS OF THE PEOPLE.

WE must go back a little to give the account of the siege and Ciro's capture.

The *masserie* or farmhouses of Apulia [we are told] are all built on the same plan, and capable of defence. They date from the period when the incursions of pirates were frequent, and the people shut themselves up with their cattle and valuables when an attack was apprehended. A square solid wall surrounds the dwelling-house, which is built on one side of the enclosure, and contains two or three rooms. The stables and outhouses form a right angle to the dwelling-house, also within this wall. A tower of two storeys stands apart, and is ascended by stone steps, or by a ladder or drawbridge. . . . Ciro, worn out with fatigue, took refuge with a few companions in the Masseria de Scaserba. He had previously provided it with provisions and ammunition. When he saw the militia of San Marzano searching for him he was not alarmed, thinking he could easily cut his way through them. He shot the first man dead who came within his range. The militia of San Marzano sent information of his presence to the nearest troops, and Ciro found himself surrounded. Seeing that a vigorous assault was intended, he locked up the people of the *masseria* in their straw-magazine, and mounted the tower with his companions.

A very few well-armed men could hold the tower against hundreds, and the brigands defended themselves vigorously till nightfall. Ciro tried to escape in the darkness, but the neighing of a horse apprised him that reinforcements of cavalry had arrived, whose pursuit it would be hopeless to elude; so he returned, having killed one of the *voltigeurs* stationed under the wall from which he had meant to descend. He shut himself up again in his tower, and spent the rest of the night in making cartridges.

At daybreak the besiegers tried to break open or burn the gates of the *masseria*, but the besieged repulsed them with a rapid and well-directed fire, killing and wounding several assailants. Then a 4-pounder was pointed against the roof of the tower, and the tiles and bricks came rattling down, forcing the brigands to descend to the lower storey. Worn out with fatigue, tormented by burning thirst, Ciro called a parley. Upon this the troops ceased firing, and Bianchi came forward. Ciro showed himself at the door of the tower.

"Good morning, gentlemen. I wish to speak with the General."

"Impossible, Don Ciro."

"But I am willing to treat with him! What kind of a man is this, who refuses to speak with me?—with *me*, Ciro Annichiarico!"

"Not even with you, Don Ciro."

"I have had the honour of speaking with many generals—and I have many things to say to Generale Giorgio."

"That may be, Don Ciro."

"But I wish to treat with him, I tell you. Good heavens! what a man is this, who refuses to see me!" He stood there, a wild figure, his eyes glaring fiercely from his powder-grimed face, showing his teeth like a wild beast, and trembling with rage—then, "Water, water!" he gasped, "for the love of God, let me have a drop of water!"

Bianchi signed to a soldier, who ran forward with a pitcher. Ciro drank greedily, and would have handed it back.

"Give the rest to your comrades," said Bianchi; "and now, Don Ciro, defend yourself as long as you choose, but you can't escape. We don't care if we have the tower to-day or to-morrow, but have it we will."

"We are rich, *signore maggiore:* those who serve us are wise!"

It was an unlucky speech to make to one of General Church's officers, and Bianchi's wrath blazed out, "Rascal, assassin," he shouted, "get back to your tower! The parley is it an end."

With a curse Don Ciro withdrew, and as he did so a rattling fire came from the loopholes of the tower, killing two *voltigeurs* who were standing incautiously exposed.

The firing went on till evening, and then another parley was called. Ciro appeared again at the head of his ladder.

"Conduct me to the General, then."

"Only as a prisoner, Don Ciro."

"So be it, then;" and ordering his men to cease firing and lower the drawbridge, he crossed it rapidly, and in another moment was disarmed and bound. On being searched they found on him several amulets, some French songs, and a red pocket-book which contained a packet of poison, and his diploma as chief of the Decisi. It seems strange that, knowing his certain fate, he had not courage at last to "end all" by self-destruction.

Soon the whole band of brigands, strongly fettered and closely guarded, were on their march to Francavilla. Ciro kept a gloomy silence all the way, except once, when he suddenly broke out, rolling his eyes and gnashing his teeth. "For eighteen years I have been absolute master of the province. I have made fools of many generals—French, Italian, Swiss, German, Neapolitan—and now at last I have been made a fool of by this accursed Englishman!" After this he did not open his lips till he and his escort reached Francavilla.

Francavilla was illuminated that night—not for joy at the capture, but because the soldiers were few and the disaffected many, and it was safer that no corners should be left in darkness. So, by military order, every house and street and square blazed with light. The houses opposite the prison were occupied by soldiers, four *gendarmes* kept guard in the room where the fallen chief of assassins lay, four hussars kept the door, cavalry patrolled the street outside, and very glad and thankful were his captors to hand over their prey to the General when he arrived early in the morning.

Both the civil and military authorities would have had Ciro put to death then and there as an outlaw; but "No," said General Church. "I am quite aware that he is beyond the pale of the law, but he shall have a fair trial for all that. Oh yes, I daresay he has been tried and convicted a dozen times, but his friends shall not say we don't dare bring him to justice publicly, or that we fear a rescue." So Ciro Annichiarico was arraigned for his crimes, according to the usual forms. When he was first brought in he made a speech, which he addressed, as he thought, to General Church. Being told that the General was not present, and refused a private interview with him, "*Ho capito*" (I understand), he said, and from that time, all through his trial, never answered a question or spoke a word.

On the 8th of February 1818 he was led to his death through the streets of Francavilla, which were crowded with spectators, as were the roofs and windows too. The church-bells tolled, the black coffin was carried along, preceding the criminal, who walked between two files of soldiers, carrying himself with an air of haughty defiance, and turning scornfully from the Mission priests, who followed, anxious to call some feeling of repentance to this hardened soul. The piazza was filled with troops and guarded by cannon. In the centre waved the banner of the Decisi—black, with the insignia of death's-head and cross-bones—and close beside it stood a row of soldiers, carbine in hand. Ciro took his place, asking for wine-and-water, which was given him, and then turning to the priests with a snarl, "Away!" he said. "Am I not a priest? Am I not the

Abate Annichiarico, and your superior?" and to one kindly old priest, who, holding out the crucifix, begged him at least to give one sign of penitence, he added, pushing away the sacred sign with an impatient gesture, "Come, these fellows would as soon shoot you as me—so be off."

The crowd looked on in shuddering silence; then there was a murmur, "It is he—truly it is Don Ciro;" but there was no thought of a rescue, the people being overawed. A soldier came forward to tie a white bandage over his eyes.

"Ah, bah!" he said, with something of his usual swagger, "I will not die so; I will die like a soldier, my eyes open. Here is my breast —fire, my friends!"

"Not so, not so, villain!" cried the soldiers with one voice: "you shall die the death of a dog! You a soldier! Never, never! Murderer, prepare to die!"

These words rang loud and clear through the silence, and were taken up and repeated, first by two or three of the crowd, then swelling to a kind of groan—"*Scelerato! assassino! maladetto!*" reaching the ear on all sides. Then Ciro's courage forsook him; his head sank on his breast; passively he submitted to be blindfolded, knelt as he was desired to do, with his back to the file of soldiery. A blast from a trumpet, a volley of musketry, and he fell to the ground. But though twelve balls took effect, he still breathed, and a second volley was necessary to put an end to his sufferings. "As we perceived," said one of the soldiers, "that he was enchanted, we then loaded his own musket with a silver bullet, and this destroyed the spell." In another moment his head was severed from his body and held up before the spectators with proclamation, "This is the head of the chief of assassins, Ciro Annichiarico of Grottaglia."

It was over. Ciro was dead. There was an awestruck silence, such as follows the crash of some tremendous thunder-peal. Then heads were lifted, some one in the crowd cried, "*È ben fatto!*" (Well done!), and the crisis was over. "*Evviva, evviva il Generale!* we are free, we are free!" cried the multitude, waving their hats, and pressing round with shouts of joy; while General Church, riding forward, addressed the crowd, thanking them for their loyalty, and exhorting them to show its sincerity by helping him to clear their beautiful Apulia from the robbers and murderers who had so long infested it.

The head of Ciro was carried to Grottaglia, and placed in an iron cage over the gate of the city.

CHAPTER X.

THE CHIEFS OF THE DECISI.

GENERAL CHURCH'S MILITIA—TALK WITH COLONEL SCHMERBER—MARTINA—A WARNING—LECCE—AN ENVOY FROM CIRO—ARREST OF THE COUNCIL OF THE DECISI—THEIR EXECUTION—SCENE WITH DON FELICE.

THERE is no general rule without exceptions; but in the main it is true that sympathy begets sympathy, trust begets trust, and this seems to have been the reason that General Church and his little force were always so successful. They trusted him, and knew he trusted them—they would follow him anywhere; and he, on his part, cannot say enough in praise of his officers, and of those soldiers who had served with him, especially the troop of hussars whom he himself had formed, and his Greeks, who followed him here with the like devotion as in after years.

The militia, he says, were "sometimes very bad"; the *gendarmes* fine-looking men and well appointed, but so many of them belonged to various secret societies that they were not altogether trustworthy. In his own words, "the stuff to work upon was not so bad as had been represented," and he made the best of it.

There are many incidents which show how the frankness and trustfulness of the man appealed to those with whom he came in contact. Stern he could be, but it was when he met with cruelty or double-dealing. He was evidently on the most friendly terms with the gentlemen of the province who answered to his call, and he again and again refers to their loyal co-operation and friendliness.

Don Ciro could make nothing of this adversary, and even his own officers were puzzled sometimes at his apparent *insouciance*.

"I can't understand you, General," quoth Colonel Schmerber one winter's dawn, as they rode together down a steep and stony defile which led from Martina to the plain of Francavilla. It was bitter cold, and the long files of the troops were winding their way through the narrow Apennine road, with steep cliffs rising on either side. Here and there, through the semi-darkness, on some shelf of the rock, or where the space widened out, gleamed ghostlike one of those curious conical huts which the peasants build for shelter, of white stones without mortar; walls and roof alike of stones piled together, looking something like large ant-hills, and white as snow. General Church and his chief of the staff had halted, and were watching the troops filing by. The General smiled.

" What can't you understand, Schmerber?"

" Why, General, we have been for a week at Martina on the look-out for Don Ciro, knowing it was one of his favourite lurking-places. Nevertheless, you have been about among the people without precautions, and never asked a question about the fellow all the time we were there! Oh, people were surprised at it, I can tell you!"

" I learnt everything I wanted to know. Besides, asking questions is your business, *mon cher*, not mine."

" Well, General, it was only Don Ciro's native modesty which prevented his dining with you. He was in Martina all the time, and probably is not far off from us at this moment."

" Very likely," tranquilly replied General Church; " let us hope that we may make him wish himself farther off before long."

" And," continued the colonel, impressively, " he was much astonished that you never mentioned his name at Martina."

" Oh ho! he thinks he has soft hands to

K

deal with, no doubt! But let us see what Bianchi says;" and Major Bianchi was summoned.

"Well, Bianchi," said the General, "I am anxious to hear what Don Ciro said about me."

The major's eyes twinkled, despite an attempt to assume a solemn and deprecatory air.

"Indeed, *Eccellenza*, I dare not. I positively can't repeat the language he made use of in speaking of your Excellency. Pray excuse me!"

"Bah, Bianchi, out with it!"

"Well, General, it comes to this: Don Ciro is equally astonished and mortified at your want of interest in him; he declares that you and your officers are—*con rispetto*—a pack of asses; and of you especially he observes, '*È una bestia, è una bestia*, who knows nothing about affairs of importance! But I'll pull his house about his ears,' he said, clenching his fists and swearing in a manner which I would not repeat to your Excellency for worlds. 'As to his officers, what good are they but to eat and drink? I'll have their lives, every man of them! Could you have believed it? It is incredible, yet it is perfectly true, that this fool of a General'—*con rispetto* again—'has never once mentioned my name in Martina. Never spoken of me—me—Don Ciro Annichiarico! Better generals than he have trembled at my name. But he shall pay for it! He shall pay for it! *Bestia!*'"

"All right," said General Church; "the rascal's vanity will prove his downfall, and we shall soon have him rush upon his fate. Then, when he is in the middle of the net, we'll pull the strings, and—*addio*, Don Ciro!"

But this conversation took place as the troops rode *out* of Martina. Let us go back a little, and accompany the General as he rode in to this same place, on his way to Lecce, in the early part of the year 1818.

Martina, he says, is a little town of 15,000 inhabitants, lying on the top of a hill, about five miles from Lecce. The place was friendly to Don Ciro Annichiarico, who often made it his headquarters, appearing fearlessly in its streets at mid-day. On the other hand, the Duchess of Martina was a great friend of the General, and was now residing in Martina; and Colonel Schmerber, chief of the staff, had received private letters from two principal inhabitants of the place, expressing anxiety for the General's arrival.

The troops halted on a hillside opposite Martina, while General Church took out his spy-glass to reconnoitre the place. The troops shouted, "*Evviva nostro Generale!*" while he gave orders that they should form in line of battle and march down the hill, and then up the opposite hill into the town. But just then a stir and movement was visible at the gates of the little city, and a halt was called, while the spy-glass was put into requisition again. "They are coming out to meet us," said General Church; and so they were. Down the opposite hillside they came, a picturesque though not very orderly procession. The bishop, a stately figure, in mitre and cope, his cross borne before him, followed by his clergy; the *sindaco* and the principal citizens; and pressing round and behind them, as many of the inhabitants of the city as could find any excuse for doing so—men and maidens, women with babes in their arms or brown-eyed toddlers clinging to their skirts, old men staff in hand, wild-looking lads,—some following, some in groups and knots outside the gate, watching with anxious curiosity. On the other slope the troops descended to meet them, flags flying, drums and trumpets sounding,—and a very fine show they made, says General Church.

At the bottom of the hill the two parties met, and then came the alighting from horseback, the mutual compliments and salutations, the bishop's benediction to the troops as they filed past; and then they all entered the city, where the General and his staff were most hospitably received in the house of Don Martino di Ricupero; and the people, seeing them on such friendly terms with the bishop and the *sindaco*, even raised a *Viva* as they rode through the streets.

General Church's account of his first evening at Martina affords us a glimpse of the man, and may show what gave him his power over all who came in contact with him.

Imagine, then, the great rooms of Don Martino di Ricupero's house all ablaze in honour of the distinguished guest,—the tables of the dining-room loaded with wines and viands of all kinds; the dancing-room crowded by the good citizens, their wives and daughters; the light of innumerable wax-candles falling on tapestried walls, and fair faces, and the gay uniforms of the soldier-guests; and all the company anxious to see the Englishman, who moved about, slight, alert, keen-eyed, thoroughly enjoying it all, the music, the conversation—he was an excellent Italian scholar—and though not dancing himself, encouraging his officers to do so, and watching the fair dancers—Martina is famous, he tells us, for the beauty of its women—with delight. "Enjoying it," he says, "with all his heart, and especially the conversation of the every-way interesting duchess and her sweet young daughter!"

Therefore he was by no means pleased to be interrupted by a sinister-looking individual who, edging his way through the crowd, murmured a request for a few moments' private interview on a matter of great importance. It was annoying; but business before pleasure! So, excusing himself to the charming duchess, the General followed the man into a little side-room which was empty, and requested to know what he wanted.

"*Eccellenza*," he began in a hesitating voice.

"Speak, signore," was the answer.

"Take care!" with an impressive shake of the head and raised forefinger.

"Take care of what, signore?"

"Has not your Excellency heard? This house——"

"Is an excellent house—I can see that."

"But—but—your Excellency, the *padrone!*"

"The *padrone* is a man of honour."

"*I* did not say so, your Excellency."

"No matter; *I* say so."

"He is a friend of Don Ciro's."

"May be so, signore."

"Your Excellency knows it! and you dare trust yourself in his house?"

"Why not, signore?"

"But, *Madonna mia!* consider, your Excellency! What could be easier? A bowl of soup—a cup of coffee—a dish of olives——"

"Oh, I see! But why not a glass of good rosolio, signore?" and the General laughed.

"Your Excellency treats the matter lightly," said the man, amazed that his suggestion of poison had taken so little effect. "I hope you may not repent it. At any rate, you have been warned, and I can say no more."

"You have said quite enough, signore— rather too much, in fact. Well, Don Martino shall hear of the matter."

"For the love of God, don't betray me!" gasped the poor man. "If you do, I am a dead man. If Ciro knew that I had spoken to your Excellency—it was with the best intentions——"

"Oh, don't alarm yourself, my friend," said the General, recovering his good-humour; "I don't mean to mention your name, and, to set your mind at rest, I will promise not to say a word of the matter till I have left Martina. Ah!" as a knock was heard at the door, "does that say that supper is ready? And so am I!"

The General adds that, though not a supper-eater in general, on this occasion he did not spare Don Martino's soup, nor his olives, nor the delicious *ricotta* sent from his farm outside the town, nor his excellent coffee, and that he finished up with a glass of rosolio di Bari. Neither did he choose to hurry away from Martina, but spent three more pleasant days there, and tells us that it was with great regret that he gave the order to depart, leaving the brightly lighted ball-room at four o'clock on a bitter winter's morning, and marching out, not as they entered, but silently, without blast of trumpet or beat of drum.

From thence they went to Francavilla, where their reception was not gratifying. The streets were thronged with a scowling rabble, wrapped in their long cloaks, and not a single high-peaked hat was lifted to salute them as they rode along. However, one gentleman ventured to receive the General and his staff for the night, and next day they rode to Lecce.

For [says General Church] Francavilla is an open town, with wide streets, and standing in the plain, so that we could take possession of it at any moment, while the Governor of Lecce was urgent in sending messenger after messenger to say that he could no longer maintain himself there without protection.

So to Lecce they went, the bright little capital, with its white houses, and the little streams running through the streets, and were received there, not very cordially, but without open show of resistance. It is true that the inhabitants had sent a deputation desiring the General *not* to enter into their city; but, fortunately for themselves, the deputation took the wrong road, and never met the unwelcome visitors at all! and when the good people of Lecce heard how well things had gone off at Martina, the courage of the Filadelfi, Patrioti Europei, Filosofi, and other secret societies, cooled somewhat, in spite of their boasts of what they meant to do should the English General presume to set foot in their city.

Here came Don Martino di Ricupero to join the General, riding over one evening to pour out his thanks because the General had trusted him, and refused to listen to evil tales. "True, he had been a protector of Don Ciro; but what could he do? The Government does nothing to protect us, and if a man is not Ciro's friend, one dare not stir out—nay, one is not safe in one's own house, one is no longer master of one's own estate, of one's own servants even; but as to being a *friend* of Don Ciro! signore, he has no greater enemy than I! Your Excellency has trusted me, has refused to believe the calumnies brought against me. I am yours; command me and all that I have!"

At this time [General Church says] murder was the

order of the day, and the number of assassinations committed weekly was from twenty to twenty-five. The magistrate's report always ended with " The assassins are unknown." The assassins were not unknown, but fear prevented their being denounced. People dared not travel unless they belonged to some secret society or other. The local authorities were thoroughly frightened, and law was paralysed.

Such was the state of things during that January 1818, which General Church spent for the most part in Lecce, and during which he met with some curious experiences. Let us relate one from his own papers, first saying that there was a great deal of gaiety going on in Lecce,—balls and banquets, masquerades and theatrical performances, in all of which the General freely joined, giving and receiving hospitality, mixing frankly with the people, and becoming, as well as his troops, very popular with them.

One day after dinner General Church retired to his private room to study reports and meditate upon plans, leaving his officers and aides-de-camp to their own ways of amusement and occupation. Presently there was a knock at the door. A major of militia, said the aide-de-camp who knocked, desired a private audience with his Excellency. He was admitted, for the General never refused audience, in spite of many warnings from anxious friends, who feared that the assassin's stiletto might lurk under the long cloak. The General did not much like the appearance of his visitor—a down-looking man, with a restless uneasy way of moving—and addressed him sharply, " Now, sir, what is your business? We are alone, and you can speak freely." The major seemed thoroughly taken aback by this abruptness, and falteringly replied that, "*Con rispetto,* he had desired to speak with his Excellency—not that he had anything very special to communicate."

The General turned upon him with haughty displeasure, fixing his keen eyes on the major's face. "How is this, *signore maggiore?* Let me know at once what brought you here. Why did you ask for a private audience? Answer me that, signore."

"That poor *abate!*" The words came out in hesitating fashion, accompanied by a furtive glance, to see how they were taken.

"Oh ho!" said the General, his eyes still on his interlocutor; "and what of him, pray?"

"Why, perhaps your Excellency looks on him with an unfavourable eye."

"Pshaw, *signore maggiore!* Can you deny that the *abate* Annichiarico is a scoundrel?"

"Perhaps, your Excellency, he is not so bad as you think. If your Excellency would just listen to explanations."

"Go on, signore; I am listening."

"Signore, he was in Lecce a day or two ago."

"I know it; and what of that?" And as the major stared at him, dumfounded at hearing that this fact *was* known, the General added in a louder key, "I repeat my question. What did you come here to say about Don Ciro Annichiarico?"

The major looked as if he wished himself elsewhere, and his mission at an end, as he faltered, "He is a brave man, your Excellency—much beloved in the province."

"I pity the province with all my heart, if it has any liking for such a ruffian."

"He has powerful friends."

"Including yourself, no doubt, signore."

"All the district of Taranto is for him."

"And your own town of Ciglia, and the militia, of which you are so worthy an officer."

The poor major was making nothing by his mission. How did this strange Englishman come to know all these facts, which were to have been used by degrees, to impress him with the desirability of making an ally of Ciro? Yet to go away having done nothing was to turn the terrible brigand chief into an enemy; so he said in his most insinuating tone, "If your Excellency would have him as a friend—remembering that he is powerful—and rich."

The General sprang to his feet, his eyes flashing with anger. "What is your name, signore?" he demanded.

"Il Maggiore Vitali, at your Excellency's commands," was the trembling reply.

"A charming mission this of yours, Signore Maggiore Vitali! I wish you well out of it. Now then, a question or two. What have you to say about the murders committed by Don Ciro? the robbing of houses, the plundering of the country?"

"Oh, your Excellency, he is calumniated! All lies, your Excellency; he is an honest man."

"How about his firing on my troops?"

"*Pazzia*, your Excellency, *pazzia, pazzia!*"

The General looked down upon him, and his voice became quiet and stern. "How about the murder of the young Princess of Martano?"

"That—I assure your Excellency—it was altogether—it was a lie to say he did it."

The story of this cruel and brutal murder has been told in Chapter VII., and at this answer the General's anger, which had been smouldering, burst forth into fire. "Get out of this house instantly, vile messenger of an infamous assassin!" he shouted, and suiting the action to the word, he seized the unfortunate major of militia by the nape of his neck with one hand, opening the door with the other, and, with a judicious kick, sent him spinning along the gallery outside, which was filled with officers and gentlemen of the town! What a break to the friendly conversation which was going on between hosts and guests! How they must have stared in amazement at the appearance of the unlucky messenger in such wise! The General, the most courteous of men too, who would have expected him thus to dismiss a visitor?

"Take this fellow to the castle," shouted the angry chief, "and see him in safe-keeping there till I send for him again." And so it was done, and the luckless envoy had full time for reflection before the day of his relief arrived.

Let us relate another story which will also show General Church's mode of dealing with the people under his charge.

In this same pleasant little city of Lecce there dwelt at this period, and had dwelt for some time, a certain Don Felice, a lawyer, rich and prosperous, in spite of hard times and a large family to support and place out in the world. How had Don Felice grown so rich? How was it that his voice was always the loudest and boldest at any assembly? that his fellow-townsmen listened to him so deferentially, and seemed so anxious to keep on good terms with him? Just for this reason—and a very good reason it was at that time—that he was known to be a leading man in the sect of the Filadelfi, one of the secret societies of Apulia, and a personal friend of Don Ciro, the dreaded chief of the Decisi. So Don Felice could swagger along the streets and give loud greetings in the piazza, and be listened to with eager deference while he declared his opinion that this new English General was as great a fool as his predecessors, and that the free people of Apulia would have none of him.

There was a great meeting — *campo*, they called it—of the Filadelfi one January evening, 1818, presided over by Don Felice, at which he proposed, amid loud applause, that the murder of the English General should be decreed. No sooner said than done. The trumpet was blown, the decree was read aloud dooming to sudden and violent death Il Generale Giorgio (their rendering of General Church's name), as a traitor to humanity: the decree was dated January 4, the fourth year of the Salentine Republic, and signed by Don Felice and others. Then came the question, How was the decree to be carried out? There had been plenty of bluster till that was asked; but when the president called upon the brethren to volunteer for the deed which would clear Apulia of this foe of the human race, his impassioned eloquence seemed to fall flat. Nobody responded, and after several vain appeals, he proposed that the decree should be forwarded to Don Ciro Annichiarico, who doubtless would find an instrument to carry it into execution. This was thought a delightful idea, and the assembly broke up with the comfortable feeling that somebody else would be found to bell the cat, while they remained safe and snug at home.

The decree, therefore, was sent by sure and secret messenger to Don Ciro, who very willingly undertook to see it carried out, and, as the first step, sent it on to his principal lieutenant, Gaetano Caffieri, who dwelt at Don Ciro's own town, his birthplace, Grottaglia, desiring him to call together a *Decisione*, or solemn meeting of the officials of the Decisi, to pass this and some other like decrees. By this time Ciro's affairs were becoming desperate, and his last attempt at a general rising and combination of forces at San Marzano, and his flight thence and subsequent wanderings and capture, have been told before.

If General Church could be got rid of by

assassination, the whole face of affairs would be changed. His army would disperse; the Government would go on in their former way, temporising and shutting their eyes to the misery of the province; Don Ciro would reappear triumphant, and more than ever the real ruler of Apulia. However, the decree never had a chance of being promulgated; for the news of the rout and taking of San Marzano reached Grottaglia the same day, and at night one of the citizens, taking heart from the news, crept to the quarters of the English General, and told him of the *Decisione* to be held that night at Grottaglia, and that the principal officers of the Decisi would certainly be there, as not only the General, but all the gentlemen of Lecce who had joined him, were to be sentenced to death by assassination.

Hardly had Signore Giosotti departed, furnished with full instructions from the General, when a despatch arrived from Captain Montorj, from San Marzano, giving an account of the capture of the place, and begging leave to pursue those of the brigands who had escaped. In reply the General sent a public letter of thanks to his brave troops, desiring them to march at once to a place which he mentioned, some twenty miles away. But there was also a private despatch, directing that when San

L

Marzano was left well behind, the troops should make a sharp turn, and march as silently as possible to a *masseria* (farmhouse) about half a mile from Grottaglia, where they would meet a guide, and receive further instructions as to their movements.

At nightfall, then, they started, a large body of horse and foot, well armed, and led by some of General Church's most trusted officers; and at the *masseria*, half a mile from Grottaglia, were met by Signore Giosotti, masked and wearing the uniform of a *gendarme*.

The night was cold, moonless, starless. It was midnight, and Grottaglia was wrapped in sleep. Not a man was to be seen, not a dog barked, as the foot-soldiers threaded their silent way along the narrow streets which led to the Piazza; while the cavalry, by Signore Giosotti's directions, guarded all the entrances to the town, especially the byways, which were generally used by the *contrabbandistas* and brigands.

The cavalry were desired to remain quiet unless they heard firing, a good deal of firing — not just a few shots, but fifty or sixty volleys — in which case they were to enter the town, and ride straight to the Piazza.

The infantry, commanded by Captain Fusco,

meanwhile had crept, almost on tiptoe, along the narrow, silent streets. The people of Grottaglia had heard nothing of the fight and capture at San Marzano, and slept in fancied security, unwitting of the neighbourhood of any foe. So a platoon of infantry was posted in the Piazza, small parties were placed to guard the ends of the streets leading to it, and Fusco with some twenty picked men was guided by Signore Giosotti to the house where the Council of Blood was sitting, and the slumberers of Grottaglia remained undisturbed.

It was a large house, and most of its windows looked out into the street. So did the front door, before which Signore Giosotti and a dozen men were posted, with orders to remain quiet in the shadow, unless any one attempted to leave the house, in which case he was to be arrested and held fast. Fusco and his men —his picked twenty—crept round the corner of the street until they reached the back-door. The front door had been securely bolted, but to their surprise the back-door was not only unbolted, but standing a little ajar, and on gently pushing it and slipping inside, Major Fusco found the sentinel—fast asleep! There he sat, his hand on his pistol, his carbine beside him, the silver death's-head hanging round his neck, his high-crowned hat shading his swarthy features. It was the work of a moment to seize him, and a few energetic and expressive signs made him aware that his only escape from instant death lay in his silently showing the way up - stairs to the council-chamber, which he accordingly did, being gently urged thereto by the bayonets of the soldiers.

Let us take a glance at the council-chamber up-stairs, and at what is going on there.

It is a large gloomy room, scantily lighted by one brass lamp, which stands in the middle of a long table covered with black cloth. On the table, in front of the lamp, is a human skull, and scattered about are books and papers, pistols and stilettoes; against the wall, at the head of the table, hangs the famous black standard of the Decisi. Ten armed men sit round the table; and an evil-looking set they are. These are the officials of the *Decisione*—not the paid plunderers and assassins who swept down over the country, but men who took rank in Grottaglia as respectable citizens, who lived in their own houses, and had their own professions. They had grown rich upon the terror they inspired, these officers of Don Ciro: it was their business to levy contributions, to sign decrees of assassination, to fix the amount of a subsidy which would avail to spare the life of some wealthy citizen. There were even cases when some harmless gentleman received a decree calling upon him to surrender some piece of land or house which had taken the fancy of one of these mysterious despots, and to refuse meant that homesteads might be burned to the ground, cattle stolen, women seized, their hair cut off (a common mode of punishment), themselves subjected to every indignity; there were instances even of women being stripped naked and left bound to trees by the highway, as a warning to their families who had hesitated to comply with the threats of these wretches, who now sat round the table to sign their infamous decrees.

The door opened, slowly, silently; through the semi-darkness, forms entered and took up their places between the Decisi and the door; bayonets gleamed darkly in their hands as they moved. The Decisi turned their heads and watched them with a kind of fascinated silence, too utterly surprised to rise or speak : they sat pale, rigid, as if turned to stone; their shaking hands could not grasp their weapons; the cold drops of perspiration stood on their brows; they made not the slightest attempt at resistance. In perfect silence they were seized, disarmed, bound hand and foot, chained two and two; their papers, their manuscripts, the silver trumpet and the black banner, were thrown into a chest which stood there, and securely locked up therein, to be sent to headquarters; and before the people of Grottaglia were awakened from their slumbers, the troops, their captives, the arms and papers, were well on their way to Francavilla, where, it is needless to say, they were welcomed warmly by General Church.

At Francavilla the Military Commission was sitting, and there was no difficulty in finding witnesses to the evil deeds of the prisoners, and they were all condemned to death.

General Church gives an account of their execution, which, he says, struck terror into the hearts of the disaffected, and was the deathblow of Ciro's power. He tells how he sat on horseback in the market-place of Francavilla, crowded with country-folk, and how his eye fell upon thousands of figures wrapped in their long cloaks, their peaked hats hiding sullen, downcast faces; and how he remembered that his soldiers were but 500 in number, among all that surging multitude! But if they were few, they were well armed and trusty, his true and tried comrades, and they sat their horses sword in hand, ready to charge at a moment's notice; and the approaches to the Piazza were commanded by cannon, and by each stood gunners, the matches burning in their hands,—and the people knew their man, and feared him. All the more necessary were these precautions, because the General had been warned that arms were hidden under the long cloaks, and that friends of the prisoners had been in and out among the people, urging them to a rescue.

Presently the crowd parted as the condemned men were brought forth, chained, and marching between files of armed soldiery. A priest accompanied them, and as he held aloft the crucifix he exhorted them to repentance, and promised pardon, even at the last hour, if they would confess their crimes and pray for pardon.

All their glory was departed. These men, who had held in their hands the power of life and death a week ago, before whom their fellows had cringed for protection, now, poor wretches, shuffled along chained, with blanched cheeks, looking round with wild, eager eyes among the crowd for a friendly face, and seeing none, no hope of rescue, crying out to one and another for pardon. "I killed your father—your brother—pardon me! I caused the death of such and such a one—pardon, pardon, for Jesu's sake!" and the murmur of forgiveness from the awestruck crowd was the only sound in reply.

No, there was no hope for them in this life,

though they had offered 20,000 ducats to the judge of the tribunal, and had thought such a bribe would surely have been effectual in saving their lives.

Now they were placed in line, the musketeers facing them, and the judge-advocate read in a loud clear voice a list of the crimes for which they were condemned to die: then followed a blast from a trumpet—their own trumpet, blown when a decree of death was promulgated. The people listened in shuddering silence. Another blast, and another; and then, following the third, a volley of musketry, and the ten criminals fell dead to the ground.

There ensued a pause of horrified silence as the bloody heads, struck off by the executioner, were held up before the people— afterwards to be set up in the various places where their chief crimes had been committed —and then the crowd melted quietly, gradually away. Not a murmur was heard, though there were sullen looks on many faces at first; and those who lingered began to venture to lift their hats in greeting to the General as he rode slowly round the Piazza, accompanied by his staff. Finally, the people gathered in groups and looked with interest on the band of veterans who, at the word of command, paraded before their chief, while he addressed them in a few ringing words, and then dismissed them to their quarters.

Let us shift the scene to Lecce, and see what is going on there some months after the execution of the Decisi took place.

It was summer-time—bright, clear, burning-hot. The grass was brown, the bushes were dusty; the cicalas chirped day and night; the little streams ran refreshingly through the streets of Lecce; the white houses were blinding in the sunlight, and the green jalousies were fast closed for a great part of the day. Don Felice went on his way as usual, with a cheerful feeling that whoever else was in danger, he at least was safe. Who could whisper a word against this virtuous citizen and hard-working lawyer? His name has never been mentioned in connection with the assassins who had paid the penalty of their crimes. Ciro Annichiarico, who might have told tales, was dead. Nothing had been heard of that decree which had been forwarded to him months ago — therefore, presumably, it had been destroyed, without ever reaching the hands for which it was *not* intended; and Don Felice wended his daily way to the courthouse, pleaded for his clients, bullied his adversaries, talked of the past crimes of Ciro with virtuous indignation, uttered the most patriotic sentiments, preached law and order to his fellows, and came home to his siesta and his cigar, to eat his dinner and play with his children: and all these civil duties and domestic pleasures took an added zest from the secret consciousness that he had had a lucky escape! "And oh, what a fool was this General Giorgio! Truly these English *are* fools, and mighty easy to hoodwink! We could tell him, if we would, a thing or two; but how well for us that he is blind! Why, he loves me as—as I deserve! He consults me even, and thanks me for my opinion, as indeed he should do, for who can advise him on matters of law better than I?" and with a chuckle of superior sagacity Don Felice would bid farewell to the friend who had accompanied him so far along the shady side of the street, and take the turning which led to his own comfortable house.

So Don Felice was gratified, but by no means surprised, when one day he got a message through a friend from the General, with his compliments. "You will see Don Felice? Very good. I should be glad of his valuable opinion—a legal matter: who could advise me better? Beg him to favour me with his presence early this afternoon."

"Ah, but certainly—with pleasure. As his Excellency is pleased to say, who could advise him better? My poor endeavours will be always at his Excellency's service." And early in the afternoon he went off to headquarters, scrupulously attired in black, his legs encased in black silk stockings, and his knee-buckles and shoe-buckles resplendent with brilliants, not to mention a handsome diamond ring on his finger.

People greeted the successful advocate as he strutted along the street with his head well thrown back, but he could only spare for his acquaintances a hasty wave of the hand, a passing word—"Business, my friend; pardon me—but his Excellency sends for me — a little matter — my poor advice — always glad to be of service;" and thus he reached the General's quarters, and, after a courteous reception, was soon holding forth on the differences between English law and the Code Napoléon.

Don Felice got quite excited over English laws, English ways, Englishmen. He adored them all! In truth, he was almost an Englishman himself, in heart! As for the General, he was his servant for life, in gratitude for all he had done for the country. Ah! the wretchedness that had been; and now (spreading forth his hands, and raising his eyes to heaven) his Excellency could not imagine—no one could who had not groaned for years under the yoke of the detestable Ciro Annichiarico. A man!—a demon rather! No words could express Don Felice's detestation of the fallen chief, or his admiration and gratitude for the man who had overthrown him.

To all this General Church listened in silence—an ominous silence, if Don Felice had only known it—his head a little raised, and his keen blue eyes looking out from beneath their dark brows, somewhere over his companion's head. Presently he interrupted him somewhat abruptly: "Don Felice, pardon me—shall we go into the next room? I have something to say to you which will be best said in private, without fear of interruption. So—sit down, signore—no, not there," as Don Felice was about to dispose of himself on a comfortable couch—"oblige me by taking that chair, and giving me your fullest attention."

He spoke in a stern tone, and Don Felice's sallow cheeks flushed a dull red; then they turned ghastly pale, as the General stepped to the door, locked it, and put the key in his pocket; then he laid his loaded pistols on the mantelpiece, within reach of his hand,

and turned to the unfortunate advocate, who sat trembling, and wiping the drops of perspiration from his brow, while his brilliant buckles flashed with the shaking of his limbs.

The General watched the frightened wretch, and contempt was mingled with his wrath, and a certain sense of the comic too, which stood Don Felice in good stead.

"How many children have you?" he asked.

"Ten—at your Excellency's feet."

"And what will become of them when you are—gone?"

At this question Don Felice threw himself on the ground, and could not articulate a word.

"Get up, you dastardly villain!" said the General, as he drew out a paper; "do you know this handwriting?"

It was the decree, which had been found among other papers at Grottaglia, some six months before.

"*O cielo,*" groaned the advocate, "I am lost!"

"Let me read it to you," said the General —"'Fourth year of the Salentine Republic. Fourth of January'—are you listening?"

"*Pietà, pietà!*" groaned the unlucky man, flinging himself anew on the floor, and grovelling at the General's feet.

"Get up, I say, and listen. 'Tis your own production, your own handwriting."

"Spare me, spare me, your Excellency, for my poor children's sake!" and Don Felice sobbed like a child. "An Englishman is always brave, always generous!"

The General looked down on the wretch grovelling at his feet, and laughed contemptuously. "To think that such a paltry scoundrel as that should have tried to compass the death of any man! Now, Don Felice, listen to me. Take pen and paper and write another decree," said the General, grimly. "You expressed yourself very well and clearly in ordering my death, and now you shall write your own sentence. Come, get up and write it."

"Oh, your Excellency—a glass of water!"

"Not a drop till you have finished your task. Remember, your life is in my hands."

At this Don Felice fairly fainted away, and the General rang the bell, and called his aide-de-camp, Captain Quandel, to fetch a glass of brandy-and-water and a cup of coffee. The door having been unlocked and these refreshments brought, "Lift him up, Quandel," said the General. "The rascal would have murdered us all, and is half-dead with fright at being found out."

"Upon my word, General, I believe he's dead altogether," said the aide-de-camp, as he tried to lift up the body, which lay a senseless heap apparently, with arms and head hanging helplessly down.

"Dead? not he! or at least I know a spell which will bring him to life," answered the General; and in a low voice he pronounced the words, "I pardon you."

Immediately the limbs stiffened, the head was a little raised, and the eyes opened. "Pardon! did your Excellency say pardon?" gasped the dead man.

"Yes, but on conditions. Drink that brandy-and-water; and now take the coffee. Now listen to me. As far as the attempt on my own life is concerned, I pardon you fully, and that for two reasons: first, for the sake of your children; and secondly, out of pure contempt for a man who, while he is a bully and a demagogue in public, can't look the man whom he would have murdered in the face! But you must make full confession of your evil deeds—reveal the plots—give up the papers—let me have a list of your accomplices—give information about the secret societies with which you are connected."

Don Felice was only too glad to do anything, to reveal anything, which might save his own skin; and Quandel accompanied him to his house to make a thorough search for compromising documents. What a difference between the going out and the coming home of Don Felice! How meekly he followed at Captain Quandel's heels! how eagerly he pulled out drawers, and unlocked chests and cabinets, and displayed all the documents contained therein!

A few days later General Church sent again to request the honour of his presence. Don Felice obeyed, dejected and trembling, not knowing what fresh agony to expect. What was his relief when, after a severe lecture, delivered in presence of the discreet and trusty Colonel Schmerber, chief of the staff, and Captain Quandel, aide-de-camp, the General tore up the fatal decree, with all the signatures attached thereto.

Happy Don Felice! With what expressions of eternal gratitude for the future and penitence' for the past, with what asseverations of loyalty to the State, did he take his leave and go his way! And oh, the joy of treading again the familiar streets, and finding himself at home among his family, with the consciousness that that terrible piece of paper was no longer in existence!

CHAPTER XI.

CIRO AND THE VARDARELLI.

CASTEL DEL MONTE—*RENCONTRE* WITH VARDARELLI—SENDING OUT A SPY — MEETING BETWEEN CIRO AND DON GAETANO—THE SPY'S NARRATIVE.

WE have said that Don Ciro Annichiarico had two meetings with Don Gaetano Vardarelli. This was towards the end of his career, when he was trying to gather together all the different secret societies—Carbonari, Calderari, Filadelfi, &c.—under the black banner of the Decisi, and to get himself acknowledged as head of them all. It was a last desperate move on his part, by way of making head against the enemy whom he had learnt to fear, the first man of whom he had said, "He will be too much for me!"

The first meeting between the chief of the Decisi and the chief of the Vardarelli took place in a deserted chapel, where Don Ciro, in his quality of priest, opened proceedings by celebrating Mass! Of the other meeting we must give a fuller account.

Not far from the river Ofanto (the ancient Aufidus) stands the Castello del Monte, built by the Emperor Frederick II. in the year 1238. From its great octagon tower one may overlook the battle-field of Bayard and Gonsalvo di Cordova; one may see Barletta, where the challenge was fought in 1503, between twelve French champions on the one side and twelve Italians on the other; many other towns, too, catch the eye—Trani with its flat roofs, and Andria, and Bisceglia, Covato among the olives; and beyond the green plain, dotted with the white towns and villages, one sees the blue waters of the Adriatic.

When General Church visited Castel del Monte, this ancient dwelling of many a gay and gallant knight of yore was half in ruins, and deserted by all but the brigands, who had made it their haunt and stronghold. He speaks with enthusiasm of the glorious view, and conjures up visions of those who had stood on those battlements long, long ago; especially his favourite hero, Manfred, the brave and beautiful; and then of those who at different periods had strained their eyes to watch pirate fleets turning their prows landward, Normans or Saracens, French or Turks or Spaniards, all bent on plunder. All have ravaged that fair plain in turn, he says, and now (in 1818) the traveller, as he traverses it and comes in sight of the brigands' stronghold, crosses himself and hurries along trembling.

Within the castle (at that time at least) are traces of its former magnificence, in the lofty chambers, the inner courtyard where 300 men could easily be drawn up in order, the columns and mantelpieces of pink marble, the wide portals and noble halls. Here it was that the second meeting between Ciro Annichiarico and Gaetano Vardarelli took place, in the end of the year 1817.

Two officers returning from a confidential mission were overtaken by the darkness on their way to Barletta, where at that time General Church had his headquarters. One of these officers was a captain in the Neapolitan army, the other, named Viti, a brigadier of *gendarmerie*, and they had with them a peasant to act as guide, but who, just then, was as much perplexed as they were to find the right road. So they dismounted, and began to thread their way among scattered trees and brushwood and a maze of turfy paths, hoping to strike upon the highroad which led to Barletta. The guide was sure it must be close at hand, and once find that, he assured them that the way home would be easy enough; but meanwhile the night was dark, the rain fell fast, and the gusty wind would not let them keep their cigars alight!

Presently they saw a light shining at some distance, and the two officers with joyful exclamations were about to mount and ride in that direction; but they were met by vehement protestations from their guide, who declared that the light was probably a jack-o'-lantern, that the country about there was haunted by evil spirits, and sagely reminded them of the proverb, *Piano, piano, sano, sano!* The discussion was closed by the brigadier holding up a warning hand; and, sure enough, voices and horse-hoofs were heard at a distance along the road of which they were in search. Feeling that it was fortunate for them that the night *was* dark, and they off the highroad, they held a hurried consultation, the guide, half out of his wits with terror, crossing himself and murmuring, "O Madonna, Madonna! *O povero me!* It will be the Vardarelli!"

"Hold your tongue," said Viti, "or we shall all be dead men," and rapidly they withdrew with their horses deeper among the trees; but curiosity proving too strong for the two soldiers, they left their horses under charge of their guide, and crept cautiously and noiselessly over the ground, all broken with turfy mounds and brushwood, until they found a safe lurking-place, not far from the shady highroad, but divided from it by a thick hedge. By this time the ringing of horse-hoofs and voices and laughter was distinctly audible, and the riders had evidently no thought of unfriendly listeners within earshot. They rode slowly, talked loudly; they jested and swore and called to each other; two or three women were with them, strapping *brigandesse*, armed likewise, and as ready to bandy blows and jests and oaths as the rest of the company.

" 'Tis the *comitiva*, without doubt," whispered Viti : " that's Gaetano's voice," as a tall cavalier stayed his horse just opposite to them, and so near the hedge that they could hear every word he said. " Bah ! " he was saying, with a laugh, " they're afraid of us." " Let them come," said another voice; " we'll soon make fritters of the whole lot of them." " Bravo, brother ! " answered the first speaker; "but I wish I could get to the bottom of the English General's schemes all the same. Unluckily all the *gendarmes* are on his side, and those fellows can fight if they choose." " *Bagattella !* " cried a third; " why, they are all Good Cousins " (the name given to the Carbonari); " they are bound to join us when the time comes." " What news from Bari, Giovanni?" asked the chief from some one behind, who rode forward and answered, "I saw the new general there. He was buying horses and organising fresh troops of cavalry." "That's bad." "And I think he has some plan against us." "Oh, as for that, every new general begins that way!" "I saw him with my own eyes," persisted Giovanni, "buying horses and marshalling his men. I could not hear much, it is true; the devil himself does not know what that man has got in his head!" "We'll cut it off one of these days and find out," laughed another; and then, at the chief's command, the *comitiva* rode on, with direction to go to Castel del Monte. But Don Gaetano stayed behind, and we may imagine that the pulses of the two officers beat faster than was pleasant when they saw his dark figure riding close on the other side of the hedge and heard him say, "Giovanni, a word with you." Did he suspect that enemies might be lurking anywhere at hand? Had any involuntary sound caught his ever-watchful ear? No, thank heaven! he had only stopped for a few words of private consultation with his favourite brother Giovanni, and the two officers from their hiding-place had the full benefit of the conversation.

"What do you think of Don Ciro, brother?

We shall meet him to-night." "He is a stout fellow," was the answer, "and has killed a good many in his time." "But can we depend upon him?" "Can he depend upon us?" "What do you mean?" angrily. "When did I, Gaetano Vardarelli, ever betray a friend?" "But is Don Ciro a friend?" "I suppose so. Are we not fighting for the same cause?" "*Per Santo Diavolo!* once a traitor, always a traitor, and Don Ciro has known how to leave a comrade entangled in the net, while he slipped through the meshes himself. But that is your affair, not ours. You order, we obey; and I believe the path you lead us will bring us to the devil one of these days." There was a pause, and then the same voice went on again, "But, *signore comandante*, remember that you are a bigger man than Don Ciro. You command almost the whole of Apulia, he is only master of a province or two: so don't be in a hurry; and if any one is to be—you understand— rather he than you." "Well," answered the Vardarelli chief, "we must find out what his strength is, and if it is worth our while, we can enter into a league with him." "You would be wiser to mind your own business and let Ciro alone," growled the other. "Keep thy wisdom to thyself, brother, and help me to wrap my cloak round me," said Gaetano; and at that moment another brigand came clattering back, to say the *comitiva* had halted at the cross-roads, and wished to know which they were to take. Evidently the expedition to Castel del Monte was not a popular one, and they wished to enter their protest against it. Whereupon Don Gaetano swore furiously, telling his liegeman to go to the women if he was afraid, and not come there preaching, for go to Castel del Monte he would, if he went alone; to which Giovanni replied, "As you will, brother; I have said that you are leading us to the devil, but no matter,"—and they all three rode away.

How delightful to the ears of the listeners behind the hedge must have been the receding sounds of the horse-hoofs! and soon all was silent save the faint patter of the rain among the boughs, and they rose, stretched their cramped limbs, shook their wet cloaks, and went back to the place where the guide and the horses were patiently awaiting their return.

The two officers held a colloquy apart as to the safest way of getting home, and the best means of acquiring some information about the movements of the brigands.

Clearly, the light which had so puzzled them must have been a signal to inform the Vardarelli that Don Ciro had reached Castel del Monte; and how welcome to the General would be any news of his doings and intentions! Viti suggested that the peasant guide might go and spy out the land without much risk to himself, and addressing him with a most insinuating air, inquired if he had a purse. Oh yes, he had one, he said, a large one, but—with a shake of the head—it was empty, and he had nothing to put in it!

Would he like to fill it? It must be a large purse, a very large one, to hold the ducats which would be his if he chose to earn them. What would he say to forty ducats? Forty real, solid ducats! And for such a little thing! Just to go to the castle there, use his eyes and ears, and report what he heard and saw!

At first the peasant shook his head, averring that ducats would be of no use to a dead man; but yet—how many did the gentleman say? and were they hard money, or paper?

"How many fingers have you?" asked Viti.

The peasant counted them with exceeding seriousness: one—two—three—and then with an air of conviction, "I believe, signore, that I have ten!"

"Well, my friend, you may count them again, and then again, and then again. All shall be yours—as many ducats as you can count on your fingers four times, if you will do this errand, and meet us to-morrow at Barletta."

"But, signore, you have not told me in what way the money will be paid. There have been many generals in our country, and they have all been uncommonly ready with promises and paper, but when it came to cash—*altra cosa!*"

"Never fear for that, my good fellow. Our General is a man of a different sort; he doesn't pay in words or paper. Forty solid ducats down in your hand, and to show that I mean it you shall have these ten as a first instalment."

"I feel my courage beginning to come," said the peasant, as he listened to the chink of the money which Viti displayed, "but it comes slowly, signore, slowly. What would you? for, do you see, my stomach is quite empty!"

"Take this then, and perhaps it will come quicker," said the captain, tossing him a lump of bread and a sausage, and holding out a flask of rum; but the brigadier caught the flask from the guide's hand, exclaiming—

"Don't drink it if you value your life! The Vardarelli have keen noses, and they will know that a beast of a peasant does not get *rummo Inglese* unless he has come from the General's headquarters. You shall have a whole bottle all to yourself, if you perform your commission to our satisfaction."

So the matter was settled. Viti offered to take charge of the ten ducats, lest the possession of so large a sum should cause the guide to be either robbed or looked upon with suspicion; but no, he was too wily for that, and preferred to deposit them in a hollow tree which he knew of, a little distance off. So they parted, and went their different ways, Viti taking charge of the guide's horse, and charging him to say, if he were questioned, that the General had been recalled, and was even now on his way to Naples.

It was close upon noon next day when the peasant made his appearance at General Church's headquarters at Barletta. He was at once brought in, and here is his own account of his interview with the brigand chiefs, taken from the notes of Colonel Schmerber, who, by the General's desire, was present for the purpose of taking down the deposition.

"*Eccellenza*, I reached the castle all wet, for it rained furiously; and I went straight to the great hall—that is, they had a guard set at the *masseria* [farmhouse] below the castle, and mounted sentinels at the castle gates, and sentinels on foot at the door of the tower, all armed; and they arrested me, the guards at the *masseria* first, and sent me on to those at the gates, and one of them marched me up to the tower, where I found all the Vardarelli—I counted forty-six of them with my own eyes—eating and drinking round half-a-dozen great fires. The fires looked pleasant enough, but I had no mind for the company sitting round them! Not that I had much choice about that, for one of the brigands marched me straight to the room where were Don Gaetano Vardarelli and the ladies—and that Other," and the peasant crossed himself and dropped his voice. "They were sitting round a large fire, and on the table were food and wine, and plenty of it too; a feast, *Signore Generale*, such as my eyes don't often behold! A nice ham, and fowls, and a fine piece of cheese, and oysters and shell-fish, besides apples and olives and chestnuts, and *ricotta* [curds of sheep's milk] and cream, and *salami* [sausages] *belle, belle salami*, and four bottles of *rummo Inglese*—that would be one for each person, you see—and a couple of barrels of wine. Truly, I should beg your Excellency's pardon for mentioning the dinner before the guests, but it was a dinner to make one's mouth water! Well then, there was Don Gaetano Vardarelli, a handsome man, as your Excellency knows as well as I, sitting with his carbine across his knees, and his pistols in his belt, talking and laughing, while he cut up the meat with his stiletto, and drinking often out of a silver cup. He joked and played with one of the women, who answered him back, and drank with him merrily. As to the other woman, she neither ate nor drank, and must surely have been a bad woman, for she never opened her lips; and was that ever known to your Excellency, that a woman should not talk! Truly there must have been something wrong about her! Who was the fourth guest? Oh, your Excellency, I can hardly speak of him without trembling. If he knew I had mentioned him, I should be a dead man—for it was—your Excellency knows his name. Yes," and he crossed himself again, and the word came out in a frightened whisper, "the *abate* himself—the outlaw—none other.

"Am I sure of it? Am I sure that I am the son of my mother? Besides, Don Gaetano treated him with great respect. Better than he would have treated your Excellency, doubtless. You laugh! Ah, *per Bacco*, it is not well to laugh when that man is in question."

"Go on, my friend, and fear nothing," said the General, encouragingly. "How was Don Ciro dressed?"

"Like an officer of *gendarmerie, Signore Generale*, as true as I live! Yes, in blue pantaloons and silver lace, and armed with pistols and sabre. Heaven knows, I wish I had never set eyes on that man, and may the Madonna grant that I never set eyes on him again! His face is dreadful to behold, and I can't get it out of my head. They say, *Eccellenza*, that it resembles the face of the devil himself, and that he can change it into three colours! And his eyes are red, as red as blood. What did he talk about? Why, he never said a word while I was there, not even to the women. One of them, the silent one, who seemed to belong to him, peeled an apple now and then, and gave it him, and he sucked a little of it, and threw the rest into the fire. He ate nothing, in spite of all the good things on the table, and only drank from his own flask, which he carried in his belt. Sometimes he took a book from his pocket, and muttered something, and sometimes he frowned, and sometimes he grinned, and the grin was more dreadful than the frown! I thought he looked like the devil sitting in judgment; while Don Gaetano, on the contrary, was gay and noisy, and—*parlando con rispetto*—was boasting that he was the champion of the kingdom of Apulia, and telling Don Ciro that your Excellency had once nearly fallen into his hands, but that you had outwitted him and escaped. When he said this, the *abate* frowned and shook his head. Then Don Gaetano drank the health of Don Ciro, and said he must go back to his own country to-morrow, but would soon return, and hold another meeting at Taranto. Then Don Ciro said something to him, and he looked at me, and asked what I was doing there, and the brigand who had brought me in pushed me forward, saying, 'Here, *signore comandante*, is a peasant from Spinazzola.' 'Beast of a peasant,' said he, 'what brought you here?' 'Hunger, signore, and the rain, and the light which burns from the castle.' 'What light?' said he, looking sharply towards the *abate*. 'Are there others here, then?' Don Ciro did not answer, but he shook his head, and that seemed to satisfy Don Gaetano, who asked me again whence I came, and where I was going. 'Wherever you like to send me, Don Gaetano *mio*,' said I, wishing to please him, you understand. 'Then go to Barletta,' he said. 'You can tell the people there that you have seen me, and that we are on the road to the Abruzzi. But not a word of this gentleman, mind, if you value your skin!' Upon which I crossed myself, and bowed, in sign of obedience. 'Now tell me,' said Don Gaetano, 'what is the English General going to do?' 'In truth, signore,' I answered, 'I heard it said that he was recalled to Naples, and that all his fine cavalry are going there too.' 'Is that the truth?' and he looked hard at me. 'It is what I have heard said, Don Gaetano *mio;* but whether true or false, how can I tell?' At this the *abate* too turned his eyes upon me, and my very heart seemed to grow cold and die within me, and when he grinned and shook his head, I gave myself up for lost. But, by the blessing of the saints, no harm came of it. Don Gaetano repeated his orders to me to go to Barletta, and what I was to say there, and then he put his fingers in his mouth and whistled. Were his brothers there? No, *Eccellenza*, not in the room; but I think they must have been with the women, for I heard loud laughter and singing, and the twanging of a guitar. But as I was going to tell you, Don Gaetano whistled, and one of his brothers came in answer to his call. He was armed too, like the rest, and a tall fellow, as tall as Don Gaetano himself, who said to him, ' Giovanni, see this beast of a peasant outside the gates.' Then he asked me if I was sure I understood his orders, and I repeated what I was to say as fast as I could, upon which he threw me a couple of ducats and bade me be off. Glad, in truth, was I to follow Don Giovanni out of the room and through the hall where the *comitiva* were feasting, and all my hunger was gone before I reached the door.

Una vera Babilonia, Signore Generale! and at every step I was saluted with such compliments as *Bestia! Maladetto!* and many other epithets which I would not repeat before your Excellency. Then Don Giovanni marched me across the courtyard, gave me a kick, and said, 'Off with you, rascal of a peasant! and if I catch you here again, it will be the worse for you!' I had no mind to stay for any further civilities, and took to my heels with a thankful heart. What then? Why, then I went straight to the hollow tree to find my ten ducats, and, praise be to the saints, they were there safe! So now behold me, *Eccellentissimo Signore Generale*, having performed your orders, and ready to receive as many more ducats as it may be your Excellency's pleasure to bestow upon me."

Viti was called in and desired to count out the thirty ducats more which made up the sum promised, with a couple added. Two bottles of *rummo Inglese* completed his felicity, and the peasant retired, kissing the General's hand, and bowing to the ground.

CHAPTER XII.

A DEADLY FEUD.

NARDELLI AND DE BERNARDIS—THE FATE OF DON BLASI—DE BERNARDIS'S BARGAIN WITH CIRO—MURDER OF NARDELLI—DE BERNARDIS'S CONCEALMENT—BETRAYED BY HIS GREED—CAPTURE—A DEVOUT BRIGAND.

THERE are so many stories of Ciro! It seems difficult to keep him out of the page, however unwelcome his presence there may be! He seems to have been literally "the head and front of the offending," and with his fall, evil-doing soon collapsed. The following story is a specimen of how readily private revenge was worked out through his agency.

There is a quaint little town, clustering round the top of a conical hill, and overlooking the sunny plains of Apulia, which bears the appropriate name of Locorotondo. Here, about this date, the two principal inhabitants were the Signore Nardelli and the Signore de Bernardis. They were rivals, and cordially disliked each other, and the reason is not far to seek. Not only each one considered himself, and wished to be considered by his neighbours, as quite the most important citizen of the little town, but the two men were so different in character, in principles, in the way they were regarded by their acquaintances—in everything, in fact, but worldly possessions—that they could not possibly have been friends! Signore Nardelli was justice of the peace for the district, a wealthy, kindly, honourable gentleman, somewhat hasty in temper perhaps, and a little autocratic, but much beloved and respected by all his neighbours, gentle and simple, rich and poor. Signore de Bernardis, on the contrary, bore an evil name among the little community, as a man dark and revengeful, avaricious in money matters, and, moreover, known to be closely connected with the secret societies, especially the worst of all, the Decisi.

It was a strange and terrible state of things in Apulia at that time, as has been said before. You had an enemy. Well, you had but to make your bargain with the robber priest, the terrible chief of the Decisi,—so much for himself, so much for the assassin,—and everything was speedily arranged, to your perfect satisfaction. Your enemy might be guiltless, beloved, loyal—the support of his home, the friend of his fellow-citizens. No matter, since he had offended you, and you wanted him punished and could afford to pay! Without warning, as he crossed his own threshold, or turned the familiar street-corner, or sauntered leisurely through his fields, or stopped for a few minutes' friendly chat with an acquaintance, the blow was struck: a shot from behind yonder wall, which he had passed, unthinking, scores of times; a swift, sudden blow from a stiletto, struck by one who seemed only a chance loiterer. The body was found with a thrust in the side, a musket-ball through the heart, and was carried home and wept over in secret by those who loved him; but no one dared ask aloud, "Who has done this thing?" for to be suspected of enmity to the secret societies was certain death.

Was not the story well known, and many stories besides, of the fate of Don Blasi, a man of high character and fearless courage? He had dared to express in public his disapprobation of the terrorism in which his country was held, and what happened?

One summer evening he was riding home from his country house to the little town where he usually dwelt, with his young son and daughter: a sweet summer evening, following a day of country delights in their much-loved *villeggiatura*. Slowly they rode, with happy jests and gay talk, enjoying the perfumed air, the nightingale's song, the dry chirp of the cicala, all the scents and sounds, as they had so often done before, without a thought of harm or evil. The children rode first—they were but fourteen and sixteen—and the father followed. Suddenly a hand was laid upon his bridle; a man in the uniform of a *gendarme* bade him stop. Don Blasi recognised the voice.

" Don Ciro ! "

" Yes, I am Don Ciro," was the stern reply. There was a click, a flash, a report, and Don Blasi fell from his horse to the ground without a word, shot to the heart. " So perish all the enemies of Ciro Annichiarico," said the murderer.

Half-a-dozen ruffians rushed from the bushes and seized the fainting, horror-stricken girl and boy, but Ciro spared their lives, and left them, after warning the lad that the slightest attempt to avenge his father's death would prove his own doom.

The poor children crouched there in the darkness, numb with terror, and were found a few hours later by some peasants, sitting by their father's corpse. The girl had quite lost her wits, and never recovered, but died within

the year. The lad dared take no steps to
bring the murderer to justice till, years after,
General Church came into command of the
province. Then he went straight to his headquarters and volunteered to join the force
which was engaged in hunting down the
brigands. But of this hereafter; and now to
return to our story.

De Bernardis, as has been said, bore an
evil name. A bad man they called him, in
whispers, in the little town of Locorotondo,
unscrupulous, revengeful, avaricious — a man
equally feared and detested. And Nardelli
had been cautioned to look to his safety, and
told that his life was not secure from such
a man. But he laughed at warnings, secure,
he said, in his own good conscience and the
esteem of his neighbours, until one evening,
as he came home from a friendly visit, a ball
whizzed past him. He was close by his own
house, and rushed in, and a bullet struck the
door which he slammed behind him, and buried
itself in the panels.

Of course this incident caused a commotion,
and everybody said that De Bernardis was at
the bottom of the affair; but they said it in
hushed voices, and there was no proof, and
no one was likely to try and find one.

Long afterwards, the whole story came out,

and it was known that, having failed in this first attempt, De Bernardis had sent to Don Ciro Annichiarico and bargained with him for Nardelli's murder. Then, one dark night, he brought the assassin into the town behind him on his horse. De Bernardis went to his house, and soon after, on pretence of business, left the town and went on a journey.

The murderer lurked about Locorotondo, but a fortnight passed and Nardelli had never stirred outside his own house, alarmed at the attempt on his life, and moved by the tears and entreaties of his beautiful wife, whom he dearly loved, to prudence.

But there came a day of heavenly beauty and freshness, and Nardelli, as he looked out of his windows and up into the unfathomable blue of the Italian sky, felt that he could bear the imprisonment no longer. Besides, he had heard that his enemy was absent, and that fact seemed of itself a promise of safety.

"My love," said he to the fair woman who stood beside him, " this life is unbearable! I have been shut up like a bird in a cage long enough. Let us go out and breathe the air."

"Is it wise? Is it safe?" she answered,

anxiously. "O *caro mio*, I fear even my own shadow! I would rather never quit this house again than that your life should be endangered."

"Nay," he said, "look out for yourself. Not a dog is stirring in the street below. Besides, our enemy is absent. Trust me, he has given up the game. Let us go to our garden and see what this fortnight has done for our roses and carnations."

"But they say that bad man has sworn to have your life, though you have never wronged him by so much as a *soldo*," cried the wife.

He laughed and laid a caressing hand on her dark hair. "Threatened men live long, they say, and I don't fancy De Bernardis will try that trick twice. He knows that suspicion has fallen upon him, for, thank God, I have no other foe! Besides, he is a coward who dares not strike, and a miser who loves not to pay, even for my blood! Come then, our garden is but just outside the town, and I will go no farther, nor linger on the way."

"True, it is but a little way," she hesitated; "but the sight of a stranger makes me die of fear!"

"Your nerves are shaken, *cara mia*," he said,

soothingly, "and no wonder. But I promise we will go no farther than our garden. Come!" And she put her black veil over her head and they went out together: just along the narrow, crooked, picturesque little streets, and out into the country beyond, where close to the walls of the old town the gardens of the good citizens lay, walled round for the most part; and with straight walks and formal borders, well stocked with fruits and flowers, and each with its *pergola* covered with trailing vines, lovely now with their wealth of greenery, to be lovelier still when the later season should bring the rich harvest of purple grapes. The husband and wife sauntered along, stopping here and there to observe the progress of some favourite shrub or flower, enjoying the sense of freedom after a fifteen days' captivity, and feeling safe within the high garden walls.

Presently they saw a man, who held papers in his hand, approach the garden gate and open it. All sense of fear had now been dissipated, blown away by the sweet evening air, and the idea that they had been watched and followed never entered their heads.

"Some poor fellow who has a petition to present," murmured the justice of the peace to his wife, as he stepped forward. The words were few that followed.

"Are you the justice of the peace for Locorotondo?"

"Yes."

"Then die (*mori dunque*)!"

There was the flash of a stiletto, and Signore Nardelli fell to the ground, just muttered, "*È finito—povera mia moglie—vendetta——*" and died.

The poor wife stood for a moment as if turned to stone, and then shriek after shriek rang through the summer air, and the neighbours rushed in, crowding into the open gate, so that the assassin, who had turned to fly, was speedily surrounded and struck down with sticks and stones, till he lay bleeding on the ground beside his victim. He lived long enough to confess that he had been sent by Don Ciro, the mysterious and dreaded chief of the Decisi, to do the deed, and that he had received seventy ducats to slay a man who not only had never done him any injury, but was absolutely unknown to him, even by sight.

Years passed away. Ciro Annichiarico and his band of ruffians had met their deserts under the stern justice of General Church's rule, and the provinces of Apulia, relieved from terrorism, breathed a new atmosphere of peacefulness and quietude. It was like the burst of sunshine which sometimes follows a thunderstorm, when the wet flowers lift up their heads, and the birds sing like escaped prisoners. People felt that they could talk freely, without anxious glances as to who was within earshot, and loiter and laugh along the road, with no thought of a possible danger behind every wall. The plains and forests were free from marauders, the white-walled cities held no lurking assassins within their picturesque streets; and all this was the doing of the English officer, whom they feared for his quick, uncompromising temper and iron determination, yet trusted for his absolute justice and kindly heart.

One evening he was enjoying a well-earned rest after the multifarious labours of the day in his headquarters at Leece. The long shadows lay on the plain that stretches between Lecce and Otranto, with here and there a golden gleam, where the setting sun caught the tops of the great olives and carob-trees; the cloudless horizon was one mist of rose and gold, melting upwards into the blue of the Italian sky. The General sat on his terrace, a cigar between his lips, and his eyes—such keen dark-blue eyes!—gazing with quiet appreciation over the fair scene before him, with a contented sense that he had been instrumental in rendering it so peaceful and so fair.

There was a step on the terrace, and his aide-de-camp came out and informed his Excellency that a lady desired to see him. His Excellency, stern disciplinarian though he was, was always chivalrously courteous and gentle to women or little children, and he straightway threw aside the half-smoked cigar, and rising from his seat, went into the house to receive his visitor. A tall lady, closely veiled and in deep mourning, acknowledged his salutation by a low courtesy, with such an air of grave dignity that it was clear she was a person accustomed to the manners of society. "Pardon me, *Eccellenza*," she said. "I have dared to intrude upon you at this hour in the name of Justice."

General Church was a perfect Italian scholar. In fact, he was as familiar with French and Italian as with his native tongue. He answered readily, "Signora, I have not the honour of knowing to whom I am speaking, but be assured that what you ask in the name of Justice it will be my duty to grant. Speak without fear; my time is yours."

The lady threw back her veil and showed a face pale indeed, and worn by years of suffering and sorrow, yet still bearing traces of the beauty for which she had once been remarkable—the dark, lustrous, passionate beauty of the South.

"You see before you, *Eccellenza*," she said, " the widow of the unfortunate Signore Nardelli." Then she seated herself and began to relate all her sad story. She told it simply, fully, graphically, from beginning to end, and the General observed that her account agreed in every detail with the official report, which he had already carefully studied. She told how, as soon as she had recovered from the appalling shock of her husband's murder, she had tried to begin a legal process against those who were suspected of the crime; how it was said that De Bernardis, though the chief author, was not the only person implicated; nay, it was said that among those who were foremost in assailing the hired assassin, some there were whose interest it was that he should die without making fuller confession; how her attempt had failed because no one dared take up so perilous a cause, and at last she had been forced to give it up; finally how, when she heard that the Englishman had taken the command of Apulia, her hopes had revived, and she had followed his course with anxious prayers for his success, and that when the news was brought to her that the head of

Ciro Annichiarico was placed over the gate of Grottaglia, she had resolved to leave her solitude and come to claim punishment against her husband's murderers, and especially against Signore de Bernardis.

There was really no difficulty in finding out who were the authors of the attack on Signore Nardelli. They were perfectly well known, and now that the reign of terror was over, there were plenty of people ready to point them out, and before long two were taken, convicted, and executed. But where was the chief criminal? No sooner had any stir begun to be made than De Bernardis disappeared.

He disappeared as completely as if he had never existed, leaving no trace behind. Inquiries and searchings, offers of money, were alike useless. Some said he had altogether left the country—perhaps gone to Corfù; some, that so rich a man had great power in his hands! and that the judges of the Criminal Tribunal were not inaccessible to bribes, and that De Bernardis had friends among the local magistrates. Besides, the shadow of the terror which the secret societies had inspired did not quickly disperse, and De Bernardis made the most of their mysterious power while it lasted.

Powerful though he was, however, General Church's vigorous measures struck him with astonishment and alarm. He could not doubt that the spell was broken, and soon after the search for brigands began he went away and hid himself: he fancied that if he kept quiet awhile the hot pursuit would abate, and then he could come back and live quietly at home. "Bah!" said he, "we have seen all this before. I have no mind to be hanged, and this confounded Englishman is capable of anything! But it will pass, it will pass! Let him catch Ciro and his band, and go home with his glory; and then it is only to keep quiet for a while, and let the tempest blow over, and sneak back to my hole!"

So when things grew quieter, he did creep back literally to his "hole," a place of concealment where he thought he would surely be safe for as long as any danger seemed to threaten.

Underneath the floor of his house was a secret chamber, the existence of which was known only to De Bernardis himself and one or two chosen friends. It was beneath a bedroom, and reached from thence by a small trapdoor and a ladder. The trap-door was easily concealed by pushing an enormous carved wooden four-post bed against it; and as for light, he bribed two masons, Carbonari like himself, with six hundred ducats and the promise of much more, to construct a little hidden window and to keep his secret. There had been once an outer door, but he had had it bricked up, and all traces of the new work carefully concealed by these same two masons. Into this subterranean chamber, then, his wife secretly conveyed food and wine, bedding and furniture, and there De Bernardis took up his abode, only quitting it when he was sure his wife would be alone, and was so entirely lost to view that neither his friends nor his servants had the slightest idea that he had returned. Only his wife and the two masons were in the secret, and at last it became a settled conviction in men's minds that he had escaped to Corfù.

Thus a year passed, and there was no trace of the criminal. The General had hunted for him far and near, up and down the country, sometimes starting off on what seemed a promising track, and sorely vexed when it too proved fruitless. Several times he and his troops had even entered the house and questioned the servants, but all to no purpose. The search might have been discontinued but for the imprudence of the poor wife, who on one occasion offered money to the commander of a detachment of troops if he would give up searching and go away. But bribes were of no avail when offered to the Englishman's chosen troops, and the money was indignantly refused and the matter reported to General Church. "Ha!" quoth he, "to give up searching, is it? Then our friend is *not* gone to Corfù!" And thenceforth a watchful eye was kept upon that neighbourhood; and yet months flew by, and the end seemed as far off as ever.

It has been said that De Bernardis, among his other bad qualities, was avaricious, and this it was which at last caused his destruction. Month has followed month, and he was still safe. He had sat snug in his hiding-place and chuckled as he heard the voices of the pursuers, and thought how small a space divided them from him, and how little they guessed it!

His confidence returned as the pursuit abated, and when he heard that the permanent Military Commission was dissolved and the province was declared quiet again, he began to repent of the high price he had paid to the two masons for his safety. That miserable little window! To think that it had cost him six hundred ducats! Why, one hundred would have been a monstrous price, and the masons would have been lucky to get half the amount. One hundred ducats! It was a fortune. For two working men to have such a sum to divide between them, holy saints, it ought to surpass their wildest dreams!

And, positively, he was fool enough to desire his wife to go to the masons and tell them that five hundred of the six hundred ducats were only lent, not given, and that it was now time they were repaid. He even fixed a certain date when the repayment was to be made, imagining probably that the General's departure was imminent, and that he, De Bernardis, would soon be in a position to show himself, and to enforce his will upon his inferiors, just as he had been accustomed to do in the bad old times which were past.

At first the two masons took the message as a jest, and laughed heartily at the gentleman's wit; but when they found he was in earnest, their tone changed. De Bernardis had not realised how thoroughly the power of the secret societies was broken, or that the people, having once tasted of freedom, had become almost like different creatures. The two masons flatly refused payment, and when the message was repeated, "*Va bene*," said they, "we will see whose business it is to pay!"

They were careful not to let slip any word

which might rouse suspicion in the mind of De Bernardis. They answered his message humbly and civilly enough, promised payment by instalments, without any apparent reluctance, and arranged with the Signora de Bernardis as to the day and hour when they should come to her house to bring the first sum and receive a receipt. She promised that the receipt should be ready when they called, and so they departed. Then the two masons took their way to the neighbouring town of Fasano, where a detachment of fusiliers was quartered with the express purpose of looking after De Bernardis, and asked to see the brigadier in command. Where the General was at this moment does not appear, probably at his headquarters at Lecce, but he had left an officer who could be trusted to carry out this little affair, and proud and delighted he was to have the chance of doing so! The two masons laid their grievance before the brigadier, and offered to conduct him and his men in safety to the place where the enemy was to be found that very night, and the offer was most eagerly accepted.

The night was cold and dark when they set out—the brigadier, dressed like a peasant, but with arms hidden under his blouse, the fusiliers, and the two masons as guides. They reached Locorotondo at about midnight, the soldiers silently taking up their stations round the house, except four, who followed their disguised officer and the guides at a distance with stealthy steps, until they had taken a safe and secret position within easy call, under the shadow of the house.

A gentle tap at the door brought the signora to a little window overhead, asking anxiously, "Who is there?"

"Friends — you know us, signora. Open the door."

Now it happened that, as all the servants were gone to bed, Signore de Bernardis had ventured out of his hiding-place, and was sitting with his wife up-stairs.

From this room a flight of wide stone steps led to a large hall on the first floor, and from this hall a narrow, winding staircase gave access to the ground-floor. Here then, in the little up-stairs chamber, the signora stood, and, prompted by her husband, parleyed with her visitors at the door below—a great, heavy door, opening from the courtyard.

"*Di grazia*, signora, let us in. The night is cold, and it will cause suspicion if any one should chance to see us at your door."

"But the money — have you brought the money?"

"Yes, yes, certainly we have brought the money."

"But how much?"

"Well, signora, Giovanni has brought two hundred ducats; but I could only scrape together one hundred and fifty, and here they are — see, good ducats, good money, and in full number!"

"It is too little," said the signora, at her husband's prompting.

"Very well, signora. If you won't take the money, you can leave it alone. We are quite willing to keep it. Good night, *signora padrona*."

"*Piano, piano, signori miei;* how much money did you say?"

"Three hundred and fifty ducats, signora, well counted. Will you take them or will you not?"

"It is too little, too little; but, *pazienza!* Let Giovanni bring the money to the door, and I will come down and take it."

There was some delay before the signora appeared in the doorway, opening it cautiously half-way, drawing back the heavy bolts, turning the great iron key with all precaution, lest the sleeping domestics should be aroused. Meanwhile, De Bernardis had crept downstairs to his hiding-place, and lay there, as he thought, safely ensconced, till the bargaining was over. Truly things had gone well with him! Who would have thought that the masons would have acceded to his demand so readily, and have brought so large a sum, even before the date agreed upon? Well, his imprisonment would soon be over, the country would soon be rid of this pestilent Englishman, who knew so little what was due to a gentleman, and then things would arrange themselves in their proper places.

So the door was opened; but before it could be closed again the two masons and their peasant friend had pushed their way inside, muttering something about the cold, and answering the signora's alarmed inquiry with the information that the third person was a friend of theirs, a good fellow, who had joined them on the way, and who also had a little business with the *padrone*.

"Come, come—this is folly!" said the signora. "What do you mean by such talk as this?"

She was evidently alarmed. Her cheeks grew pale and her limbs trembled, though she tried to speak authoritatively, poor soul! "Give me the money, and go your ways, I say!"

"I will carry it up-stairs for you, *signora*

padrona," replied Giovanni, who took the leading part. "Don't trouble yourself about fastening the door — leave that to my comrade—and let us settle matters and get the receipt."

So they went softly up the wide staircase to the large hall, the signora first, Giovanni and the disguised brigadier following; and as soon as they were out of sight Piero, the second mason, admitted the four armed fusiliers, and they also silently crept up the stairs and took up their positions just outside the door which their friends had closed behind them, and waited there in the darkness till they were wanted. The signora seated herself in a great carved wooden chair, putting down the flickering oil-lamp, which her trembling hands could hardly hold, and tried to speak in a cheerful, assured tone, while the chill and gloom seemed to intensify and creep closer round the one spot of flickering light in the great, unwarmed, gloomy, ghostly apartment.

"Well, now," she said, "let us finish the matter. It is late and cold. Where is the money? Give it me quick, and go."

"*Piano, piano, signora padrona!*" Giovanni spoke civilly, yet there was something of menace in his voice. "I must have a receipt, if you please. Yes, we must have a receipt from the *padrone*."

"From the *padrone?*" faltered the lady. "Oh, you talk folly! Leave the money with me, and go about your business. O *Madonna mia*, will you not go?"

"*Per Bacco*—no!" and the man stamped on the ground thrice, and at the signal the door of the hall opened, and out of the darkness stepped the four armed men, and stood there silent, ghostlike, yet so terribly real. The poor signora cried out, "All is lost; we are betrayed!" and fainted in her chair. Poor soul! her life had been a hard one, yet he was her husband, and perhaps, for old sake's sake, she loved him still. Piero and one of the soldiers were left as guards and sentinels, and the rest of the party, headed by Giovanni, proceeded on their search.

Giovanni knew the way, and they had provided themselves with lights. Through a little low door, down a narrow, winding staircase, to a large bedroom on the ground-floor, furnished but unoccupied, intended apparently as a guest-chamber. There seemed no place there which might serve for a lurking-place. A large dark room, with massive oak furniture, but no corners, no cupboards, no extra doors. Giovanni surveyed the room, and then, " Help me to move that box," he said, "that arm-chair —so;" and he took the light and began a close inspection of the oak-panelled walls, pressing his finger against first one and then another, till he reached the side of the great bedstead. Then there was an exclamation, and he turned and beckoned to the brigadier. His finger had found the secret spring, and a panel flew back, disclosing an aperture some three feet square, from which a ladder gave access to the hiding-place below, where lurked De Bernardis. He, hearing the trap-door open, naturally imagined that his wife had come to tell him that the affair was concluded, and cried out at once, "What is it?" expecting an answer in her voice about the money. But it was a man's voice that answered—

"We are here, signore, with the money."

"What do you want of me? Why are you here?" he questioned.

"The receipt, signore. We want the receipt."

"Then you must get it from the signora."

"Are we to understand that you refuse to receive the money, signore?" and then there came a burst of wild, malicious laughter, which echoed strangely, fiendishly through the darkness. "*Povero signore! povero signore!* He refuses the money! Perhaps he knows he will never want money again;" and then, changing their tone, "Oh, thou wretch, come out of your hiding-place, or we will blow out your brains!"

Here, however, the brigadier interfered, putting the mason aside, and taking up the word in an authoritative tone.

"Signore de Bernardis, in the name of the law, and by virtue of this mandate which I hold in my hand, I command you to surrender yourself. We cannot wait. Make haste! Come up this ladder, and save us the trouble of coming down to fetch you. You cannot escape, and resistance is of no avail; I am here at the head of a company of armed men."

De Bernardis, as has been said before, was a coward at heart, and as soon as he understood the state of things his courage failed utterly. Repeated calls and exhortations being of no avail, the brigadier and a couple of his men climbed down the ladder, and found the wretched man crouching in a heap on the floor, half senseless with terror. They bound the abject creature, and contrived to convey him up the ladder, and then to march him off to Lecce, arriving triumphant at daybreak at General Church's headquarters.

Before going, the brigadier called up the sleeping servants, and left the poor signora in their care.

As to the people of Locorotondo, they heartily rejoiced at the capture, for they felt that the peace of their pleasant little town was now thoroughly established, and there was no one to mourn when De Bernardis suffered the fate which he had so justly deserved.

It is tempting to relate another short story which curiously illustrates the mixture of superstition and crime which went together in the lives of these people, who would commit a murder for hire on one day, and then join in devotional exercises the next. Nay, there were priests among the Carbonari and Decisi who exercised the functions of a priest in the midst of their career of murder and plunder. There was a certain arch-priest of Surbo, we are told, who celebrated Mass one Christmas eve armed from head to foot.

There was a certain ruffian, the captain of a band of Decisi—of all the secret societies they were the most cruel and bloodthirsty. This ruffian went by the nickname of Picco Pane, and among a long list of his enormities we hear of his absolutely having roasted to death a gentle, pious old Canonico Chiffi, because the poor old man did not prove to be so rich as the robbers had supposed him to be. Picco Pane went regularly to confession and Mass, choosing for his devotional exercises some little church, far away from the haunts of men, perched up among the rocks, and only frequented by the poor shepherds, or by such as himself. The times and churches he chose were only known to his intimate friends, and the hour was always of the earliest.

When the poor old Canonico Chiffi was dead, and his money and vestments carried away, Picco Pane, for convenience' sake, left these last concealed in the cottage of a relation, some miles distant from the town where the murder was committed, and then rode off, meaning on some future day to come and claim his own. But, unluckily for him, General Church had sent a detachment of *gendarmes* to search the villages around and try whether any trace could be found of this notorious ruffian; and, entering into one cottage, their eyes fell upon a vestment which one of them recognised as having belonged to the canon.

The people of the house were forthwith arrested for having the articles in their possession, and, in great fear of the consequences to themselves if they were brought to trial, they eagerly offered to give any information as to the best means of getting possession of their cousin, Picco Pane.

"Where was he?" Well, at that precise

moment there was no saying; but it was easy enough to tell where he would be next Sunday. Oh yes, he would certainly go to the earliest Mass! That was his habit, and he would certainly go to a certain little church in the mountains alone, for he would have no thought of danger. "Armed?" But certainly, he never went unarmed; and besides, for greater safety, he always wore many relics of the blessed saints on his breast. Oh, he would surely be there!

In the grey of the morning, then, Picco Pane, armed, and with his breast covered with relics, entered the little church. He cast quick glances on this side and on that as he stepped along the steep, narrow, stony path. If he had known it, every boulder or bush held an armed avenger; but he did not know it, and he went in, made his confession, heard his Mass — strange and shocking though it sounds, it is true — and came gaily forth, absolved and blessed! There, on each side of the church porch, stood a silent file of armed men. He started back, and would have turned to fly, but it was too late. Strong hands seized him, and in a few minutes he was securely bound and carried off, to be triumphantly led to the General's headquarters.

CHAPTER XIII.

A DAY AMONG THE *MASSERIE*.

THE MASKED BALL—THE MASSERIA DELL' DUCA—A NOVEL BATTERING-RAM — SULLEN PEASANTS — BOEHMER'S DISCOVERY — THE PIÈ DI MONTI — A BRIEF REPOSE — DE FEO'S DISGUISE—NEWS OF THE BRIGANDS.

IT may be amusing to give the description of a day's ride—one among many—taken by General Church and his men among the *masserie*, which were always favourite haunts of the brigands, who knew that the *massaro* was generally, either from fear or favour, a friend to be relied on.

The scene opens at Lecce, the General's headquarters, one evening in January 1818.

"Your Excellency," said Captain Quandel, the General's aide-de-camp, "Major Fusco has just arrived from Francavilla. May he come in?"

"Certainly. Ah, Fusco, *buona sera!* What do they think about Ciro at Francavilla?"

"All, all, absolutely all, are for him, your Excellency. They insult us in the streets as if we were dogs."

"We must pay our friends a visit forthwith, Fusco. And from Ostuni?"

"I have brought you a letter, sir, from Don Bartolomeo Lopez. He has just come to his house in Ostuni, after standing a siege in his tower a little way from that town."

"Bravo, Don Bartolomeo!" and the General read the letter.

(Don Bartolomeo Lopez, be it observed, had been intended for the Church, and had taken minor orders, but had got dispensation, and married late in life, on his elder brother dying childless.)

"As you know, *Signore Generale*, I was once on the road to become a cardinal, but never on the road to become a general. I hope, therefore, that you won't take it amiss, that after having defended my castle — pulled up the drawbridge, fired out of the windows till the rascals raised the blockade and rode off — I and my family retreated in good order, and took up our quarters in Ostuni, where, with all respect to you, we mean to stay, and where the best apartments are kept in readiness for your Excellency's reception."

"Very good," said the General, as he folded

up the letter with a smile. "And now, Fusco, eat and drink, sleep or dance; only be ready at two o'clock after midnight to accompany me."

It was a gay season in Lecce; people crowded to the capital for protection in those disturbed times; and besides, the worthy inhabitants were hospitably eager to welcome their guests. That night there was a magnificent banquet, ending with a masked ball, in honour of the English General, attended by all the rank and fashion of Lecce.

The General waxes poetical in talking of the fair ladies who gathered there. "The sex whose presence gives a charm to life." "Fair daughters of Terra di Otranto!" he goes on, "bright, gay, artless, confiding, all heart, all animation, quick as lightning in impulse, but not changeable in love!" And he owns that it was with great unwillingness that he obeyed Colonel Schmerber's whispered summons, "*Tout est prêt, mon Général;* the horses are ready at the Rugia Gate."

At the same moment the charming Duchess of San Cesario came up to him to take leave, so the General seized the opportunity of attending her to her carriage, and left the ball-room followed by his aides-de-camp and officers— went out regretfully from the brightly lighted rooms, the fair faces, and flattering welcomes, into a dark and drizzly January night; and he says it was some time before talking and laughter broke the silence of the ride, so full were their minds of the kindness and hospitality they had been enjoying at Lecce.

However, the rain stopped at daybreak, the grey clouds parted, reddened; streaks of gold lay along the horizon, blue patches of sky showed through the rifts of cloud; the raindrops quivered and glittered like diamonds, hanging in rows on the leafless branches. When they halted at I Castelli, says the General, "it was like a fairy scene; and when the splendid band of the 1st Foreign Regiment struck up, and the strains echoed from rocks and trees and rivulets, how calm, how delicious it was! What dreams of glory and felicity, never to be realised, presented themselves to the imagination!" The men dismounted and shook their dripping cloaks and hats, and there was much laughter at the drowned-rat appearance they presented. Then there was a passing about of wine-flasks, and bread and cheese and sausages, by way of an early breakfast, as they sat among the crags on the hillside, and the officers took up their place upon the ruinous battlements of the now deserted castle, until the advance was sounded; the light-

P

armed *cacciatori* bounded like chamois from rock to rock, the sabres of the cavalry flashed as they were drawn and carefully wiped before being returned to the scabbards, the drums of the infantry echoed from the rocks, making them sound double their real number, and the troops began to file down the winding, stony paths, which led to the green and fertile plain.

Suddenly a long shrill whistle was heard, and Colonel Schmerber was still exclaiming, "That's Don Ciro's whistle, we had better clear out," when a discharge of muskets came rattling down among the walls and rocks where they stood.

"If they can't shoot better than that, we may as well stay where we are," remarked the General.

"They are pretty close, though," said a young officer. "Look up, sir; there are half-a-dozen rascals just over our heads."

"*Bagattella!*" laughed Colonel Bentz; "I took them for crows. If you stand there, General, I wager they'll hit you."

"I wager they won't!" he replied, while Schmerber clapped his hands and cried—

"Bravo! Look, General, the rear-guard has got on the rocks higher up."

"Splendid! The sergeant commanding that battalion shall have one hundred florins. You have lost your wager, Bentz!" cried the General.

A peal of laughter was heard from the brigands.

"Softly, softly, gentlemen. Let them laugh that win," said Fusco, raising his carbine; but General Church put it aside with his cane.

"No, no, Fusco; leave the rear-guard to settle the matter."

And as he spoke, two of the brigands fell, and the rest leapt away among the rocks and were lost to sight.

This little interlude over, all rode on gaily to Cellano, where, in the absence of the Marquis of Lizzano, the *intendente* entertained them at breakfast, and where they were overtaken by a band of the gentlemen of the province, come to join in their ride. The old *intendente* received them most hospitably. "*Benvenuta, Benvenuta mille e mille volte, Eccellentissimo Signore Generale!*" Then turning to the gentlemen and officers with gracious salutation, "*Benvenuta a tutti loro signori cavalieri! Che gioja, che piacere!*" So the kind old man bustled about, interspersing compliments and felicitations, with remonstrances for having taken him by surprise, so that he had nothing in the house, nothing fit to be offered to such honoured guests, "*niente, niente affatto,"*—though a sly peep into the dining-room set the young officers' minds at rest on that score, for the tables were laden with good things—fish, flesh, and fowl, mountains of jelly, oceans of cream, fruit, salad, pastry, wines of all kinds. The hungry cavaliers did ample justice to the fare, and jests and laughter went merrily round, rejoicing the hospitable heart of their host, who perambulated the room, heaping plates and filling glasses, and only distressed because General Church, always a small eater, did not, as he expressed it, "*mangiar generalmente. Coraggio, Signore Generale,*" he coaxingly said, "*bisogno mangiar molto per star bene!*"

Then suddenly darting off, he reappeared followed by a servant, and bearing a dish of hot smoking potatoes and a bottle of rum, his face beaming with the joy of one who is conscious of having hit upon really the right thing.

"I am acquainted with your English customs, you see, *Signore Generale,*" he cried. "Yes, yes, I know that you can never finish a meal without these," pointing to the tray. "See, a few potatoes and a couple of glasses of *rummo Inglese.* Now, your Excellency, this at least you will not refuse!"

What was to be done? To refuse the kind

old man was impossible. Equally impossible to gratify him! The General cast imploring glances upon the circle of aides-de-camp and officers, but there was no help for him there. They would follow him to face the foe any day, but they were enjoying his present dilemma too thoroughly to wish to help him out of it. There they sat in their places, with grave faces and dancing eyes, to see what their chief would do. He says he thought of pleading his Irish birth, but the plea seemed incongruous somehow, and would have been certainly incomprehensible, and attempts at excuse were of no avail, only bringing a doubting question, whether then his Excellency was *not Inglese?* So he seized and swallowed a potato, and then, with smarting throat and tearful eyes, gulped down half a glass of the potent rum; whereat his host clapped his hands gleefully, exclaiming, "*Evviva, evviva, è in verità un' Inglese,*" which was echoed by the servants, and a delighted giggle ran round the circle of aides-de-camp.

Now the work of the day must be begun: that was to visit some of the *masserie* which lay perched among the craggy slopes of the Monte di Martina, and which were favourite lurking-places for Don Ciro Annichiarico and his band of brigands. The first they visited,

Masseria dell' Duca, was a very good specimen of its class. It was backed by steep wooded hills, which rendered escape and concealment easy on the first alarm. Its thick walls dated from the middle ages, and were loopholed and protected by great solid gates and an avenue of trees, which was now effectually blocked up by carts with the wheels taken off, and logs and tree-trunks laid crosswise. At one corner of the enclosure rose a square tower, from the top of which you might overlook the great plain, dotted with white towns and villages, patched with brown leafless vineyards, green meads, silver-grey olive-orchards, and bounded by the shining sea. But at present the view was not before the eyes of the visitors, as they were outside the walls, within the avenue.

In the first place, it was necessary to remove the obstacles which blocked the avenue, and this took some time. The dragoons stood by meanwhile, carbine in hand, to guard against attack. Having reached the outer courtyard, they found the gates fast barred, and these being broken open, they entered: not a sign of life appeared. The grey old tower, the square building, lay silent and apparently deserted, though it was close upon noonday. The oaken doors were fast closed, and no reply was returned to knocking. It might have been the castle of the Sleeping Beauty, as it lay there in the sunshiny silence!

A soldier laid his ear to the door.

"Sir," said he, "I think I hear whispering within."

"Bianchi," said General Church, "your men command those loopholes?"

"A mouse, sir, daren't show his nose!"

"Good. Don't fire if you can help it. Fusco, knock again."

Three thundering knocks followed, with shouts of "*Aprite, aprite!*" but there was no sound in reply.

"Come, we must get in somehow," said the General. "Let us see what the heels of the trumpeters' horses can do for us."

He explains that as the trumpeters ride in front they are not often in close contact with the other troopers, and that therefore the wickedest horses are likely to fall to their share, and that this was the case in the present instance, these horses being known as furious kickers. The idea was received with a shout of laughter. The three black beasts were backed against the door.

"Fire the train!" cried the General, and a cut of the whip across their heels set the horses plunging and kicking so furiously that in crashed the door, and half-a-dozen *gendarmes*, carbine in hand, rushed through the opening thus made.

They found themselves in a very large room, comfortably furnished after the manner of these Apulian *masserie*. Great chests, some for holding meal, some for holding clothes and linen, a heavy oaken table, some stools and benches, were on the floor; jars of olives, figs, raisins, stood upon a shelf against the smoke-dried wall; strings of onions, sausages, and dried fish dangled from the rafters. Cheeses there were too, and huge jars of olive-oil, and half-a-dozen demijohns (great stone bottles), stoppered with oiled cotton, and containing the wine of the country, stood under the table. There was provision for a garrison, but apparently not a soul to make use of it! But, on examination, a small door leading to an inner chamber was discovered, and on opening it two sturdy peasants were discovered lying on a bed, and apparently so sound asleep that it required a good deal of shaking and shouting before they sat up, rubbing their eyes with portentous yawns, and asking—

"*Che volete, signori?*"

"Come, get up, and come along to the General. Here they are, General."

"Ah, my friends, you sleep pretty soundly, methinks. Who lives in this *masseria?*"

To which the only answer was a sullen "*Chi lo sa?*"

"Why did you not answer our summons?"

"I suppose because we were asleep."

"Are there any people here besides yourselves?"

A shrug of the shoulders and another "*Chi lo sa?*"

"You rascal! Is that the way you answer his Excellency?" cried Fusco. "Though, in truth," he muttered, "it is your Excellency's own fault. They think their lives are safe in your hands, so they won't speak a word."

"Yes, yes, I know. We'll try another plan." Then raising his voice, "Bianchi, blow open the door of the tower and let us see what's within. Where's the powder?"

Whereupon the door of the tower was flung open from the inside, and out rushed half-a-dozen men and women, crying, shrieking, gesticulating, wringing their hands.

"O Madonna, Madonna! *O misericordia! O perdona,*" they cried, "*O poveri noi!*"

It was impossible to get any information out of anybody in such a din; so after examining the tower and finding it empty, some of the *gendarmes* took the men in charge and marched them into the courtyard, while the women were shut up in the tower, under charge of Captain Viti, the tallest and handsomest of the *gendarmes* ("a body of men," says General Church, "remarkable for their good looks"), who was recommended to treat them civilly, and try whether he could get any useful information out of them! Meanwhile the General set patiently to work to examine the men in the courtyard, especially the two first found, but to very little purpose, "*Chi lo sa?*" being the burden of their replies.

"Where were the brigands? How should they know? They were poor peasants, who minded their own affairs, and never stirred beyond their own farm. Poor? Yes, truly. So poor were they, in fact, that the brigands passed them by, and their safety lay in having nothing to lose. Why did they bar their doors and refuse to answer when summoned? Ah, *chi lo sa?* From fear, certainly. His Excellency was merciful, his Excellency would understand. What did they know whether it was the brigands who knocked or not? As to Don Ciro—yes, they *heard* of him, without doubt. How old was he? *Chi lo sa?* How tall? Dark or fair? How could they know when they had never seen him?"

The General began to lose patience, but tried another tack. "What will you drink—wine or rum?"

Still the elder man answered only "*Chi lo sa?*" but the other, a less sullen and determined-looking fellow, looked up with a twinkle in his eye. "A glass of wine, if your Excellency pleases."

His fellow pushed him impatiently aside. "*Scusi*, signore, we are not thirsty at present."

"Look you, my friend, do you know that you are on the way to be hanged one of these days?"

"Very likely, signore," was the cool reply.

Just then a diversion was caused by the sudden appearance of the General's orderly, an old soldier, Boehmer by name. Boehmer was a very good servant if he could be kept from the wine-flask, but because of this weakness he was always getting into scrapes, being threatened with dismissal, and then forgiven because he was so faithful, so affectionate, so zealously devoted to his master, and withal such a quaint, amusing, good-humoured fellow. Now behold him, rolling forward, with the most ludicrous attempt at steadiness, and saluting with preternatural gravity.

"What do you mean, you drunken scoundrel?" cried his angry master. "Get along with you, and don't dare to appear before me in that state!"

"If your Excellency will let me speak——"

"You are not likely to say anything worth hearing. You ought to be ashamed of yourself."

"As your Excellency pleases. I thought it my duty to take a turn round the place—to see that all was right—and if your Excellency will follow me——"

"Boehmer has wit in his wine. Let's go and see what he has found," said General Church; and they went, prisoners and all, Boehmer marching in front, very stiff and straight, and muttering "*Con rispetto*—never soberer—as sober as any of you!"

He led them through a little gate in the wall, and there in a corner he pointed dramatically to a huge heap of feathers and freshly picked bones, and asked, "Where did those come from? *Mon Général, v'là les brigands—le dîner des brigands—c'est-à-dire*——"

"Right, right, Boehmer," cried the officers who pressed round; "they must have dined here within the hour. What a feast they have had!"

"You live well in this *masseria*," said the General to the two peasants who stood stolidly by.

"Alas! signore, no: bread and water—a few olives—perhaps now and then a fowl, or a kid from our own flock."

"Come, come, this has gone far enough! We must teach you to speak the truth. Look there! Lambs, capons—a feast for a prince! Twenty people have dined here. Tell me who they were, or——"

"Perhaps it was the wolves," suggested the younger man, with an insinuating air. "We are much troubled by wolves at this season, your Excellency."

The General had to pass his hand over his mouth to hide a smile at the fellow's effrontery.

"Nonsense, sir! No more lying. Bianchi, get ready, since these fellows won't tell the truth."

They were marched back into the courtyard, and made to kneel with their backs to the wall, while a file of soldiers stood opposite with levelled carbines. The women, who crowded to the windows of the tower overhead, set up a dismal wailing, mingled with entreaties to their friends to tell the truth.

The younger man cried out, "*Eccellenza*, sooner than be shot I will tell——"

"*Bestia!*" interrupted the other. "Don't listen to him, your Excellency. He lies, he knows nothing. I will speak. What does your Excellency desire to know?"

"Desire to know, fellow! Who dined here to-day? I ask for the last time."

"Well then — if I must speak — it was — the *intendente* of the province — on his way to Martina. He left an hour before you arrived," said this cool personage, smiling and smacking his lips as if he remembered the taste of the feast; "and he enjoyed his dinner amazingly!"

"As you seem to have done!"

"Just so, your Excellency. Yes, yes; there have been fifteen or twenty people here, as you said."

"You mean to say that is true?"

"But surely, *Signore Generale*"—in a tone of candid expostulation — "ask my comrade. The *intendente* left Bari this morning; and since in these times one has to be cautious, he bade us say nothing about his being here."

"Now look here, you rascals! — it would serve you right if I had you shot out of hand. Perhaps I might, if there was a priest handy! So, Bianchi, you keep the fellows safe till I ride a bit farther and come back here."

The General knew that the peasants were more afraid of Don Ciro's vengeance than of his, and that he should get no more information at that moment. So he rode off to another *masseria*, called the Piè di Monti, where the only inhabitant was a slim, dark-eyed, curly-haired lad, who uncovered with a frank open countenance, which took the General's fancy at once.

"My boy, is it not true that Don Ciro dined here to-day?"

"Not here, *signore mio*. He dined at the Masseria dell' Duca—and then he came here, and carried off our wine!"

"Is this really the truth?"

"*Per Cristo, si, signore!* I would say it to their faces."

"Do so, my boy, and fear nothing. Mount behind that dragoon."

"Will your Excellency protect me?"

"Certainly I will."

"Then I am ready."

"You will speak out?"

"Your Excellency may depend upon me. I have given my word!"

Soon they were back again at the Masseria dell' Duca, and very black were the looks of the other peasants when they were confronted with the handsome lad.

"Speak out, my boy. Where did Don Ciro dine to-day?"

"Here, signore. Here in this very *masseria*."

"Oh you liar! oh you rascal! oh you son of a lying mother!" cried the other peasants, "how dare you tell lies to his Excellency?"

"Who lies? not I," said the boy. "Do you mean to deny that he dined here, and Palma too, and all the *comitiva?* A fine *festa* they had, for I heard them say so—only they were disturbed over their drink, so they came on to us, and carried off six skins of wine, curse them! It was all we had. They said their scouts warned them that General Giorgio and the cavalry were close at hand."

"Oh thou liar, and son of liars! Hold thy tongue. The *comitiva* has not been here at all to-day, and the only people here have come from Taranto."

"From Taranto? What people from Taranto? *Bagattella!*" said the lad, with a toss of his curly locks.

So the matter ended. The two peasants were marched off under escort to Francavilla for further examination. The lad went with them for protection; and the General and the rest of his men rode to two more *masserie*, before starting home to Francavilla.

The sun was going down. The cavalry horses were tired with a ride of nearly forty miles. Francavilla was twenty miles distant, and General Church was bound to be there that night, and wanted, besides, to visit his chain of posts on the way. The officers remonstrated, declaring that the road was too unsafe for travelling by night without the cavalry, and entreated their chief to take up his quarters till daybreak at the Masseria dell' Duca.

"Send me a couple of orderlies, then," said he. "Tell those fellows to get everything prepared for me and my staff at once." Then in a lower tone, "That will surely be handed on to Don Ciro. So now, good night, my friends! Who will ride to Francavilla with me? Of course the officers of cavalry must stay and look after their men, and you will all meet me at breakfast to-morrow morning."

So he started with the aides-de-camp, the now sober Boehmer, and the gentlemen from Lecce, who, in spite of his protestations, refused to stay behind, and after three hours of "riding in the dark over execrable roads, broken ground, and swampy fields," reached Francavilla in safety, the only stoppages being caused by the challenges from the vedettes posted along the road. Near Francavilla the heavy rain had so flooded the low-lying ground that ditches were undistinguishable from dry banks, especially in the dark. Presently there was a tremendous splash, followed by a laugh, and the General's voice exclaiming, "*Avanti, signori*, a little water more or less can't make much difference!" The fact was, he had been riding along a bank, followed by the faithful Boehmer, when both fell slap into a now invisible ditch; "and the compliments which Boehmer paid to the stream," says the General, "we cannot exactly repeat!"

"You fool! what did you do that for?" asked his unreasonable master, when he had scrambled up on the bank.

To which Boehmer pertinently replied—

"*Vous avez y passé, mon Général, et c'est mon devoir de vous suivre partout!*"

"*Depuis quand est-ce que tu mets de l'eau dans ton vin*, Boehmer?" laughed one of the aides-de-camp.

"*Depuis que le Diable—je veux dire le Général—m'en a donné l'exemple!*" answered Boehmer, as he drew out and carefully wiped his sword; but as he remounted, off flew his shako. "*Brigand de shako*," &c., &c., he cried, and with his sword dexterously picked it out of the water, and placing it on his head, trotted off to regain his place behind his master.

Wet and weary, they came to Francavilla, where they were hospitably received and magnificently feasted by a gentleman of the place, and after dinner the celebrated improvisatore, Don Angelo, was announced, requesting leave to recite some verses in honour of the distinguished guests. The General was charmed to see Don Angelo—would be charmed to listen to his improvising—in ten minutes' time, when he had held a short conference with Colonel Schmerber on matters of immediate import. Would Don Angelo and the worthy host excuse him for this short space? Then, business over, pleasure would have its turn. So the General and his chief of the staff retired to a private room, and were soon so deep in their maps and reports that poor Don Angelo and his verses were clean forgotten.

Two hours later an aide-de-camp entered.

"Oh, De Nitis, is it you? Upon my word, I forgot! What became of the improvisatore?"

"Oh, he spouted for an hour, and very good his verses were. Then he went home, hoping to pay his respects to your Excellency in the morning."

"It is not quite certain that he will find me here to-morrow morning. Schmerber, I don't think you will object to a couple of hours' sleep, and I am sure I shall not. We must be in the saddle at daybreak. So now, good night, gentlemen."

Next enter the master of the house on hospitable thoughts intent, bearing a tray of wine and biscuits with his own hands, to do the more honour to his guest. Oh, horror! The General, booted and spurred, was calmly wrapping round him his military cloak in preparation for taking repose on a wide old-fashioned sofa, while there lay before him the mighty best bed, elaborately carved, curtained with crimson velvet, furnished with mountainous feather-bed and pillows, and snow-white, lace-fringed sheets and coverlet.

"How, how, your Excellency?" gasped the old gentleman, almost letting fall the tray; "in my house! I should never forgive myself, and what's more, my wife would never forgive me either! See, your bed is ready, and it has been her pleasure to prepare it with her own hands for your Excellency. And you would sleep on the sofa? No, no, that is impossible —you will not do us such a wrong."

"Only for this one night, dear Don Bartolomeo," pleaded the General, in his most insinuating manner; "when I return, how happy I shall be to occupy your most beautiful bed, but in two or three hours I must be off again, and how could I persuade myself to leave so comfortable a couch in two hours' time? Indeed, I must resist the temptation, dear Don Bartolomeo."

"But my wife; ah, if your Excellency had a wife!"

"I should doubtless say to her as you, dear friend, will say to the signora—'How kind! but it is impossible.' When I return I will myself make my excuses to the signora, and obtain her forgiveness. I will sleep in that magnificent bed for a week with pleasure then; only to-night I positively must have my own way."

"Ah, it is the same as saying that your Excellency is an Englishman," answered the host, with a sigh and a shrug. "It is an Englishman's nature to love freedom and to be set on having his own way! So, *felice notte, caro Signore Generale.*"

But the General was not to have the sleep for which he longed, for no sooner had the door closed behind Don Bartolomeo than it was opened again by the General's orderly, with the information that an ill-looking fellow insisted on coming in to see him.

"And I can't allow such a fellow to enter your Excellency's presence unless I may remain in the room," said the faithful Boehmer.

"Thank you, my friend; but bring him in, whatever or whoever he may be. I am accustomed to queer visitors, you know, and you must leave us alone. But never fear," and he significantly touched the pistols which lay close at hand.

"As your Excellency commands; but it is much against my will," grumbled Boehmer.

He went out, and returned with a bronzed and bearded man, wrapped in the universal cloak, and with his felt hat well slouched over his face.

Very unwillingly the orderly obeyed his master's sign and left the room, leaving the door a little ajar; but the stranger stepped back a few paces and quietly closed it. Then he took off his hat, and a smile stole over his swarthy features as he asked—

"Does not your Excellency know me?"

"In truth, my friend, I do not."

He rubbed his hands and showed his white teeth with an air of delight.

"Is it possible! Am I already forgotten? *Povero me!* His Excellency positively does not know who I am?"

"Not I. You might be Don Ciro himself with that beard. Come, none of this foolery, sir. Who are you, and what do you want?"

"*Perdona, Eccellenza;* I thought you would have recognised De Feo."

He pulled off a half-mask, which disguised the upper part of his face as effectually as the beard had done the lower, and stood revealed as a certain officer of *gendarmerie* who had been for the last two or three weeks on a mission to watch the movements of the brigands. He was a hardy, reckless, dare-devil sort of a fellow, who was suspected of having had dealings with the brigands on his own account in former times, and who had certainly managed to get into the bad graces of former commanders; but General Church had taken a fancy to him, and always found him a faithful and honest officer, prompt and eager when any adventure was forward, and, on the principle of "Set a thief to catch a thief," particularly useful when there was looking after Don Ciro and his banditti to be done.

"I am very glad to see you, De Feo. Well, what have you done?"

"Spent time enough among the brigands to count against all the sins I have committed when I come to purgatory."

"Let me hear—but have you supped?"

"Not even breakfasted, *mon Général.*"

"Call the orderly then, and tell him to get you something to eat. Now then, while it is getting ready, give me a sketch of your proceedings. First of all—where is Don Ciro?"

"In Francavilla at this moment."

"The devil he is!"

"Fact, your Excellency. He rode here with you to-night, in the uniform of the regiment Reale Corona."

The General used an expression for which he would certainly have reproved Boehmer, before he asked, "Where did Ciro dine this morning?"

"At the Masseria dell' Duca. He rode there from Grottaglia last night. Your Excellency was at Grottaglia yesterday, and he left the town as you entered it."

"And he is here now, of course, in some other disguise."

"Of course; and as to finding him in this infernal city, which is full of his friends, and where we are a mere handful——"

"Yes, yes. Not to be thought of. Do they mean to make a stir?"

"Not unless Taranto, Ostuni, and Lecce will join."

"They won't. And where have you been?"

"About the woods of Girifalco, where I came across the whole *comitiva*. Luckily I was mounted and they were not, at the moment. But I had a close shave for my life. They were lounging in a little glade among the trees, drinking, laughing, quarrelling, and I crept up as near as I dared behind the brushwood. One said, 'Why shouldn't we laugh?' and another voice growled out, 'Because a couple of balls may send the laugh down your throat.' 'Softly there,' said the first; 'two can play at that game.' 'Come, come,' said a third voice, 'if you must shoot, shoot the rascally soldiers.' 'What do you mean? I have been a soldier myself,' said the laugher. 'Come on, you dogs! I defy you!' 'You talk big enough; but it's not the dogs that bark loudest that are quickest to bite,' was the answer. Another voice spoke in an authoritative tone, 'What is this? Rascals that you are, how dare you quarrel together when there is business in hand? Join hands and be friends if you value your lives.' 'Here is my hand'— 'And mine'—'And mine'—'And mine!' they cried. 'It is well, and I forgive you this time; but remember, you are warned. Brothers, be careful in future.'

"When I heard this, in the deep authoritative voice, I knew it must be Don Ciro himself who spoke, and I thought it wisest to mount and ride off as silently as possible. But they caught sight of me, the villains, and half a dozen started up to bar my way across the opening of the glade. However, I dashed through, while the balls whistled past me. One went through the high crown of my hat, though luckily it did not stop in my head. Here it is, General," and he held up the hat.

"Truly a providence," said the General, examining it. "Well, what next?"

"Oh, when I got clean away, I left my horse with a friend, and skulked about a bit in the disguise which puzzled your Excellency. By the by, you had a narrow escape on your way to Lizzano this morning. Ciro had posted a strong detachment in ambush on the San Marzano road; but your Excellency went another way. For the love of God, don't run such another risk as you did in to-night's ride."

"Oh, nonsense! But how did Ciro know I was going to Lizzano? I thought I had kept that a secret?"

"Your Excellency did so, but the Marquis had ordered preparations to be made for guests, though he mentioned no names. Fish and oysters were ordered from Taranto, *confetti* from Manduria, cream and *ricotta* from different farms, and a wild boar from the Armeo woods. I have told you that Ciro is here to-night. He is come on purpose to find out what you mean to do to-morrow."

"He won't find out much."

"Certainly not; for not even your Excellency's officers know whither they are bound, when they mount. But remember, Don Ciro has sworn to kill you, General, and——"

"And your supper is ready, De Feo; so go and eat it, and do wash your face. Good night."

So ended a busy day, one of many like it.

CHAPTER XIV.

THE MAN OF THE SEVENTEEN MURDERS.

GENERAL CHURCH'S PROGRESSES — NOTICE BY SIR JOHN RENNIE—A NIGHT IN A *MASSERIA*—CAPTURE OF OCCHIO LUPO — EXECUTION OF THE LAST CAPTAIN OF THE DECISI.

AFTER the capture and execution of Ciro Annichiarico, Francavilla regained its normal condition as a quiet little country town. The crowds who had gathered from the country round dispersed to their own homes; no trace remained of the ghastly scene in the little Piazza; churches, there and everywhere, resounded with *Te Deums;* the city gates were adorned with triumphal arches; the troops had a couple of days' holiday; the General's brother came from his home at Florence to pay him a visit, and rode with him, and other friends, in an almost royal progress from city to city, welcomed everywhere with speeches and shouting, presented with the freedom of the city here, with a sword of honour there.

Some extracts from old family letters tell us of this time. On February 15, 1818, the brother writes to his wife :—

As I told you in my last from Francavilla, the army marched on the following morning. You can have no idea of the manner in which the General has been received. About a mile from the town all the authorities met him in a procession of carriages. At the gate he was met by the commandant, the governor and officers of the port, and served with a salute of artillery, the people shouting "*Evviva il Rè ! Evviva il Generale !*" as we reached the house prepared for our reception. We sat down to a sumptuous banquet, followed by a brilliant ball. We have been to several towns, and have been met everywhere with the same enthusiasm and joy. People come miles to meet Richard—the king himself could not have been better received: but for him this province would have been the theatre of a dreadful rebellion. We have gone through beautiful country, the most fertile in the kingdom. Our march to Lecce will take three days. We have ridden about three hundred miles from place to place, through woods and over rocky irregular roads, accompanied by two hundred cavalry and about twenty gentlemen of the country.

A week later he writes from Lecce :—

Have finished a campaign of twenty days, fifteen on horseback, but none the worse, and have met the same enthusiastic reception everywhere.

Once they fell in with a party of young hunters in a wood, who presented the General with a huge wild boar which they had just killed. Rather a weighty present, one would think, to carry about on a march! The weather was fine, the country beautiful, every one looked gay and festive, coming out with music, with addresses, with flags and garlands. Bishops and clergy headed their flocks, and gave solemn benedictions to the troops as they rode by. The city of Lecce received them at the Gate of Rugia, which was decorated with wreaths and with flags inscribed *Pace—Sicurtà—Onore—Gratitudine;* and as they rode slowly along through the streets, flowers were showered down upon them by fair hands from the gaily draped windows and balconies.

People were almost afraid to speak to one another, [says another letter], but now all is changed. Richard gives a ball every week, and the *intendente* gives another. . . . Richard's commission makes him completely despotic: people hope it will continue, for he has saved this country from a reign of terror. Every day wretches are brought in from the woods and caves. . . . Though the brigands are pretty well got rid of, Richard will not let us travel without an escort. I have much enjoyed this visit.

There is an interesting notice of General Church at this time in the 'Autobiography of Sir John Rennie,' F.R.S. He says:—

We reached Lecce, the capital of the province, February 8, 1820. Next day I called on General Church, the Governor of the province, and was most kindly received by him, he insisting on my making his house my home. . . . General Church was an extraordinary man. He was below the middle size, about the age of five-and-forty [his age at this time was about thirty-six], extremely well-built, spare, sinewy, and active, with a well-proportioned head, sharp piercing eyes, rather aquiline nose, and a closely compressed mouth, denoting great firmness and resolution. He commanded a regiment of Albanians and Greeks as an auxiliary corps in the British employment during the great war, and in that position assisted the operations of the British cruisers on the coast of Italy, and hence became subsequently attached to the army of Lord William Bentinck after his conquest of Sicily. Church was a proficient in the Greek, Italian, and French languages, and having considerable military talents, and being a great disciplinarian, soon brought the rough and savage elements of which his corps was composed into tolerable order, and rendered them of considerable service in the wild warfare in which they were engaged. At the conclusion of the war he retired on half-pay to Naples, where, being well known to the Government, he was made Governor of the province of Otranto, at that time overrun with brigands. Church was appointed to the command with unlimited control, and by his vigorous and energetic conduct soon spread terror and dismay among them: he was here, there, and everywhere; when they least expected, he came upon them suddenly, dispersed them, and destroyed the leaders without mercy. He had many narrow escapes himself. . . . In a short time he extirpated brigandism, the province regained its tranquillity, and the people pursued their several employments in peace, without fear of molestation, blessing the General who had relieved them from their oppressors.

THE MAN OF THE SEVENTEEN MURDERS. 255

Being particularly desirous of seeing Brindisi, from my recollections of Horace, I obtained an escort of two dragoons from General Church, "For," said he, "you may meet some unwelcome visitors on the road; but if they see the uniform of my dragoons they will not trouble you with their acquaintance."

There is another letter, dated May 1820, from which a passage may be quoted. It is from John D. Church, Richard's elder brother, whose letters have been quoted before. "I reached Lecce through a country where I had an escort of eighty soldiers when I was here last. Now all is quiet, and no escort is needed."

On this occasion he was accompanied by his wife and little son, five years old. That child, who clung to his father's hand and listened with wistful half-terrified eyes to the talk of his elders, grew up to be Dean of St Paul's; and in later life he always had an impression that he had seen and shuddered at the grim blackened heads fastened in iron cages over the gates of the cities. But this must have been the impression left on his lively childish imagination conjuring up pictures of what he had heard described till they seemed reality; for in September 1818 we find that the General had proclaimed "an amnesty for the past to include all those who from ignorance or fear have consented to belong to criminal associations;" publicly announced "that he will receive no accusations against the individuals of this province on the subject of the principal or secondary part which they may be accused of having taken in the late unfortunate events;" and finally, in April 1819, orders a letter to be read in all the churches of the province commanding that "the heads of the malefactors executed by the Military Tribunal shall be taken down from the different gates and towers on which they had been set up, and buried, so that their memory may be altogether extinguished."

For some time stragglers from the brigands were found by the peasants, and brought in from caves and forests; and there are curious stories of such captures, of which one shall be related here.

Two officers were returning from Taranto to Lecce one night. A dark and stormy night it was, and very glad were they to see the twinkling of a light at no great distance, as they were crossing the plain not far from Manduria, famous for its holy well, "della Madonna di Misericordia." Also, we are told, "the inhabitants of Manduria are distinguished for their love of order, urbanity, and hospitality." The twinkling light led them to a poor little *masseria;* but poor though it was, the two officers were glad of shelter. So they put their horses into the stable and entered the house. The only inhabitants were an old man and his little granddaughter. An "old, old man," bent and bowed, with a queer brown face, all seamed and crossed with wrinkles, who regarded the uninvited guests with small favour, muttering to himself and shaking his head, as he shot furtive glances at them out of his little ferrety eyes; and after informing the officers that he had nothing to give them to eat, and no beds to offer them, he threw a log on the hearth, lay down on a heap of straw in one corner of the room, where the child was already asleep, and appeared to follow her example.

The young officers took it very coolly, shook streams of water from their hats and cloaks, pulled a bench in front of the fire, devoured such refreshment, in the shape of bread and sausage and wine, as they had with them, and then pulled out their cigars and prepared to make a night of it. An hour had passed, when the door of the *masseria* was pushed open, and another guest, after standing silently for a moment on the threshold, came forward and joined himself to their company. He was very tall, with a muscular sinewy frame, showing great strength and activity, gaunt, brown, with dark glittering eyes which reminded the officers of those of a hungry wolf, and hands disproportionately large, even for his great height. Also, one finger was wanting on the right hand. All this the officers were able to note as he shook his long brown cloak and slouched hat, before putting them on again. They saw also that he carried a carbine, and that in his belt were stuck three pistols and a curved and curiously embossed hunting-knife; while round his neck and on his breast were hung several relics— a small black cross, a silver death's-head, and two figures of the Madonna, embroidered in crimson silk.

The officers glanced at one another: they did not like this apparition; but what was to be done? They were far away from head-quarters, there were no other inhabitants of the *masseria* than a feeble old man and a child. Besides, they had no commission to arrest suspicious wayfarers, and it was by no means certain whether a whistle might not fill the house with armed confederates, if they showed mistrust of the stranger.

So it seemed best to salute him, to make way for him on the bench, and to take out fresh cigars. The stranger returned their civilities, and remarks upon the weather followed, while the thunder growled, the lightning came in fitful flashes, and the rain pattered steadily on the roof. Presently the stranger tried a new topic. "*Signori miei*," he asked, while his wild glittering eyes seemed to gleam from under his slouched hat in a way to make one shudder, "do you know General Giorgio?"

The officers turned and looked at him at this unexpected question. "*Sì*, signore," answered they.

"Ah, he is a fine man!" The mysterious stranger kept his face in the shadow of his hat, but "held them with his glittering eye" as he spoke. "He has rid the country of robbers, and we travel in safety by night and by day."

"Signore, do *you* know General Giorgio?"

"Oh yes; but perfectly! In fact, I am in his service."

If these had not been young officers, new to their work, they would have recognised by the silver death's-head round his neck, and the curious characters traced on his long black-handled knife, that this was no follower of General Church, but a *guapo*, a brigand, and, worst of all, one of the sect of the Decisi. But as it was, though they doubted whether any amount of sheep's clothing would make him anything but a wolf, there was the possibility, they thought, of his being a *gendarme* in disguise returning from some secret mission to headquarters, like themselves. At any rate, it seemed best to accept the statement.

"Signori," he said, "when next we meet, I hope you will bear witness that you found me busy in the General's service." To this they answered with a gesture, and the stranger went on: "Yes, yes, I have done good service against Ciro Annichiarico. Ah, his time is over now! Eighteen years he was king of these provinces and more, but, *per Santo Diavolo*, his head is off at last, and his reign is over! *Che briccone!* what a rascal! And now we are free, thanks to General Giorgio. And I have served him so well! Ah, when we meet at headquarters you will see, you will see!"

They made some reply to this, and the conversation dropped. Now and then one or another threw a fresh log on the hearth, and lit a fresh cigar. Now and then the two officers made some remark to each other in French, but otherwise they sat still and silent, till the crowing of the first cock made them all start.

"It will soon be daybreak. What kind of

night is it now? The thunder has ceased," said one of the young men, rising; and, followed by his comrade, he went to the door, opened it, and stepped outside. It was still raining, and "dark as a wolf's throat," and they returned to the fire to wait till daylight. But where was their strange companion? They had left him sitting on the bench, staring at the smouldering fire, cigar in mouth, carbine in hand. They stirred the logs till flames shot up and lighted the room. They seized a splinter, and, using it as a torch, searched every corner. He was not there! Yet the room possessed but one door, and its only window was but a few inches square, and, moreover, full fifteen feet from the ground. They looked in vain for a ladder, or even a chair to mount by, and the bench stood exactly where they had left it. As to the old *massaro*, he was snoring on his heap of straw, and there was not a cupboard or chest or corner which offered any chance of concealment.

"What do you think about it?" asked one, with an involuntary shudder.

"*Per Bacco!* I don't know what to think," answered his companion gloomily. "Brigands in flesh and blood are all very well, but as to this——"

"Since Ciro is dead, upon my word I think

it was the devil himself," said the other. "Could any mortal have escaped in such a fashion?"

They went to the door again and looked out. The rain had ceased, and a faint greyness showed that dawn was on its way. Every now and then a gust of wind shook the trees, bringing down a shower of drops. Otherwise, everything was still and quiet.

"Let us leave this place," said the two young officers. "*Holà, amico!*" to the sleeping *massaro*; "wake up and tell us our way to Lecce."

The old man got up and came forward, glancing timidly round him, and hurried off to fetch the horses. The little girl crept after him, and both listened with frightened eyes as the officers told the adventure of the night. Then exclaiming, "O Madonna, protect us! It was doubtless the devil himself. If he should return? *O poveri noi!*" the *massaro* seized the child by the hand and hurried off into the woods which stretched like a belt round his house, leaving the two young men staring after him in amazement! However, as there was no use pursuing him down unknown paths, they saddled their horses, took the widest road, and arrived at Lecce in safety in time for breakfast.

Presently they were summoned to General Church's room, and found him, map spread on table, ready to listen to their report, which they gave, winding up with a full account of the night's adventure, and an inquiry as to whether the mysterious stranger was really in the General's service.

The General leaned back in his chair and laughed. "Why, gentlemen," said he, "don't you know the meaning of the death's-head? Have you never seen the black-handled dagger of the Decisi, with emblems inscribed on the blade? Well, you never saw the papers and things found at Grottaglia and San Marzano, so how should you? That fellow, from your description, must be Occhio Lupo of the Seventeen Murders—a nice name, is it not?—and you must go after him. Come to me at sundown for instructions, and each of you provide a dozen men. You won't want more, now that Ciro is dead."

When they returned, General Church showed them on his map that there were two roads which reached the *masseria* from Lecce, and directed that each of the officers should take one, with his little company of men, and reaching the fringe of wood that surrounded the house, at two o'clock in the morning, should take up their positions on either side of the door in silence, and wait there till the crowing of the cock.

"But if the fellow has not dared to come back to the same place, General?"

"He will, and he will leave it as soon as the first cock crows. I know the ways of those gentry," answered their chief. "Only mind that your men make no noise of any kind."

So said, so done. And sure enough, as soon as the first cock began to crow the door of the *masseria* opened, and the dull glimmer of light within showed a dark figure stepping swiftly and silently across the threshold. But half-a-dozen strong arms were round him, and in a moment he was thrown to the ground and securely chained, his evil eyes glancing from one to another, till he saw the faces of his companions of the night before. Then an angry gleam and an oath showed that he recognised them, but he said not a word more.

"And now, friend *massaro*, what have you to say for yourself? Harbouring brigands in your *masseria*, eh? You will come along with us to Lecce, and see what General Giorgio has to say to you."

The old *massaro* threw himself on his knees, and the child wept piteously, turning with clasped hands from one officer to the other, and entreating pardon for her *povero nonno*, her dear *nonno*, until the young men consented to hear the old man's story.

"He harbour the robbers? But no, no, the Madonna knew better than that! It was true that this bad man had taken shelter in his house at night; but what then? How could he, a poor old man, help it, if such a one opened the door and walked in? Could he drive him out by force? See then, let the gentlemen ask the little one, if what he said was not true." Ah yes, but it was true, and the Madonna knew it. And the child chimed in, bringing to the rescue a pair of artless blue eyes, and many pretty gestures of appeal and coaxing, which quite softened the hearts of the two young officers. But how did Occhio Lupo escape? Let the *massaro* tell that, and then——

Certainly he would tell all. To such kind signori it was a pleasure to tell everything! The signori thought he was asleep; but no, not exactly asleep—on the contrary, he appeared to sleep, from fear, and thus he could see what happened. The signori went to the door—well. And opened it—well. And returned to find the *guapo* gone? Had the signori happened to turn their heads, they would have seen that he followed at their heels, so close that at the moment they stepped outside, just at that moment he stepped outside too, and slipped into the shadow, so that when they returned, the door that shut them in shut him out! He, the old *massaro*, prayed for the good gentlemen to all the saints, when he saw the Wolf-eye creeping behind them — so — with his carbine in his hand. For, you understand, there might have been a shot from the carbine, a blow from the dagger—but why speak of those things, when it was past, and, blessed be the Madonna, they were safe?

"And the kind signori will not hurt the poor *nonno?*" cried the child, clinging to him, and turning her pale wistful little face towards the questioners.

"No, little one, we will not hurt him. But see here, friend, you may get your neck into the noose if you don't give up the habit of harbouring assassins; so be warned. Now let us march!"

The two officers returned with their captive to headquarters, where of course he was tried by the Military Commission, and met with the fate which his name shows that he deserved. There was no longer any difficulty in finding people who would witness to his crimes, now that his chief was dead; and he was taken to a village where one of his most atrocious murders had been committed, and there shot, behaving like the hardened ruffian he was to the last. "Ah!" said he to Colonel Bentz, shaking his head and grinding his teeth, as the place of his doom came in sight, "if I could only burn the whole village!" When, according to custom, the coffin which had been carried before him as a condemned criminal was laid on the ground beside him, he shuffled round it in spite of his irons, in an uncouth dance, called for a glass of brandy, and grumbled when wine was given him instead. A priest came near, holding forth the crucifix: the wretch spat upon it, pouring forth a flood of oaths and foul language. Then turning to the soldiers, who stood with levelled carbines, he said, "I go then. It is my turn. Good. I have killed seventeen and more, and it is only fair that I should die for that. I had thought I could venture on one more night in the *masseria;* but never mind, I can die as well as others have done. So now let us go—*addio, addio, addio!*" and the words were cut short by a volley which laid him dead on the ground, the last of the captains of the Decisi, if not the worst.

CHAPTER XV.

THE PACIFICATION OF APULIA.

GOVERNMENT INGRATITUDE — DON LUIGI GENTILI — A COMPLAINT TO THE KING — THE GENERAL'S FIRMNESS — GENERAL CHURCH AND THE TAILOR.

FOR the next two years General Church lived at Lecce as commandant of the province of Apulia. Lecce, which for some years had lost its old reputation for gaiety and light-heartedness, again became "one of the pleasantest cities of Italy." He "enjoyed the agreeable society and splendid hospitality of the inhabitants of the provinces of Bari and Otranto." "Not a single murder or robbery took place during this time." He was flattered and fêted, the Government gave him thanks, and promised him rewards which never came. His brother writes:—

Richard is promised a post of great honour and eminence, so now his fortune is made; [and a little later]: he has not yet got his reward, but before long (*entre nous*) we shall have a Marquess in the family with a fine estate! So attached are the people to him that his recall would cause a rebellion. Will you believe that such has been the state of the country for years under the sway of the terrible brigand and his band, that many people have not ventured outside their doors, and even the *sindaco* of the place and the *intendente* of the province have not ventured outside the gates of the city?

Meanwhile the General has expended his own little fortune, and has borrowed a large sum from his devoted brother, in paying his soldiers, and returning the hospitalities offered him, but is unable to get from the Government even his arrears of pay.

The work was done, and done well. But as to paying the workman, that was another matter. And as time went on, and other claims were pushed to the front, the Government was glad to forget old promises, and throw aside their no longer needed instrument.

Even during this period of General Church's prosperity there might be heard the grumbling of the coming storm. It was impossible that it should be otherwise. He was a foreigner, set in a high place over the heads of native governors; this of itself would naturally cause jealousy and dislike. He was uncompromising, determined to do his work in his own way, to hold to his rights—very likely a bit arrogant in asserting them, very likely not so courteous as prudence would dictate towards those whom he disliked and thought badly of.

Two stories will illustrate his methods of dealing with those who were not worthy of respect or trust.

There was a certain Government spy in Lecce, Don Luigi Gentili, who for years had lived and grown rich by his infamous trade. Everybody detested him, but everybody feared him too much to show it. He was almost as powerful in the city as Ciro Annichiarico himself. His mode of action was equally simple and ingenious. He merely sailed with the stream. When King Ferdinand reigned, Gentili furnished him with lists of the disaffected people who were on the side of Napoleon. When Ferdinand gave place to Joseph Buonaparte, Gentili was equally ready with lists of those who were plotting to get the old Government back. The same game was played under Murat; and when Murat was shot, and Ferdinand IV. of Naples came back as Ferdinand I. of the Two Sicilies, who so ready with protestations of service as Don Luigi Gentili? And each Government in turn seems to have accepted his services, and paid for them too! The Government registers revealed this fact on inspection.

Most extraordinary papers they were [says General Church]. Long lists of the most respectable people of the neighbourhood were found, denouncing them as favourers of first one party, then another, year by year, month by month; and subjoined were the punishments inflicted—shooting, fines, imprisonment for years—and the records of money received, from whichever Government was in power, for information given. His own receipts, in his own handwriting, bore witness against him. More than a hundred families had suffered from the infernal calumnies of this wretch!

Don Gentili was a great ally of the *intendente* of Lecce, a timid man, and no friend to General Church, who got him displaced and recalled to Naples; also he was a member of half-a-dozen secret societies, which would account for the respect shown to him by the same *intendente* and other authorities. Some time before this date, when the General first came to visit Lecce, Gentili had tried to stir up the people to attack the troops on their way from one city to another,—thus, as he put it, "freeing the country, driving back the foreigner, and establishing the Salentine Republic." The idea was responded to with acclamation, and a body of armed citizens were placed in ambush on the Bari road, the day the General was expected to enter Lecce. Perhaps it was as well for them that he happened to come in by a different road, so no harm was done! Then Don Gentili went off to the authorities and denounced several people as having been concerned in a plot to attack the royal troops—and was duly paid for the information by the Government.

"The fellow deserves hanging," said the General, pulling his moustache, and pacing the room perplexedly, as he listened to all these details. "Yes, the world would be well rid of him, no doubt. But then, there are probably half a dozen nearly as bad; and he has a wife, you say, and a whole tribe of children. What is to become of them? Can't we keep him out of doing any more mischief without going to extremities? If I send him before the court he is doomed. Suppose he is banished, and put under surveillance for the present, so as to give him a chance of mending his ways?" So Don Luigi Gentili was sent to Barletta, out of his own province, and with stern warnings and threatenings if he should venture to leave the place without express permission from headquarters; and for a short time he kept quiet enough. But he had a friend in the displaced *intendente* of Lecce, the Marchese Pietracatella, now living at Naples, and brooding over his displacement, which he set down as the work of the meddlesome Englishman.

THE PACIFICATION OF APULIA. 273

One fine day King Ferdinand, in his state carriage, was taking his usual drive along the Chiaja. The four fat horses pranced solemnly along, conducted by the gorgeous coachman in royal livery. The lazy, good-humoured, self-indulgent king sleepily returned the salutations of passers-by. The sky was blue, the sea was blue, the air was golden, dazzling; early summer made the Chiaja of Naples into an earthly paradise; bright-eyed, bare-legged boys played *moro*, sellers of macaroni and lemonade cried their wares at every corner, flower-girls showed their white teeth in ready smiles when likely customers came by — all was pleasure, ease, light, colour, movement, amusement. Suddenly King Ferdinand rubbed his eyes; a respectable-looking man, dressed in black, darted forwards, seized the handle of the carriage-door with one hand, and waved a paper with the other, wildly gesticulating and exclaiming, "*Giustizia, Maestà—giustizia, giustizia!*" The carriage was stopped. The king ordered a lackey to open the door. He was fond of posing as the father of his people, when it did not entail too much trouble; and in his best "*Rè di lazzaroni*" manner, "*Ebbene, amico,*" he said, "*che volete? Parlate, parlate.*"

Upon this Gentili fell upon his knees, seizing the king's hand and kissing it effusively, while

S

he poured forth most lamentable complaints against General Giorgio, who was persecuting an unfortunate gentleman of Lecce to death! The king shook his head at this. "How? how? Persecuted by Giorgio! Can't believe it; can't believe it. I know Giorgio well—too well to believe that he would persecute one of my people!" Gentili, still on his knees, swore by everything in heaven and earth that he spoke the bare truth, and that he and his innocent family would die of want unless his majesty would interfere to protect them from this grasping foreigner. "Well, well," said the king, "give me your paper; the matter shall be seen to;" and taking the petition, Ferdinand ordered the lackey to shut the door, and the carriage drove away, leaving Gentili, with clasped hands, invoking blessings on the head of the father of his people.

A few days later the petition reached General Church, having been forwarded to him by the Minister of Justice, Tommasi, and accompanied by a request that he would explain what it all meant. The General's reply is characteristic.

> I am not a little surprised [he says] at hearing from your Excellency that Don Luigi Gentili is at Naples, he having been placed by my orders at Barletta, under surveillance. I shall be happy to give your Excellency information about the man when I hear that he has

returned to Barletta. Till then you will, I am sure, understand that to do so would derogate from the respect due to the *alter ego* with which his Majesty has invested me.

On the next Council day the king inquired what reply had been received from General Giorgio, and the letter was produced and read aloud. "Let me read it myself," said Ferdinand; and having done so, he threw it on the table, and a frown gathered on the royal brow. The white-haired Marchese Circatella next took it up, put on his spectacles, read it through, and put it down in silence. Then the Cavaliere Luigi di Medici took the missive, read it aloud, glanced at his companions, and observed deferentially, "It is very well written, sire!" and the others chimed in assenting to this fact, though observing that perhaps the General was a little — a little — the English were a stiff-necked race! Doubtless he *might* have replied differently, since the query was made in his Majesty's behalf, yet — "Yet, knowing the General as I do," quoth old Circatella, "I say, depend upon it he won't give in!"

"And after all, he has right on his side," put in De Medici.

The king's little fit of temper had gone by; he laughed and rubbed his hands in easy-going fashion. "What a fuss about nothing! What have you to say, Tommasi?"

"I say, your Majesty, that the General saved Apulia."

"Yes, yes, quite true. I know I owe him half my kingdom; but he might have sent me an answer."

"The English are fierce and intractable, but they are honourable, and hold fast to their friends," said the old Marchese.

"Well, well, we have had enough of it," said the king. "Tommasi had better write and tell Giorgio I never doubted he had done right about that fellow. I only asked for information."

So Tommasi wrote again, but to no purpose. Naturally General Church felt that he, being on the spot, knew a great deal more of the intrigues and malpractices which had been going on for years than did the Government at Naples. Besides, he felt the necessity for making his authority felt, so he replied thus:—

I beg to inform your Excellency that I am perfectly well aware that it was his Majesty who required information; but no information can be obtained from me till Gentili is sent back to Barletta. What will people think if a person of Gentili's character can set at defiance the authority of the Crown? It would be no less, since the *alter ego* was intrusted to me by his Majesty himself. I think your Excellency will see that either this man must leave Naples, or I must beg leave to resign the command with which I am at present intrusted.

This settled the matter, and a few days later the General received an official despatch informing him that Gentili had been sent back to Barletta, and also the following letter from Prince Zurlo:—

Caro Amico,—I congratulate you. Your firmness has broken up the plot. This affects the security of every household in the province, for those who have been injured by this infamous man will now venture to witness against him.

As to Don Luigi Gentili, he had better have trusted to the General's clemency, and kept quiet in his banishment, for now he was handed over to the royal courts of Naples, and sent to the galleys for ten years.

The second story relates the fate of Maestro Longo, tailor and citizen of Lecce, — a very good tailor, but a very bad citizen! It was an evil day for Maestro Longo when he dropped the tape and scissors and took to politics, attended meetings of the secret societies, and stuck a stiletto in his belt. He never murdered anybody, but he talked as if he were ready to slay the whole Government! He had a ready tongue, and loved to use it in furious declamation. The applause of the rabble was sweet to him, and much more sweet the feeling that his betters were afraid of him. So he talked mysteriously in corners, gave it to be understood that he was on intimate terms with the chiefs of banditti, was always a principal speaker at patriotic meetings, gave weekly receptions at Lecce, and insisted on the young gentlemen of the place attending them, if they valued their safety; and it shows how great was the fear caused by these secret societies that his noble customers dared not disobey his mandate! The then *intendente* was a special patron of the tailor, and fed his arrogance by treating him familiarly, until Maestro Longo gave himself airs as the most important person in the town.

But this glory ended when General Church took up his quarters at Lecce. His coming was heralded by a grand ball, where Maestro Longo appeared, swaggering among the best; but, alas! times had changed, and before long he found himself taken up by a couple of tall youths, and fairly tossed out of window —by which means the poor little man broke his arm.

"It would be quite a pity to harm the fellow. We must teach him to attend to his trade," said General Church to a group of young gentlemen of Lecce, who were paying their respects. " He is a good tailor, is he not?"

"None better, your Excellency. Did your Excellency ever hear of the tailor and the marchese's pantaloons? No? Then, *con rispetto*, you must know that the Marchese Pietracatella one day sent for his friend Maestro Longo, who arrived with scissors and tape to take his patron's order, and found that patron lying on his bed, much in need of some new diversion. 'Have you ever seen me dance?' said the marquis. 'It is something worth seeing, my friend. I believe I could dance down any man in the Two Sicilies.' And springing off his bed, he began a tarantella to his own whistling, snapping his fingers, springing half-way to the ceiling, whisking round faster and faster, until at last he sank panting on a chair. 'Give me one minute to recover my breath, Longo,' said he, 'and then you shall measure me for a pair of pantaloons.' 'Certainly,' said the tailor; 'but first it is my turn. I have waited for your Excellency — it is only fair that you should wait for me; and, in truth, I flatter myself I can do better than that!' So he began to dance, and went on dancing as if he was bewitched!. The marchese begged him to stop, ordered him to stop, stamped, swore, threatened: still the tailor danced on to his own whistling, serenely ignoring his patron's anger, until in despair Pietracatella called his servants to put the fellow out. But for months after the marchese had to wear his old clothes, for the angry tailor flatly refused to make him new ones, and the other tailors of the town dared not disoblige Maestro Longo!"

"Look here, gentlemen," said the General, when he had done laughing. "I have determined to give a ball at my house every Monday during my stay here. I am afraid—I am really very much afraid—that this will clash with the weekly ball which I understand is given by Maestro Longo. But pray observe that you are perfectly at liberty to take your choice and go where you will. I would not interfere with the tailor for worlds! Only, unhappily, it will be quite impossible for you to be in two places at once, and you will clearly understand that it is at your own choice to attend one or the other—not both."

The young men looked at one another, laughed, and declared that they had not the least intention of entering Maestro Longo's house in future except as customers, but they hoped to attend the General's receptions.

The next day the tailor received a summons

to wait on the General. Softly and sadly he went, with his arm in a sling, and meekly he sat in the anteroom for a considerable time before he was admitted to the great man's presence. The General fixed his keen blue eyes on the round, little, black-eyed person, who fidgeted and bowed nervously, and expressed his desire to serve his Excellency.

"Measure me for a coat, *signore sarto,* if you please," said General Church.

"Uniform or plain? But pardon me, your Excellency, I have not brought my measure. With permission, I will run and fetch it, —though indeed"—and he shook his head mournfully and looked at his arm—"an accident, your Excellency. *Poco, poco,* but for the moment it causes me difficulty."

"No hurry, Maestro Longo. Let us talk of something else. Though you have never worked for me, I have a pretty long account to settle with you, I find," said the General, locking the door as he spoke, and seating himself in an old-fashioned arm-chair. The tailor's ruddy face grew pale, and his teeth positively chattered. Down he went on his knees, protesting that he was a guiltless man, a good citizen.

"I believe, as far as I know, you have never committed a murder; so much the better for you," said the General. "Get up. Now tell the truth, for you will gain nothing by lying."

"It is true that I have been guilty; but I will tell your Excellency all. I throw myself on your Excellency's mercy," gasped the poor little man.

"Good, so far. Get up, and answer my questions. And mind, you must alter your ways, if you don't want to spend some years in the galleys. You have become uncommonly expert of late with the small sword, I hear. How many stilettoes have you on your premises?"

"Oh, your Excellency knows everything! Pardon, pardon, and my life shall be devoted to serve you."

"Look here, my friend. I happen to know that you have the diplomas of the Filadelfi and the Patrioti Europei. Lucky for you that you have had nothing to do with the Decisi! Now, how many men have you in your squadron of Filadelfi?"

"Sixty, *Signore Generale*."

"All armed?"

"*Sì*, signore."

"How many altogether in Lecce?"

"About 300."

"All armed?"

"But no, signore, only about half."

"Any assassins among them?"

"Not to my knowledge, signore."

"Under what supreme authority do you, or rather did you, act?"

"Under the Salentine Republic."

"Your own rank?"

"Prefect of the city of Lecce. Your Excellency knows that it is the same as *intendente*."

"Have you a diploma as prefect?"

"*Sì, Signore Generale.*"

"What do you aim at?"

"Equality, your Excellency. No man to have more land than another."

"Very good. And now, *signore sarto*,"—the General's eyes twinkled in spite of himself,—"pray, what was your fancy for giving those weekly balls?"

Poor Maestro Longo hung his head, and looked like a boy caught in an apple-tree and brought face to face with the headmaster. He cast piteous looks at the General, and stammered out, "I—I wanted to—to break the pride of the gentry, *Signore Generale*."

"And did many of them come to your balls?"

"A good many, especially—that is——"

"Well, go on. Especially?"

"When the invitations were signed by me—with four dots after——"

"Four dots! What does this mean?"

"They were bound to comply—else——"

"Speak out, man; else what?"

In a very low voice, and with eyes fixed on the ground, the tailor finished his sentence. "It meant—that they would die, your Excellency."

There was a pause, long enough for the last remains of courage to ooze out of the tips of the poor tailor's fingers. He stood, limp, pale, and shaking, with the feeling that two stern eyes were fixed upon him, that lies were of no avail, and that—O heavens! if he should have to leave his pleasant house, his admiring friends, his chats on the Piazza, his speechifyings at meetings, for the galleys! Presently the questions began again.

"Who paid the expenses of these balls?"

"The Government, *Signore Generale*—that is, the Salentine Republic. The money was raised by—by forced contributions."

"Did you collect the money?"

"*Per Dio*, no, no, no, your Excellency! I had nothing to do with it, and it went to the Directory."

"Where is your muster-roll?"

"In a priest's house in Surbo."

"Is Major Farini your superior?"

"In the military line, *sì*, signore. I am the superior in the civil line."

"How many officers of the *Reale Corona* Regiment belong to you?"

"Twelve or fourteen."

"Any other regiment?"

"Not to my knowledge, your Excellency."

"Now, Maestro Longo, attend to me. Can I depend on your good conduct in future?"

"Oh, your Excellency, pardon me, save me! I swear you shall have no cause of complaint against me!"

"Will you go back to your tailoring, and keep your fellows to their proper work?"

"*Sì, sì*, signore."

"Will you go round to all the gentlemen you have insulted, and ask pardon, one by one, for your former insolence?"

"I will, signore, I will, and gladly!"

"Will you give your associates clearly to understand that these secret societies must be broken up?"

"They are so already, your Excellency; and in truth the majority of the people are delighted at it, and feel safe under your Excellency's protection."

"And are you of that opinion?"

"Ah, signore, I am a reformed man! I am yours for the rest of my life."

"If that is so, you need fear nothing for the past, and I am sure you will find tailoring a much more profitable trade than sword-exercise. But you must hand over all your weapons to Colonel Bentz, and all your papers to me."

"*Per l' amor di Dio!* but there is enough to hang us all!"

"*Signore sarto,* you will please to understand that I am not admitting you to a capitulation. I am giving you commands, which you will disobey at your peril."

Poor Maestro Longo was crushed again. "Certainly, certainly," he murmured. "My life is in your Excellency's hands. I will give up all, all. I trust to your Excellency's generosity."

Thereupon the General unlocked the door, and desired two officers to go with Maestro Longo to his house and seize all his arms and papers. It was a wonderful find! Six hundred stilettoes, 260 stand of firearms, were handed over to the military authorities, and Maestro Longo himself brought the papers, books, and diplomas; and what was his joy and relief when he saw them blazing in the grate, while he, with tape and scissors, was employed in measuring the General for two new uniform coats and several pairs of pantaloons!

CHAPTER XVI.

REVOLUTION IN SICILY.

GENERAL CHURCH APPOINTED TO COMMAND OF TROOPS IN SICILY — OUTBREAK IN PALERMO — OPEN REBELLION OF MILITARY — IMMINENT DANGER OF THE GENERAL — HIS IMPRISONMENT — PETITIONS FOR HIS LIBERATION.

Two years later, a family letter from Naples says :—

I expect Richard here in about a month. He has been selected by the king for an important commission in the island of Sicily, a most honourable and flattering appointment.

A very unfortunate appointment for the General it turned out, as we shall see; though at the time it was considered a matter of congratulation.

You speak, my dear General, of returning to England [says the Minister De Medici]. You don't expect me to agree to *that*, I hope. You may leave the province of Lecce perhaps, but the king counts on you for another mission. . . . You, who are so attached to the king and your other friends, will surely put by the thought of going away, out of kindness to both.

And again :—

You will see in the new commission destined to you by his majesty a striking proof of his affection and confidence. Let me be the first to congratulate you.

While Sir William à Court, British Minister to the Court at Naples, writes :—

I was very glad to hear from De Medici that you were to be sent to assume the command at Palermo. It is an honourable thing for you, and I hope will be attended with *solid* advantage.

When King Ferdinand was in exile in Sicily he had been ready to promise anything—civil liberty, reduced taxation; had flattered the Carbonari, and promised oblivion for all past offences against the law; but at the same time, when the Sicilian Parliament refused to give him as much money as he asked for, he sold the Communal lands; and when the Parliament protested against this infraction of the old Sicilian Constitution, he put several of the members into prison. When he was brought back to his kingdom, "having learnt nothing and forgotten nothing," he had a heavy bill to pay to his Austrian allies, who had put him there, and that of course meant fresh taxation to his already overburdened people. "There are fresh difficulties at Palermo," writes Sir W. à Court, April 1819. "Another regiment was sent off in a hurry yesterday. The king's journey is postponed *sine die*. The Hereditary Prince returns as Viceroy to Palermo as soon as the Emperor [of Austria] is gone." But apparently it was thought wiser that the Hereditary Prince should keep out of the way; and in the following year General Naselli, a Neapolitan, was appointed Lieut.-General of Sicily—a post equivalent to that of Viceroy—and General Church to have command of the troops. The chestnuts were in the fire, and it was convenient that foreign fingers should pull them out!

General Church pressed for permission to take with him his own foreign troops, well known and trusty, as he was aware that no dependence was to be placed on the Sicilians; but this was not allowed. They were wanted at Naples; but they should be sent, he was assured, early in the autumn. Before that time the revolution in Sicily was over, and the General in prison.

He reached Palermo July 5, and found "the force in Palermo quite insufficient for garrisoning that city, and the discipline of the troops lax. No military system whatever, no public place of parades, no regular mode of transmitting orders. The officers always dressed in plain clothes, and were scattered in different lodgings in and out of the town. Nothing like military regularity was to be seen in Palermo. A spirit of insubordination reigned in several of the corps, and all of them were in some degree infected with Carbonarism." Palermo was crowded for the great national festival, the Feast of Santa Rosalia, which lasts, we are told, five days; and just as it began, a despatch from Naples brought the news of the revolt there, of the new constitution for the kingdom of the Two Sicilies. The sailors of the boat landed, all with tricolour cockades in their hats; and in a few minutes, as if by magic, all the crowd in the streets had mounted the tricolour, instead of the royal white ribbon, and were cheering for the Constitution, Liberty, Independence.

In July 1820, the 'Constitutional Journal' of Naples publishes an article giving an account of what happened. It laments the excesses which took place, but throws all the blame on the "foolish and stupid conduct of General Church, a stranger to us by birth and feeling, who tore from the breast of a peaceful citizen the yellow ribbon. The tumult would not have occurred but for his folly and imprudence."

This yellow ribbon was added to the tricolour as the sign of independence. The General replies :—

It is a fable, an absolute falsity. Never did prudence

so abandon me that I should risk my life among the infuriated mob. . . . It was my singular fate [he adds, evidently smarting under the sense of failure and injustice], that precisely what I did to fulfil my duty is imputed to me as a crime, and the pride and honour of a soldier cruelly wounded for the first time in my life.

And he gives his own account of what took place.

At 8 o'clock P.M., July 14, the Viceroy, General Naselli, sent to General Church with news of the revolution and new constitution at Naples. "My first act was to tender my resignation to the Viceroy, who refused it, begging me not to abandon him in so critical a position, until the arrival of his successor, General Fardelli, who had been appointed by the revolutionary Government." General Church consented to withdraw his resignation, but begged for definite orders. Getting none, and finding that his officers were "all thunderstruck at the prospect of affairs, and indifferent to anything but their own safety," he went home, desiring Marshal O'Ferris, chief of the staff, to call on the Viceroy at six next morning, and request definite orders *in writing*. These proved to be "to announce to the troops the king's acceptance of the new constitution, and to order them to wear the tricolour cockade, as worn by his majesty and the royal family."

The troops were, however, forbidden to add the yellow ribbon for the independence of Sicily.

The orders were given out, and at 10 A.M. all functionaries, military and civil, went in state to the Cathedral Church to assist at the great national festival of Santa Rosalia. The streets, the Piazza, the Cathedral itself, were crowded with people wearing the four-coloured ribbon, and shouting for liberty and independence, but there was no disturbance; and the service over, all went their way, to meet again at the Palace of the Senate that evening according to custom, and see the fireworks and processions from the windows.

At first all went well. The Viceroy, the generals, the magistrates, and their friends chatted together and watched the crowds coming and going, with singing and laughter, bandying of jests and shouting, under the soft, starlit July night. But presently there was a rush and a tumult, the crowd swayed and parted; a noisy procession, headed by a number of non-commissioned officers and soldiers, marched into the Piazza, stopping under the palace windows, waving their hats, and shouting, " *Viva l' Independenza di Sicilia! Viva la Libertà! Viva Robespierre!*". Then they marched on, the people following and joining in the cry, out into the Cassaro, the principal street of Palermo. The Viceroy looked uneasy. "This conduct on the part of soldiers is infamous! It will lead to mischief," said he, addressing General Church; and as soon as the Piazza was clear, he took leave and went home with his guard of honour. Most of the other guests slipped away, and Generals Church and Coglitore and Lieutenants Quandel and De Nitis were left alone.

General Church proposed to follow the procession, and order the soldiers back to barracks. General Coglitore demurred to this, as useless and dangerous; but when his friend replied, "It can't be helped: it is my duty: we had better show the people that we share their pleasure," he agreed to the plan, and the four soldiers went out together. They reached the thronged and brightly lighted Cassaro, and found some difficulty in making their way. The soldiers had been the instigators of these riotous proceedings, and General Church contrived to approach one of the non-commissioned officers, and asked him to "tell his comrades not to make so much noise, to conduct themselves with more regularity, and when they had reached the end of the street to return to their quarters; adding that I had no objection to their sharing the general joy on the last night of the festival, but that the manner in which they were acting might lead to disturbances." This had no effect. The soldiers moved on, the crowds closed round, the four officers were pushed and hustled, and threatened with death, unless they would join the popular cry. General Church consented to cry, "*Viva il Rè! Viva la Costituzione!*" but as to anything else, in spite of General Coglitore's advice, "*Jamais!*" said the sturdy Briton. "*Pas un mot!*"

The tumult rose higher, daggers were brandished, cries arose of "Down with them! Death to all tyrants! Kill them! away with them!" Fortunately General Coglitore's carriage was waiting at the entrance of the Piazza, and, extricating themselves from the crowd, they managed to reach it and jump in, though not before General Coglitore had been wounded by a dagger, and General Church half stunned by a stone. Off they drove, full speed, followed by execrations, threats, showers of stones, and beating with their swords those who climbed upon the carriage. I have before me an old print representing the scene: the open carriage, the coachman whipping up his horses, the mob clinging on or following with brandished daggers and uplifted stones; the occupants of the carriage in their cocked-hats; while at a little distance stands another carriage-and-pair and coachman, with the utmost placidity!

After a while they distanced their foes, and stopped to hold a consultation. General Coglitore went to his sister's house, promising to send disguises to his friends; but they heard no more of him. In fact, he was forced to remain in hiding for several days, and could do nothing for them. They were close to a small fort, and a house by the roadside was inhabited by an artilleryman. Lieutenant De Nitis borrowed this man's clothes and went to Palermo. Church and Quandel took refuge in the fort, which stood on a rising ground, above the sea, and consisted of a loopholed wall, and open-rail gate, without even a lock. The artilleryman stood sentinel, and the officers, still in dress costume, took shelter within.

So the night passed, and the summer morning broke blue and golden. People began to pass to their business, singing and whistling; fishing-boats came out from the neighbouring villages, but would not come near, in spite of signals, for fear of the *Sanità* (health officer). Groups came from Palermo, and the fugitives could hear them shouting information about what happened in the town, and threats as to what they would do to General Giorgio when they caught him. Once some lads ran up the slope, looking everywhere round the battery, but not *into* it. The two officers gave themselves up for lost, and determined to sell their lives dearly. They crouched close to the wall; and after a good deal of shouting to a group of men on the road below, the lads ran away, and the fugitives could breathe again. At last an officer in plain clothes came to them, saying that a gunboat, sent by General Naselli, was on its way to rescue them. It soon appeared but dared not land, for a throng of people assembled on the shore, evidently watching its movements. At that moment, most fortunately, a little fishing-skiff slowly passed beneath the rock on which the fort was built, and immediately the two officers sprang over the parapet and into the boat, " much to the terror of the poor fisherman, whom we obliged to row us to the gunboat, where we found De Nitis awaiting us."

The gunboat carried the Viceroy's orders that General Church should be taken to Trapani. The General, on the contrary, wished to return to Palermo, and try his authority with the troops there. He persuaded Captain La Rocca to wait a while, and sent letters by a sailor to General Naselli; but the man came back, reporting that the troops had fraternised with the populace, that he had had great difficulty in gaining admittance to the palace, and that the Viceroy had ordered him to go back at once and tell General Church that it was impossible for him to write, and that the gunboat must instantly proceed to Trapani.

"The man is quite right, General," said De Nitis, in French; "I was in the town this morning, and the people were in a state of fury. It is useless to expect any help from the troops; there is no confidence to be placed in them. They would have given you up to the mob, had you been in Palermo."

Meanwhile the sailors were getting up the anchor and putting out to sea; whereat General Church seems to have lost his temper, and rated the captain soundly, calling him a traitor, and declaring that he meant to throw the fugitives into the sea.

"I am not a traitor, General," said Captain La Rocca; "I am your friend. I dare not disobey my orders, which are to go to Trapani; and I can give you no better proof of my fidelity than the assurance that I and my crew have left our wives and families in Palermo, in danger of being murdered, in order to save your life!"

So to Trapani they went, but found no welcome there. The commandant told them that the soldiers openly declared their intention of deserting as soon as they got outside their barracks, that the officers had set free and brought into their *vendita* (club) certain Carbonari from the province of Lecce who had been condemned for murder by the Military Commission there of two years ago, and whom " the misguided clemency of the Government" had exiled to Sicily. They sailed on to Marsala, where they were most hospitably received by a Mr Wodehouse, who had a house near the sea, on the outskirts of the town. He ordered wine, and food, and ammunition to be got ready for provisioning their boat, and brought them all home to dine with him, assuring them they need fear nothing either for themselves or for him: for, in the first place, the people of Marsala owed him too much to wish to offend him; and in the second, he had workmen enough to defend his house against the whole population! He wanted them to remain with him a day or two; but before dinner was over, a messenger from Palermo brought the news that the galley-slaves had been set free, and that the troops had quarrelled with the people, and were fighting them in the streets. Upon this the General thought he saw a chance of recalling the soldiers to their allegiance, and, in spite of all remonstrance, insisted upon hurrying off with the gunboat in the direction of Palermo. This was on the evening of the 17th July.

On the way they called at Trapani, but were received with threats that the fort would fire on the gunboat if she came closer. So they went on their way, till at dawn they came to the point of S. Vito. Here were three gunboats and an armed boat at anchor. Quandel was sent to parley with them, and returned with the captain, who, in answer to the usual inquiry how things were going at Palermo, said all was lost. The galley-slaves were let loose, the Viceroy had fled, the Palermitans had armed a number of boats, and no one was allowed to land. Then, turning to Captain La Rocca, "Your boat is under my orders," said he.

"I *was* under your orders," was the answer; "but having been sent on a special service by the Viceroy and General Staiti, I can obey no orders but theirs, or those of his Excellency here, for whose safety I am answerable."

The other captain scowled at this reply, and getting into his little boat, took a hasty leave and returned to his gunboat.

"I don't like his manner," said La Rocca, "and those sailors are mostly Palermitans. We are much better without them."

While they were discussing what was best

to be done, they suddenly observed that the gunboats had left their moorings, and were approaching them — in fact, were but forty yards away. The sailors seized their oars, muttering *Tradimento*, and began to row as hard as they could. The other side shouted to them to stop, or every one of them should be cut to pieces; but the brave fellows took no notice of the threats. They were outnumbered three to one, says the General: no blame could be attached to them if they yielded to so superior a force, and to give up their stranger guests would ensure them personal safety and large rewards. However, they entered into the race gleefully, shouting defiance at their pursuers, while every epithet that Sicilian wit or rage could invent was bandied from one to the other. "Trust us," they cried, in answer to the General's words of encouragement; "those are rascals, traitors, Carbonari! We have better hearts, and God will be on our side. We will sooner die than give you up;" and they rowed with all their might out of the line of fire, for they had no idea that their foes happened to be short of ammunition.

It had been a perfectly still morning, hot and clear as July should be, but very exhausting for the oarsmen; and now a breeze sprang up, and they hoisted their sails, cheerily exclaiming that theirs was the fastest sailing-boat in Sicily, and that they should soon leave the others behind. So it proved — and after three hours' chase the enemies slackened sail, gave up, and returned home, and with great joy Captain La Rocca and his men refreshed themselves with Mr Wodehouse's excellent wine; then came thanks and mutual congratulations, and a few hours of much-needed sleep.

On July 23 they reached Naples, entering the Mola with the king's colours flying from the mast. What did they find?

The Government overturned, the king and prince prisoners in their palace, the tricolour flag waving everywhere. Our boat was boarded by officers of the port, and the king's colours struck by them. An immense mob was collected on the Mola, exceedingly attentive to everything going on in the port, and apparently directing all the movements there. An awning over our boat (the sun being very hot) fortunately kept the persons in her from being easily seen. In an hour Major Staiti came with orders to confine me in the Castel dell' Ovo, to which I was conveyed by water.

There he remained four months, no charge being preferred against him.

I admire the spirit of rectitude which brought you here [writes Sir W. à Court], and lament your imprudence in committing yourself into your enemies' hands. In revolutionary times the spirit of reason and justice is hushed. Why did you not go on board the English frigate in the bay? How can I serve you? I have no power or influence now. I am assured you are in personal safety; but is the present Government master of the country?

And again :—

The Parliament is composed of a set of Carbonari, over whom neither the prince nor his ministers have any more influence than you or I. I know not what advice to give you. It appears to me that you are more closely watched than formerly. I was myself stopped by the sentinel the other day, and only released by the sergeant. It is an infamous business altogether. Campochiaro himself says he is ashamed of it.

In September a protest, signed by nineteen English nobles and gentry resident at Naples, entreats Sir W. à Court, as accredited Minister of England, to obtain the liberation of their fellow-countryman, who has been in prison nine weeks without any accusation of any sort being brought against him. This, they say, is "an act of injustice on the part of the Government of a kingdom to whose prosperity General Church is universally admitted to have essentially contributed. The steady principles of loyalty and honour which have distinguished him; his tried firmness and moderation upon all occasions, especially in the late commotions in Sicily; his watchful attention over the tranquillity of the provinces under his command; the successful measures he adopted to suppress a system of defalcation in the public revenues, —claim respect from every candid mind, and the peculiar hardship of his case calls in the strongest manner for the support and protection of his country." This protest was forwarded, accompanied by a protest from Sir W. à Court himself, in which he points out that though a Commission had been appointed to inquire into the affair, nothing had been done. And in the month of November a family letter says :—

Richard is still in prison, though his liberation or trial has been demanded officially and unofficially. The Commission appointed last August of ten civil judges and ten generals gave no opinion. The Committee appointed by Parliament declared that he had done his duty; yet he remains in prison. He bears his change of circumstances with great philosophy. He lost everything at Palermo—furniture, books, papers, &c.—but the Government refuse even to give him his pay; besides, he has incurred a debt of £3000 in providing clothes, &c., for his troops.

The fact was, the Carbonari ruled in Naples, and the Government was powerless. A letter (undated, but evidently of this time) from Sir W. à Court says :—

Your affair, you may depend on it, is drawing to a close —that is to say, if the Carbonari do not overpower the Government and the well-meaning part of the community to prevent your release. Campochiaro has promised to demand an interview with the Deputies expressly for this purpose.

At last he was released, and the story may wind up with a letter from Frederick, Duke of York, and Commander-in-Chief, dated March 7, 1822:—

On the 3d instant I received with great satisfaction your letter with its enclosures, and I lose no time in congratulating you upon the result of an investigation which, if correctly conducted, could indeed be no other than honourable to you, and such as would do justice to the spirit and zeal with which you had discharged your duty under very trying circumstances. I never doubted that your conduct had on this occasion been consistent with the character which you have always maintained.

Thus end some stirring chapters in the life of General Church, perhaps a dull ending to a dashing beginning. Still, his life did not end with these adventurous episodes. Greece, which had attracted him in early years, held his heart to the last. He fought for her through the war which gave her independence, and spent the remaining years of his life in Athens.

CHAPTER XVII.

SOME NOTES AND PERSONAL REMINISCENCES BY HIS NEPHEW, CANON C. M. CHURCH, GIVE THE SEQUEL OF THE LIFE OF GENERAL CHURCH IN GREECE FROM 1827 TO 1873.

A VISIT to Athens in 1893 revived the memories of early days in Greece, which have been a "fount of joy" amid the occupations of later years.

I saw then for the first time the grave and monument of General Church in the cypress-grove of the Greek cemetery above the Ilissus.

The monument raised by the Greek people bears an inscription which is a simple and truthful record of his life in Greece. He "lived for her service and died amongst her people."

For forty-six years Sir Richard Church lived in Greece, leaving it only once on a visit to Constantinople in 1838. After the War of Independence he had settled down in Athens in the same house in which he died in 1873. It was a house of the older town, clinging to the roots of the rock of the Acropolis on its north-eastern side. Once belonging to a Turk, it had been adapted to modern use by its purchaser, Mr Finlay, in the first days of liberated Athens.

The semi-Eastern character was still kept up. A square tower of thick walls and small windows, strong to stand an earthquake or a siege, overlooked a large enclosed courtyard in which cypress-trees flanked the entrance from the street, and outer stairs led up to a gallery from which the dwelling-rooms opened. Above it rude houses in tortuous lanes and the cupola of a Byzantine church climbed up the rocky slope, and the great rock, crowned by the wall of the Acropolis, overshadowed all.

Here he was living when I first saw him in 1848. He was then an erect and vigorous man of sixty-five, with grey hair and small moustache, high forehead, a bright upward look from keen blue eyes. Cordial but stately in manner, dressed with careful neatness, he gave the impression of the refined English gentleman or diplomatist, rather than of the adventurous soldier who had gone through such rude experiences in Greek guerilla warfare.

Since the days of the Apulian Tales and the

Neapolitan Revolution he had seen and suffered much.

The life in Greece was the sequel to that romantic career which had closed in Italy in 1820.

Letters to his brother in 1822 connect the earlier and later chapters of his life, and describe the feelings and circumstances under which Greece became the scene of his later adventures.

The brothers were deeply attached to one another, and the elder had generously assisted his younger brother with money at the time of his losses by the Neapolitan revolution.

He writes from Florence in September 1822 :—

You ask me what I have on my mind. I will tell you as far as I can the future of my course. My first effort shall be by every means in my power to acquit myself of the vast obligations I am under to you. It must not, however, alarm you if you perceive with what constancy my mind follows the prospect of going to Greece. So deeply is this impulse rooted in my mind that I really believe that death alone can eradicate it, and what I have suffered by the postponement of it is neither to be described nor conceived, except by those who are conscious of a superior calling, and have conquered difficulties and carried their destinies into effect.

His purpose had long been formed. He

recalls his formation of the Greek regiments in the Ionian Islands in 1811-14, recruited in Greece, and disciplined by himself :—

I disciplined them—a new event among Greeks, to which they had refused to submit either from the Venetians, the French, or the Russians. A spirit of liberty rose naturally in the breasts of these soldiers, encouraged by the British protection and service, and these men returned to their country full of the desire to exercise the discipline they had acquired in the English service, for the liberation of their own country.

When in Apulia I formed a Greek regiment for the Neapolitan service, not only as a corps highly useful to the Government, but in order to keep up communication with Greece, and to continue the system of disciplining the Greeks and Albanians as much as possible towards the great work I had in view.

He concludes :—

I am no adventurer or buccaneer : to go to Greece I must make heavy sacrifices—must give up my position in the English service, and my commission as lieut.-general of the King of Naples, besides those prospects of home and rank, perhaps of wealth, certainly of comfort. I am willing to give up the reality or the prospect of these advantages. I feel that the glorious enterprise in a just cause has more attractions for me than these pleasurable enjoyments. You will call me a fanatic, an enthusiast, or a fool. I will allow that I am an enthusiast, in loving so glorious a cause, and in being ready to affront the dangers and difficulties attendant upon it.

But his brother could not then enter into

his exalted state of mind, and opposed his schemes.

Full of these ideas, he went to England in 1823 to ascertain the state of feeling in England towards the Greek cause. In England strong sympathy was being felt with this first uprising of national spirit, the struggle of a Christian race against the long tyranny of the Turks. He met with men with whom he had made friends abroad—Lord Exmouth, Hudson Lowe, Lord Guildford, Colonel Leake. Among his intimate friends were Stratford Canning[1] and David Morier, first met at Constantinople in 1811, and afterwards at the Congress of Vienna, with both of whom he kept up an affectionate friendship through life.[2] He was in communication with George Canning, then Prime Minister, and with other influential men, on projects for assisting the Greeks.

In 1826 he married a sister of Sir Robert Wilmot Horton,[3] then Under-Secretary for the Colonies in Mr Canning's Ministry. She entered into his feelings for Greece, and en-

---

[1] Among the letters between Canning and himself are some in verse, dated 1815, and again 1853.

[2] Among his letters of 1825 is an invitation from Sir T. D. Acland to meet friends at breakfast—"all Grecians, mostly Congressers"—naming especially S. Canning, D. Morier, Gally Knight.

[3] Afterwards Governor of Ceylon.

couraged him in his enterprise, little knowing what would be the cost of the sacrifice for both. In the first years of peace in Greece she joined him at Athens, until, struck down by Greek fever, she was ordered to England, and remained there a sufferer to the end of her life.

At last, steadfast to his purpose, he sailed from Leghorn for Greece, and arrived there in March 1827. It was apparently a desperate and quixotic enterprise on which he had embarked when he was sworn "on cross and sword," in the orange-grove of Trœzene, on Easter-Day, April 25, as General of the Greek land forces. He brought with him nothing but his name, his sword, and his enthusiasm. He told the Greeks that he had no money, and he made no terms for himself. The Greeks whom he was to lead were needy and undisciplined clansmen of chieftains jealous of one another, divided into two Assemblies quarrelling almost to civil war, with no government, no plan of action, no money or material of war.

Messolonghi had fallen, Northern Greece had submitted to the Turks, and the Greeks who were still in arms were clinging to the eastern fringe of the Morea, threatened with extermination by the junction of the Egyptians ravaging the Morea, and the Turkish army before Athens.

A friend alike to Church and to the Greeks, who knew the situation and was a man of cool judgment, Captain Hamilton, long time Commodore on the station, saw the generosity but the madness of Church's action, and tried to save him from the sacrifice. Writing to Stratford Canning at Constantinople, he said :—

Church is here: he certainly is a fine fellow, but a complete Irishman, with their great virtues and little faults. I am sorry for his sake he has come.

To Church himself he wrote :—

I advise you to refuse any command. It is evident that there is not any energy in the country against the present danger. I give you my opinion; your own feelings may prevent you from attending to it.[1]

But Church had made up his mind. The one condition he demanded before he would take any part was the union of the two factions in one National Assembly. "He did what no one else could have done," said one, writing at the time.

Very soon he had bitter experience of the difficulties of his position.

Within ten days of his appointment a crushing defeat and massacre of the Greeks before

---

[1] Captain Hamilton's letter, March 1827.

Athens was the result of false intelligence, divided counsels, and incapacity for any combined action by the undisciplined Greeks. His coolness, energy, and determination alone saved the Greeks from despair and complete abandonment of the camp. He gathered a remnant of the panic-stricken crowd round him on the Munychium hill, and held the position for three weeks in face of the Turks swarming around them, though in want of shelter, provisions, and money; and he brought them off at last without loss to Salamis, and formed a camp on Mount Geraneion. The diary of an aide-de-camp[1] describes scenes on the days succeeding the battle:—

May 7.—The camp a scene of tumult and confusion. Yells and shrieks and rejoicings of the Turks, accompanied by constant firing, lasted without interruption during the night. From Athens the whole plain to the foot of the Munychium was a blaze of light. Desertions in boats were hourly taking place through the day. The General posted a guard off the point of land near the "tomb of Themistocles," from whence the desertions chiefly take place. Lord Cochrane sailed away with the whole of his fleet last night.

May 8.—Fighting along the whole line. Turks attacking advanced posts and driving them in. The General shortening the lines of defence and concentrating on the Munychium. Panic among the Greeks.

---

[1] Diary by Major O'Fallon, A.D.C. to Sir R. Church from April 1 to May 25, 1827.

May 9.—Troops murmuring and discontented. Nothing but the invincible firmness and patience of the General could keep them in the position.

The relations between the General and his Greek soldiery were peculiar. On the first morning he called the "generals" around him, and through his Greek aide-de-camp and interpreter he told them his determination to hold the hill. A Greek letter, written on a dirty bit of coarse yellow paper (now before me), was the answer of the Greek "generals":—

Most Excellent Generalissimo,—The whole camp has decided not to remain any longer in the position; therefore we beg of you to have the boats ready to embark us.

(Signed) The Camp (ὅλον τὸ στρατόπεδον).

His answer is characteristic. He sent the boats away for supplies, and wrote:—

To the Generals and Officers.

I thought when I saw and spoke to you yesterday that I had made an impression on your minds; but if you are determined to destroy yourselves and your soldiers, whom you have encouraged in this disgraceful and seditious conduct, be it so!—let every one go who is afraid to stay in the camp; but understand that I will not leave it until, and how, I can do so with honour, and I am sure some brave men will remain with me for the honour of your country. Look to your posts and fear nothing.

They agreed to stay for three days. Finally,

in spite of numerous desertions, he retained the best of the men—Roumeliots chiefly—until he had taken measures for the defence of the Isthmus of Corinth in the passes of Mount Geraneion. Writing to Hamilton in the midst of these tumultuous scenes on May 9, he says :—

All these troubles and disappointments will have no effect upon my spirits or my efforts to weather the storm. I am at least saved from that distracting doubt whether to stay or to go away. Having voluntarily thrown myself into the torrent, I as voluntarily remain to sink or swim with the cause of Greece. I can readily excuse those who have left us, as there is nothing amusing or agreeable in what is going on here; it is stern and barbarous warfare, with all the privations, difficulties, and distressing events imaginable. Still, if one acts from principle, that principle and the holiness of the cause must give us the perseverance necessary to carry through.

He was writing again and again to the Government at Egina that he could only hold his position if they would send pay and provisions. Throughout it was always the same story—"the want of money is the permanent evil, crippling all efforts and plans."

Hamilton wrote to Canning on May 17 :—

Church wrote yesterday to entreat me to lend him secretly 2000 dollars for a fortnight, or that he should be obliged to abandon his station to-day. It was painful for me to refuse an old friend, but knowing how the money was to be applied, I thought it my duty [as a neutral] to do so.

He held on with what supplies he could get from Egina until the 27th May. Then he had arranged his plans, and the position had become intolerable from the scorching sun to men without tents on this bare and waterless rock: he had held it for three weeks, "not only against the enemy, but still more against my own men." In the night and early morning of the 28th the embarkation of about 3000 men was effected in a masterly way with the loss of only two men, in the little harbour of Munychium, in face at last of the Seraskier and the Turks, who had become aware, when too late, of the evacuation.

Church's ascendancy over these wild and savage Greeks dated from this long trial. His firmness and composure cowed the noisy and turbulent; his courtesy, kindness, and fellow-suffering with their privations won over the best to personal devotion. He attached to his person a band of 400 to 500 Roumeliots under chiefs whom he could trust, and they became the nucleus of larger and more fluctuating bands who joined him from time to time from the several cantons where his headquarters were fixed. Some characteristic stories were told of him at this time. Mr Edward Masson, who was Lord Cochrane's secretary at the time, and outlived the General at Athens, spoke to me of seeing him in his tent on the Munychium with nothing but his Bible and sword on a table, and of his patience and composure during this stormy time. One of his Greek aides-de-camp told the Davidic tale of his refusing to drink of the water of the well at the foot of the Munychium hill because it had been brought to him at the risk of life from the fire of the Turkish outposts.

Such was the prelude to his camp-life of the next two years spent with the Greeks among the mountains of Achaia, and the plains and lagoons of Western Greece. He lived with his men throughout to the end of his campaign in Western Greece in July 1829.

An English officer, the Resident of Cerigo, writes to him in December 1828:—

Dionysio, one of your Greek soldiers, has again set out to serve under you. I admire the warm devotion and affectionate respect with which he spoke of you. His tales of the war were most graphic, and every one heard with intense sympathy the extreme hardships, risks, and sufferings to which you were daily exposed while engaged in a warfare so peculiar. He gave us an account of your brilliant success at Vonitza: it shows what might have been done if you had been seconded, and if you had a paid and disciplined force. Dionysio says that a kingdom would not repay you for all you have suffered and sacrificed in the cause of Greece.

He tired out the Greeks often in marches; and by pluck and cheerfulness of spirit, in endurance of cold and heat and thirst, put them to shame for their complaints. To one of his Moreote "generals" who complained of his quarters on one of the mountain stations of Achaia in November, he wrote:—

It is true the torrents of rain drench us all by day and night; but what can I do to remedy this evil? I cannot help you in any other way than by giving you and your men the houses which are set apart for the headquarters, and take those that have been given you, of which you complain. Your time of life, my dear friend, requires care, therefore please yourself.

Alone, by force of character and personal influence and unconquerable patience, he kept his men together, without regular pay, often without rations, ill-clothed, and without proper shelter in winter and in summer, and he worked out with them the accomplishment of his purpose. He had from the first determined on a descent upon the coast of Western Greece to cut off the supplies of Messolonghi and Lepanto and to liberate the western provinces. To that purpose he tenaciously clung for two years. His progress was slow, delayed and harassed by the penury of the Government and their niggardly and fitful support. "Six months' experience," he writes, "is more than sufficient to show me how impossible it is to act with vigour when my movements depend on the caprice of others." He spent all his own money, and then was forced into the ruinous step, in his simplicity in money matters, of contracting loans in the Ionian Islands, on the authority of the National Assembly but in his own name, for the support of his army. At the end of the war the Government of Capodistrias only acknowledged their liability for a portion of this amount; they paid only a small sum, on account, and Church was thereby involved in pecuniary embarrassments for after years.[1]

A good-humoured sketch of the General's camp of wild bandit-like *palicari*, from an English diplomatist's point of view, is given in the account of a passing visit of Stratford Canning to him on the Akarnanian coast. Canning is writing to his wife on his voyage from Corfu to Greece in an English frigate in July 1828 :—

In spite of sea-sickness I am rather in good spirits to-day at having done a good action. After entering this bay I went round to a corner of the coast near an island called Calamos, and paid a visit to my old friend General Church, the Greek Commander-in-chief. I found him occupied with his army of whiskered ragamuffins in a plain at the foot of a semicircle of lofty, steep, barren hills, while a flotilla of gun-

---

[1] Cf. p. 353.

boats, headed by a Greek steamer, maintains his communication with the sea. We called him out of his hut between five and six in the morning, and had as rapturous a meeting as the formalities of the quarantine would allow. I had great difficulty in persuading him not to salute the ambassador with the two wretched pieces of ordnance of which his one battery is composed. The expenditure of ammunition would have delayed his operations.

Church's letter is pathetic in its simplicity of feeling at the unexpected sight of his friend in such circumstances :—

Nothing could have given me greater pleasure than your visit in the midst of all the suffering I have undergone for some time past. It was really the kindest thing in the world, and I thank you for it. I saw you sail off with the greatest regret. I returned to my camp with the fervent hope that Providence will crown your labours and my humble exertions with success, and that we may one day witness the solemn declaration of the independence of Greece, and have a happy meeting again.

The cultured and fastidious diplomatist might well have thought scorn of the dirty kilted Greeks, "untaught knaves, unmannerly," as they must have appeared to him. Probably he would have sniffed as much at Garibaldi's Thousand at Marsala. Nevertheless men such as these, Church with little support from Capodistrias, trained to discipline and order and humanity — with these he carried to success his plans of warfare, and added two provinces to the Greek kingdom. At the head of these men in their poor equipment, acting under the inspiration of his enthusiasm, patience, and fortitude, Church at last entered Messolonghi, the sacred spot of Greek heroism, in June 1829, the liberator of Western Greece. What was still more remarkable, he was able to control these men to keep faith with enemies. Turkish prisoners were brought into camp instead of Turkish heads; defenceless women and children were respected after the capture of Turkish fortresses, and prisoners of war were conducted in safety to the Turkish outposts by his soldiers.

The full importance of Church's military operations was shown when the line of the frontiers of Greece was determined. The occupation of the provinces of Akarnania and Ætolia by his soldiers afforded the basis on which the claim rested that those provinces should be included within the Greek State, and that the line of frontier should be drawn through the Gulf of Arta.[1]

[1] A pamphlet was published in London, 'Observations on an Eligible Line of Frontier for Greece.' By Sir R. Church. Ridgway, 1830.

For further details of General Church's campaign in 1827-1829 see 'Sir R. Church.' By Stanley Lane-Poole. Longmans, 1890.

'New Quarterly Magazine,' July 1879 : "The Greek Frontier, how it was won in 1829."

An impartial testimony to the value of General Church's services to Greece in this campaign is given in a letter from Mr Finlay written many years before the publication of his history of the Revolution :—

DEAR GENERAL,—I return your notes with many thanks. I have taken the liberty to copy them, as to me they recall the scenes and correct many of the errors of Gordon. I well recollect the landing at Dragomestre, which at the time I thought a desperate and even hopeless attempt with the small force you had. I have long, however, seen that it was to that desperate step that Greece owes the extension of her frontier. The 500 men induced Romeli to take arms, and prevented Capodistrias from making the Morea Greece. You gave him Romeli in spite of himself, and you made Agostino [Capodistrias] a hero. — Yours sincerely, GEO. FINLAY.[1]

Thursday Evening.

While the General was in the wilds of Akarnania in January 1828, his elder brother died at Florence, to his great grief and loss, and from henceforth he was lost to his brother's family for many years. His nephews, at school and college, grew up with a very indistinct knowledge of their uncle until they saw him at Athens in after years.

[1] The letter before us is without date. From ink, paper, and handwriting, it appears to belong to a series of letters from Finlay in 1831-32, in one of which he addresses General Church as "the liege lord of all true Philhellenes."

He had thrown in his lot with a fickle people naturally jealous of the foreigner. They owed him a debt of gratitude, and of money, which it was difficult to repay, and often burdensome to remember. His signal successes in Western Greece met with no recognition from the President Capodistrias. He resigned his command with an indignant protest against the neglect of his soldiers during the war, and he used all his endeavours in opposition to Capodistrias to obtain the extension of the frontier of Greece so as to include the territories he had won.

When the Allied Powers had put Otho of Bavaria on the throne, the ministry of Mavrocordato desired to make amends to Church for the ingratitude of Capodistrias. He was nominated, by a strange freak of fortune, as it seems now, Greek ambassador to the Emperor of Russia.[1] Not unnaturally the Emperor did not wish to receive an Englishman as representative of Greece. In the year before he had declined, without reason given, to accept Stratford Canning as ambassador from England, and the two friends were now united in sympathy under the like affront from the same quarter.

But honours in Greece which more fitly belonged to him, were now conferred. He was

---

[1] The appointment of Sir R. Church as "Envoy Extraordinary and Minister Plenipotentiary," fully made out and signed by the king at Nauplia, January 13, 1834, exists among his papers.

made a member of the Council of State, and in 1836 Inspector-General of the army and of the National Guard, with divers orders and decorations, and finally, in 1844, a Senator. An insurrection in Western Greece gave him an opportunity of exercising his powers of conciliation and firmness with the chieftains who had served under him in the war, and he did good service now not only in reconciling their feuds, but in interceding for them with the Government. "Wild and headstrong chieftains who proved unmanageable to all others readily and willingly submitted to his command, for he was known to be just, and to thirst after no power."[1]

Sir E. Lyons wrote to him in 1843:—

I rejoice to see such fruits of your exertions for the welfare of this country, to which you have devoted so much time, so much talent, so much energy, and for which you have, when we take the extension of the frontier into the scale, done more than any other man, be he who he may.

He was still holding this command when, in September 1843, King Otho was forced by a bloodless revolution at Athens to dismiss his Bavarian counsellors and army of occupation, and to grant the promised constitution and a representative assembly. The Council of State

[1] Words said in the funeral oration.

assumed the direction of affairs, General Church was elected to act as intermediary with the king, and he obtained the king's acquiescence in the demands of the Council without any popular disturbance.

His English name appears strangely metamorphosed in a proclamation of the Council of State which thanks the people and the garrison of Athens for their orderly conduct, orders an oath of fidelity to the Constitution to be taken by the army, and appoints the 3d September to be kept as a national festival. Richard Church, as "P. Τσώρτσης," is the fourth in the list of names subscribed, following the well-known Greek names of Conduriottes, Mavromichales, and Notaras.

But in the next year the wheel of fortune swung full round. Suddenly, and with no reason assigned, General Church was deprived by royal decree of his post as Inspector-General of the army. No doubt Church, as commander of the army, was in the way of the unscrupulous minister of the day, Coletti, an Epirote of the school of Ali Pacha, one of the most audacious and intriguing of the old klephtic chieftains, who had risen to be minister of the constitutional king. Church was a foreigner and an Englishman, and had held the command eight years, a long time in Greece. Coletti wished to appoint a Greek, and one of his own instruments. The king, smarting still under the humiliation of having been forced to grant the constitution and to dismiss the Bavarians, signed, nothing loath, the act of dismissal.

This indignity was accompanied by the gross and stupid insult of appointing in his place Theodore Grivas, one of the most lawless of the chiefs of Western Greece, and one of Church's most mutinous officers. As associate and instrument of Coletti in 1827, he had seized and held against the Government the Palamede fortress at Nauplia, and Church, with great difficulty and forbearance, had forced him to evacuate it. Afterwards he had been sent up with his corps to join Church in Akarnania by the President Capodistrias, with warnings of his mutinous spirit. Lately he had been in insurrection against the king, and his evil character was known of all men.

Sir E. Lyons wrote indignantly in an official despatch to Lord Aberdeen, November 10, 1844:—

Sir R. Church, who has sacrificed his fortune and eighteen years of his life to render most important services to Greece, who in the late occasion of the Revolution contributed more than any man to preserve the throne, not to say the life of the king, such a man is abruptly dismissed to make room for a man who has committed several murders, who was only a few months ago in open insurrection, and is now Coletti's instrument in all the injustice committed by the Election Commission.

Articles in the Greek press at the time denounced the ingratitude and indecency of the action, and repudiated it on behalf of the Greek people.

In the English House of Commons Sir R. Peel, then Prime Minister, said :—

> I cannot refrain from declaring that the conduct of Greece towards General Church involved in it a charge of grievous ingratitude. But no censure, no dismissal could make Europe insensible to the great services which that distinguished officer has conferred upon Greece. I believe he is too proud to complain. The sufferers are not the objects but the authors of such proceedings.[1]

Church at once replied by a letter addressed to the king demanding to be relieved from all military rank, and retiring from the service :—

> SIRE,—Entretenir V. M. des services que je me flatte d'avoir rendus à la Grèce et au trône de V. M. serait importuner V. M. de trop. Je me bornerai, Sire, à prier V. M., avec tout le respect dûe au Roi Constitutionel d'une nation qui m'a honoré de son suffrage au delà de mes mérites, d'accepter ma démission du service militaire de V. M. que des circonstances non ignorées de V. M. m'obligent à demander.
>
> D'ATHÉNES, à { 30 Oct. / 11 Nov. } 1844.

---

[1] 'Morning Herald' and 'Times,' March 15, 1845.

He wrote to Sir R. Peel to thank him for the honourable way in which he had been mentioned in Parliament:—

Upheld by the conviction that I had done all in my power for Greece at the sacrifice of my own personal interests, I was stung by this unmerited insult from a quarter whence it ought not to have come, and from a sovereign who, I may assert without fear of contradiction, would have lost his throne on the 3d of September had I not interfered on his behalf, and opposed the almost general wish of the Greeks in the moment of their deepest excitement. Subsequent events have left me no option but that of instantly quitting the service of the king, though suffering under the mortification of seeing such an end to my military career in Greece.

This was practically the close of his active military and official life in Greece. For ten years he lived at Athens without any military rank or pay, but holding his position as senator. Then in 1854, at the time of the Crimean war, King Otho begged General Church to return to the military service with the grade of full General, holding rank next to the king himself, and superior to all other military men.

With much reserve, and only after the persuasion of his friends and the English Minister, Sir Thomas Wyse, and with the full approbation of Lord Clarendon, the English Foreign Secretary, he accepted the proffered honour.

In a letter written at the time, March 17, 1854, he says :—

> Without the slightest application from myself, I have received this invitation from the king. It is the opinion of everybody here, that I should accept the king's propositions. In an audience I asserted my perfect liberty of political opinions and actions either in the Senate or elsewhere: the king insisted so strongly, saying at last that if I did not accept he should attribute my refusal to a personal hatred to himself, that I said I could not refuse his request.

In the same letter he condemns the folly of the king and Government of the day which allowed aggressions on the Turkish frontier by Greek military officers, one of whom was Theodore Grivas, no longer in office, against the advice of the best friends of the country.

These aggressions led to the occupation of the Piræus by English and French soldiers in 1855, which was a great distress to the General.

On this occasion Lord Palmerston wrote to him, May 29, 1854 :—

> I was very glad to hear that King Otho had made to you suitable reparation for the bad treatment which you had experienced at his hands, though I fear that this measure on his part did not proceed so much from a consciousness of former injustice as from a foolish notion that by calling you back to his service he would give countenance to the idea that the English Government was favourable to his aggression in Turkey. Out

of evil sometimes comes good, and your reinstatement is a great, and I hope will be a lasting, advantage to Greece.

But the General never after this took any active part in political or military affairs. His rank gave him a position of honour suitable to his services and expressive of the respect in which he was held in the country.

It was in the year 1848 that I saw him for the first time. His house was every morning the meeting-place of his friends. Men of the war, captains of Western Greece, whenever they came up from the provinces to Athens, paid their homage to him as their former chief and also their comrade. Senators, the leading men of the Opposition, professors of the University, nomarchs of the provinces, men from the islands, were to be found at these morning levées, "the rallying-point," as Lyons said, "of the steady and intelligent patriots." His Greek friends came to him to talk over the affairs of that eventful year in Europe, as well as the political prospects of their own country and party, and to gain information from the experience and calm judgment of the generous Englishman who had seen men and cities beyond Greece, was the friend of English statesmen, yet had fought and suffered with themselves.

It was a picturesque and polyglot company. The General, in the corner of the sofa of his drawing-room, talked quietly but freely in Italian or French, seldom in Greek, in which he was never fluent, with one or another, breaking out into good-humoured raillery of some old comrade, often into strong language at the iniquities of the Ministry and the outrages reported from the provinces. The last new thing in political scandal or insurrection was brought by some visitor and discussed—the men of the war in the Albanian dress, embroidered vest and *fustanella*, for the most part not talking much, but smoking solemnly the long cherry-stick chibouques, or playing with their amber beads; some journalist or professor in Western dress, haranguing from time to time in French. Around the room were pictures of the king and queen and of scenes in the war, and twenty-four miniatures of the General's friends and chieftains. Everything around told of the new Greek life working itself out under strange conditions beneath the shadow of the Acropolis of the old world. In 1848 the times were interesting. Greece was feeling the swell from the great upheaval of society in Europe. There were rumours of revolution, and of a *coup d'état* in the capital, and risings in the provinces here and there—at

Lamia in the north, at Corinth and Pyrgos and Messenia, in the Morea. It was as of old: here and there rival leaders of parties set up a grievance, and "went out" with a political cry, and "every one that was in distress, and every one that was in debt, and every one that was discontented"—klephts and brigands—gathered themselves for the time in bands and scoured the country, and the poor villagers were equally oppressed by the bands in revolt, and by the king's soldiery who were sent in pursuit. But there were no materials for a revolutionary mob in the little capital of not more than 20,000 people, all impoverished by the war, and all the ready money was in the hands of the king. All evaporated in tall talk and journalistic warfare. But the popular discontent made the General's warnings of danger frequent and weighty, and he took his military precautions for the defence of his Tower. Great was at first the excitement of living in this strange atmosphere and among many brigand-looking faces. But among the elder warriors who came to the General's house were also some fine fellows, with stern, care-worn faces, telling of determination of purpose, and hardihood and suffering, who had gone through with him a wild and savage war—several of large build, of handsome features and honest and good expression, whose look and bearing heightened the interest which the General's introduction often raised. They all had in his eyes some claim to distinction. One "is of the best families of Epirus," whose father and brother were decapitated by Ali Pacha; another in a coarse woollen vest, *fustanella*, and woollen leggings and large thickly soled shoes, is a naval captain who did great things in the war, and is now "a kind of Cincinnatus"; another is an old Mainote who can only speak Greek. Canaris, the great admiral and brûloteer, is also here sometimes; and the leader of the Opposition, Alexander Mavrocordato, the only Greek statesman of the time of whom Stratford Canning spoke with great respect.[1] Between him and the General there was always reciprocal confidence and esteem —a small, old, and whiskered man with large head, recalling to me the incongruous likeness of Hartley Coleridge, but with spectacles. Other public men came there, also held in honour by the General, among whom I especially remember Psyllas and Pericles Argyropoulo, his intimate friends.

The three aides-de-camp of the General, who

---

[1] "I hold him in my esteem as the most able, honest, and public-spirited man of his nation."—S. Canning to General Church, December 18, 1865.

were with him at different times, were men of note in the war, and typical in their ways.

Dangli, the tall, grey, handsome old Souliot, blind in one eye, in blue and silver embroidered vest and leggings, had been one of the Souliot hostages with Ali Pacha, and was present at his treacherous murder in the island of Joannina lake. Afterwards he had been with the General in the Ionian Islands, and was with Byron in Messolonghi at his death. Anagnostes Mostras, the man of Arta, was one of four brothers who had been in the siege of Messolonghi in 1826, and had broken through the Turkish lines in the sortie — three of them carrying by turns the fourth brother who was wounded, on their shoulders, —big and burly, honest, able, and devoted. Colonel Mostras was the General's secretary, and was alone with him while I was at Athens. Theágénes the Theban had escaped out of the Acropolis when blockaded in 1827, and hiding himself in ruins and ditches for three days and nights, had made his way through the Turkish camp to the General at Munychium. He in 1870, as Colonel Theágénes, was most unjustly the object of attack in Parliament and by the English press for the failure of his mediation with the brigand fiends at Oropò, and his life was embittered thereby. He alone survived his chief, and for three months only.[1]

These men were examples of the best soldiery of Greece, and also of that fidelity and devotion to the person of their chief which the General won from so many of his Greeks. With them he spoke always in Italian, on mutual terms of easy familiarity and of implicit confidence, and on their part always of deep respect and affection. Occasionally the imperfect political morality of his more intimate friends, and even of some in high position, roused him to chivalrous rebuke. In a note of one of these days I find :—

Mr Z. came in to-day. He was praising somebody who had insulted a fallen enemy. The General broke out upon him in wrath, and our friend the "judge of the Areopagus" caught it warmly.

It is a proof of his strong healthy influence that it could be said of him by Greeks, "He fears no one, and all the bad men fear him."

Sometimes the passing English traveller was introduced into this mixed assembly of modern

[1] Sir Thomas Wyse, some years before the event which gave such notoriety to Colonel Theágénes, describes him while on a visit at his house in Thebes: "Our host entertained us by a lively and interesting conversation. He speaks French and Italian remarkably well, and understands ancient Greek; is a humble, independent, courageous man, as his life, both political and military, proves, and of the most cheerful and obliging character."—Impressions of Greece. By Right Hon. Sir T. Wyse, K.C.B., p. 64.

Greeks, and would be struck by the courtesy and refinement of the English host who received them. Sir G. F. Bowen, one of the few survivors of those days, writes:—

I can recall that happy and interesting time of my first visit to Athens in 1847, and your uncle's hospitable house in the shadow of the Acropolis, where he would sit — every inch of him a polished English officer and gentleman — among his then surviving comrades of the War of Independence, a picturesque and historical group of wild and white-kilted *palicars*.

In later years I also frequently met him at the British Legation, where he was always a welcome guest; and I still remember the stately courtesy of the old school which made him popular with his hostesses and with ladies generally.

When travelling in the provinces, letters in the General's name were a passport to the houses of "our constitutional friends," though we were sometimes frowned upon by the local officials. We heard reminiscences of him at different places where he had been in 1827, when in command, and in progress with his soldiery through the mountains of Achaia, on his way to embark at Cape Papas for Western Greece. The tambours of his camp in the "Great Dervhen" of Mount Geraneion were then visible to the traveller through that most beautiful route from Megara to Corinth. At Nauplia friends recalled his intervention in the military broils in 1827, when Moreote and Romeliot flew upon the spoil and fought over the grapes of Argos, and Grivas was lording it and firing guns over Nauplia from his fortress on the Palamede. At Argos they told with wonder of his feat of swimming across the bay to the mills of Lerna, and the punishment which the scorching sun inflicted upon his back and shoulders. At Megaspelæon the monks honoured his name as one of their great benefactors for the support and protection he gave them when the convent nest in the rock was a fortress against the Turks under Ibrahim, and a refuge for several hundred women and children of the neighbouring cantons. At Diakopto, on the heights above the Gulf of Corinth, the news of the battle of Navarino had reached his camp, and there were those who remembered the bonfires in the camp and along the high land of Achaia from Diakopto to Patras, which woke up responsive fires from the mountain heights across the Gulf.

We were fortunate in meeting also with some representative men of semi-klephtic Greece. This is an extract from a letter of the time:—

When we were off Messolonghi divers Greek passengers came on board — among others, one of the notabilities of the war, Theodore Grivas, once of evil

fame, but now aide-de-camp to the king, and going to
pay his court at Athens. He came on board *tutto d' oro*,
in gold-embroidered vest and leggings, with a body-
guard of four picturesque *palicaris* carrying his sword
and gun and pistols and yataghans, besides each their
own gun and their belts stuffed with arms. The
chief strutted about and twisted his moustache as
if the ship was all his own and he was on his way to
glory. He soon took notice of us, and gave us to
understand that he wished to make acquaintance; and
then, after Greek bowings and salutations by hand to
heart, and finally English hand-shaking, the palaver
began. He expressed great friendship towards his
Excellency the General (ὁ στρατηγός), and all the
English, and he told of a visit which "the Great Har-
most" (*i.e.*, the Lord High Commissioner) of the Ionian
Islands, and ὁ Βωεν,[1] then the chief secretary, had paid
him at his castle opposite Santa Maura. He assured
us that it was a slander (συκοφαντέια) that it was unsafe to travel in Greece; there was now great quietness
(πολλὴ ἡσυχία) in the mountains, and brigands did
not exist. "Are there not bad men everywhere?"
All day long he has been on deck, talking interminably
and receiving the salutations (σεβάσματα) of his friends
from the shore, except when he was eating lamb and
drinking κρασί, sitting on his carpet and waited on by
his *palicari*, and smoking chibouques. In the course of
the day he showed us his arms,—a very handsome Turkish sword which had belonged to Ruschid Pacha, who
shot Ali Pacha; and his gun with his name (Θεωδώρα
Γρίβα) cut on it, and inlaid with curious rude figures
of the Panagía and of animals. Now he has had his
bed made on the deck—that is, his *paplomá*, a quilt,

[1] Sir G. F. Bowen, G.C.M.G., afterwards governor of five of
our principal colonies.

and his *capote* laid down; and he tells me the klephts like to lie out in the open, and to sleep under the moon. But he goes on late into the night talking to a listening circle about the war in "Karlili" (Akarnania), and his former deeds with Botzares against the Turks, 30,000 of them! and he fights over his battles with gestures and sounds to imitate musketry—piff! puff! boom! boom!—in most animated and truly Falstaffian style, until it becomes wearisome to listen to him, and we salute and say good-night.

It was a happy thing for us that at that time Northern Greece seemed free from brigandage. In consequence of the small insurrections going on, the sporadic bands of robbers had attached themselves either to the constitutional insurrectionists or to the king's irregulars; so the highways were unoccupied by brigands, and the travellers could pass safely even through the byways. Travelling in company with Edward Lear, his truthful and delicate pencil made captive many an exquisite combination of poetic mountain and of broad plain, or he fearlessly sketched the wild *palicari* as they strutted in the bazar or skipped down the mountain pass and stopped to drink at the wayside spring; and as we journeyed he would sing out some Italian air, or chant with deep feeling some Tennysonian verse, as "The Lotos-eaters," sitting on the yellow shore of the little bay of Aulis, or throw off some nonsense ditty, as in the mid-day halt by the hot sulphur-springs of Thermopylæ :—

> "There was an old man of Thermopylæ
> Who never did anything properly."

But, sketching too eagerly in the hot July weather, he was taken ill of a fever in the house of our friend Theágénes at Thebes. Doctors were sent out by the General in great alarm in a carriage from Athens; but after a sharp struggle of some days he rallied, and the Greek doctor was able to say with classical humour, νὰ θύσωμεν ἀλεκτρυῶνα 'Ασκλήπιῳ—"Let us sacrifice a cock to Æsculapius."

The General's daily life was simple and uniform. An early ride of four miles to the Phalerum to bathe was his almost daily habit during the summer months, starting between three and four so as to return before the sun had risen with its scorching heat over the shoulder of Hymettus. In August 1865, then past eighty, he wrote :—

We are broiling, but with the help of bathing I manage to get through the day. But, as you know, the sea is a long way off. I am obliged to get up at 3½ A.M., and then to ride to my bathing-place, as I do not go to the baths of the Phalerum, which are crowded morning and afternoon. I prefer my solitary rock and little cove, where in the sea and out of it I spend a delicious cool hour.

In June 1870, in his eighty-seventh year, when he no longer rode, he went in a carriage. "In this great heat I have no comfort but when I am in the sea."

The rocky eastern point of the Phalerum bay, the Tripyrgi, was his bathing-place. It was a historical scene in his life. There he told me of his narrow escape of being taken prisoner or sabred by the Turkish horsemen at the battle before Athens in May 1827.

There was a chapel of St George some little distance inland of this point, around which a tambour of loose stones had been raised. He and Cochrane and about forty men were watching the scene here when a charge of horsemen swept round and past them in pursuit of the flying Greeks, too eager to stop. Cochrane and the General had only just time to get off to the boats before another charge came down upon them to the water's edge.

That year (1870) was a memorable year in Athens for the intense heat and for earthquakes.

I have no recollection of a summer like this in Greece [he writes]. We had an earthquake yesterday (August 1) about two in the morning. I was in bed, and remained there, having confidence in the strength of the walls of the old Tower: it behaved nobly; its motion backwards and forwards was awful, but it soon righted itself and became again steady.

Of a strong constitution, always simple and temperate in his habits, he knew little of illness, though at times he suffered much from the old wound in his left arm shattered at the taking of Santa Maura in 1811. After breakfast came the morning visitors, or he wrote or read until the mid-day rest; dinner at five, at which the aide-de-camp was the only company; then the coffee and chibouque on the verandah, looking on the garden court, its pepper-tree and cypresses; and the evening ride in stately dignity, but in such scenes as it was a delight to linger in on beautiful summer evenings— either round the Acropolis, or to a country house at Karà where Dr and Mrs Hill lived in the summer, or along the moonlit shore of the Phalerum Bay, or in the silvered olive-groves and by the water-courses of the Cephissus. There was little general society in the poverty-stricken capital, except the occasional balls at the Palace, where the General went not; but the terrace of the hospitable English Legation, under the reign of the Lyons, Wyses, and Stuarts especially, was always open to him, and there he found his chief solace.

In the winter evenings sometimes I read aloud to him his Apulian Tales, which he would amplify and comment on with quiet humour; or I heard some recollections of other days gone by; but he was reticent of his own deeds, and I knew not enough to ask questions. He was always a great reader, chiefly of history. Some of his books—Gibbon, Grote, and indeed most of his library books, including his Bible—are scored through with pencil notes and comments, according to his usual practice of reading with a pencil in hand. He was also a great writer in verse — books full of poetical composition remained—of heroic Greek subjects in the style of Glover's 'Leonidas,' and epic poems in which such as Manfred of Apulia or Harold of England were the heroes. Sonnets and pieces devotional, he would write in bed to a late hour in these years.

CHAPTER XVIII.

LAST DAYS.

SIR EDMUND LYONS—LETTERS FROM LORD PALMERSTON AND MR GLADSTONE—THE SUCCESSION TO THE GREEK THRONE —CESSION OF THE IONIAN ISLANDS — DESTRUCTION OF THE SENATE—FINLAY'S 'HISTORY'—THE END.

DURING these years of simple and retired life at Athens, there was little to cheer him in the political state of Greece. His friend Sir E. Lyons wrote in 1849 :—

I see no comfort for the General in the political prospect of Greece, and I am afraid that, sanguine as he has always been, he has but little hope left himself. But, nevertheless, by his precept and example he keeps up the spirits of others.

The loss of Sir E. Lyons in that year, with whom he had kept up a warm and uninterrupted friendship for so many years, was a great blow to him. Lyons also felt it much.

It seems to me a dream [he wrote], that the happy and delightful daily interchange of feeling and sentiments with you which constituted the charm of my long residence in Athens should be at an end.

The letters of the two friends in after years abound in affectionate expressions. Lyons could write from the Crimea—

It is long since we have written to each other, but I am very sure that I have constantly been in your mind, as you have been in mine. Never can I forget the interesting scenes of all sorts in which we have taken part together, nor can I ever cease to remember with pride and pleasure the noble part you have taken on all these occasions, inspiring in my mind admiration, confidence, and friendship.

But there was no evidence of despondency nor even of regret in Church's mind. In the spirit of a religious enthusiast he had devoted himself to this cause for life, and had never looked back. It was thus he wrote, after twenty years of trial:—

I do not regret having sacrificed everything to the cause I embraced, and to whose triumph I hope I contributed. Once embarked in the cause, every other consideration was lost sight of. Notwithstanding what has happened, were it to be done over again, I should voluntarily undertake the same difficulties and dangers, and even with the anticipation of ruin to my private fortunes. I am not, however, the only one whom the mighty effort made to liberate this country has totally or nearly ruined. As no division of land nor arrangements have as yet been made for indemnifying the chief leaders of the country in the great struggle, every man is more or less in a state of ruin in his domestic affairs.

His letters during these later years of his life bear out Lyons's words, that by his precept and example he was keeping up the spirits of others amidst much of failure and disappointment. He was also exerting an equitable influence in behalf of the Greeks on important occasions with friends in England. Throughout he acted as the interpreter of the higher public opinion in Greece, as distinct from the Governments of the day, and he brought to bear upon the Greeks the influence of leading men in England. So it was in 1850, at the time of the English blockade of the Piræus; so it was in 1854, when he was the apologist for the Greek people, suffering, as he thought, for the sins of their rulers.

Lord Palmerston wrote to him in 1854:—

I am glad to hear confirmed by your authority the notions which I had previously entertained as to the origin and character of the incursions made from Greece into Thessaly and Epirus. You may confidently assure all your Greek friends that the British Government, though indignant at the bad faith and astonished at the folly of the Court of Athens, knows how to distinguish between the actors in the Russian cabal and the Greek nation, and the Greeks may be assured that nothing will be done to impair the independence and political existence of Greece.

If my personal and individual wishes could have prevailed at the time when the kingdom of Greece was constituted, Thessaly and Epirus would have been included within its limits; but arrangements once made cannot be reversed, and the Greeks must be content with the boundaries assigned to them.

It was in the correspondence of the year 1855 that the General for the first and only time expresses regret for the sacrifice of his life to Greece, and only for the reason that he was thereby excluded from the military service of his own country. Still eager for active service, at the age of seventy-two, during the Crimean war, and even during the Indian Mutiny in 1858, when seventy-five, he wrote on both occasions to Lord Palmerston, and also to Stratford Canning, to ask if it were possible that he could re-enter the English service.

It is only now, my lord [he wrote, September 12, 1855], when my country is at war, that I feel the full weight of the sacrifices I have made for Greece. I am oppressed by the retrospect when I think of the high position I might now have held amongst the lieutenant-generals in her Majesty's service.

At such a moment [he wrote in 1858, during the Indian Mutiny] I have thought it my duty to place my humble services at your lordship's disposal, and I fear no reproach for arrogance for stating my readiness to serve in India.

He retained so much of the generous and quixotic simplicity with which he had thrown himself into Greece thirty years before.

After 1861, when he first saw Mr Gladstone in Greece, letters to him are more frequent; he felt sure of Mr Gladstone's sympathy, if not of full agreement in opinions.

In 1862 he expressed to him the strong wish of the Greek people for the English Prince Alfred to be the successor of Otho as King of Greece; and when that was impossible, he urged the early nomination of a successor, describing the present calm, but the growing anxieties, of the Greek nation during the crisis so serious and so prolonged. Mr Gladstone in his reply says :—

> Your description of the hopes and fears of those for whom you have done so much, has a touching, almost a tragic, interest. When will you come to England, where there are many who would be glad to see you, and where you would do good to the Greeks, by showing what sort of Englishman it is that has felt so profound an interest in them for half a century, and has left his name engraven in their hearts?

On the cession of the Ionian Islands to Greece, his feelings were much divided. Welcoming the accession of that territory to Greece, where he had first trained Greeks to be soldiers, he saw also that a strong anti-English party was now brought into the Greek kingdom which would affect for a time public opinion in Greece, and he ascribed to that influence threatened changes which he deprecated in the constitution. As a military man he deplored the destruction of the fortifications of Corfu and Vido, as a selfish and unworthy course of action which depreciated the value of the gift.

Mr Gladstone answered his objections:—

As to the fortifications of Corfu, I do not think that the Government have been prompted in what they intend by any selfish fears as regards the use of these fortifications in possible cases by Powers rival or hostile to England. I am confident that this has not been the main object in their view.

But in the cession of the Ionian Islands we have had to consider the necessarily delicate relations between Turkey and Greece, and to take care that in securing a benefit for the latter Power we should not inflict an injury on the former. Now it was most unfortunate that when the Greek kingdom was constituted, Thessaly and Epirus should have been left under Ottoman rule. But so it was; and it being so, we must respect within, and up to, the limits of honour and justice the authority which Europe has suffered to exist.

I do not know whether the matter has presented itself to you in this as much as in other points of view. The Albanian coast is no match for Corfu fortified. We might perhaps have been glad if that coast could even now have been placed under the Hellenic Government, but this it did not rest with us to accomplish.

You will admit that, whether a right view or a wrong one, this was no narrow or selfish view of the subject.

Again, in 1864, the General writes in review of the policy of the advisers of the young king, and is alarmed at the threatened abolition of the Senate :—

> The late King Otho was not a bad man nor a despotic ruler, but totally incapable of government. Still the nation forced upon him a good constitution. Now there is danger that a bad constitution will be substituted for that of 1843, and the existence of the Senate is threatened, I feel compelled to make plain my own opinion on so important a subject.

Greece was called upon ultimately to try the experiment of having only one Chamber.

Mr Gladstone wrote in answer on October 7, 1864 :—

> The destruction of the Senate is a design (I hope I need not yet say an event) to be deplored. Great as are the difficulties of the existence of two Chambers in a country like Greece, they will only be exchanged for more complications by the adoption of a single Chamber. But if Ionian influence has helped to bring about this mischief, I am afraid it was partly due to the strange, incongruous, unintelligible, and wholly bastard example of a Second Chamber which we gave them in the Ionian Senate.

When Mr Finlay's 'History of the Greek Revolution' appeared at Athens, it was naturally a great trial to General Church to find his character and services so unjustly depreciated by his own countryman.

The two men had been always on terms of friendly intercourse and free communication.

Finlay had asked and obtained information from Church on points of personal history and military operations, and Finlay's letters of earlier date were appreciative and complimentary.

The General, remembering the time when Finlay had addressed him as "the liege lord of all true Philhellenes," was taken by surprise, and his letters show his sense of having received wrong by suppression of truth and concealed feelings of ill-will.

His first comment on the book appears in a letter early in 1862 :—

My old friend and very near neighbour, Finlay, has given me not a little abuse, I find. God help us if this book can be called a good history which contains in it so much at variance with truth! For myself, if truth has any weight in this world, I am not apprehensive of suffering much in public estimation from the too clearly apparent animosity contained in my friend's narrative.

He says again in another letter :—

His conduct to me has been that of an assassin in the dark. Does he forget that I have letters of very different purport to what he has now written of earlier date?

There is no appearance of his having ever taken any notice to Finlay himself of his book.

A contemporary review of Finlay's History justly pointed out that—

The manifest unfairness of Mr Finlay's judgments of his contemporaries affects seriously the weight of his judgment as a historian. We cannot help suspecting a writer who has an ill word for every one and seldom a good one—who brings the worse characteristics of a man into distinct and emphatic prominence, while he lets his redeeming good deeds appear incidentally and without comment in some casual mention. There is throughout a studied and ill-natured depreciation of Sir R. Church's character and actions, which almost suggests the supposition of personal animosity. If an historian is not bound to be generous, he is bound to be just, and it is not just to be silent, as Mr Finlay is, on the patience, the unselfish devotedness, the constancy under reverses and difficulties, the disregard of personal considerations, with which Church threw in his lot with the Greeks, shared their fortunes, and tried to make the best of the enormous disadvantages under which he laboured.[1]

The General's friends in Athens were more concerned than he was, and Lord Lyons [2] wrote :—

I burn with indignation when I think of the unworthy detraction of the great services of one of the most noble-minded men I ever knew.

The General employed himself in putting his papers in order, knowing that they presented another side which would demand a juster judgment; but as time went on he felt content "to rest on truth," as he said. The two men were of different temperament, but their courteous relations were never broken. Two

---

[1] Guardian, February 5, 1862.
[2] Afterwards Ambassador at Paris.

notes from Finlay a few days before the General's last illness express thanks for kindness received. The two old men in their last days parted as friends.

The end came at last to the hale old man by an attack of bronchitis in March 1873. He was in his ninetieth year.

During the few days of his illness he was nursed by the Sisters of St Joseph, who lived in a house adjoining, and whom he had always taken under his care. His good friend Colonel Theágénes watched over him to the last, and the king and many mourning friends were by him in the ante-chamber of the little room in his Tower in which the old warrior passed to his rest with the prayers of the Church. The national funeral, and the words spoken at his grave in English by the son of an old Greek friend bearing the honoured name of Gennadius,[1] expressed with feeling and just discrimination of character the nation's gratitude for this unique devotion of a life to her service.

After all was over, and the General's papers and the records of a long life were examined, one circumstance brought to light the completeness of his sacrifice. Among his papers

[1] His Excellency John Gennadius, then Secretary of Legation; afterwards Greek Minister to England.

a memorandum was found dated "18th May 1861," in which he left on record his claims, officially certified, upon the Greek Government, and at the same time his renunciation of those claims except in the event of his leaving any personal debts in Greece at the time of his death. His only object in placing these claims upon record was that others might thereby be secured against loss in the event of his actual property being found insufficient. These papers showed that the claims of the General were, *not* in compensation for services in Greece, for which during his whole career he never once had asked; they were, *not* for repayment of any part of his private fortune, the whole of which was sunk in supporting the war; but they were for repayment of losses by loans contracted by him for the support of the war, on the authority of the National Assembly, the justice of which had been acknowledged by successive Governments, but a small portion only had been paid on account, up to the year 1858.[1] In his lifetime he would never allow these his claims to be put forward by the British Minister among other private claims of English subjects; he now only claimed the

[1] Documents in verification were deposited in the Chancellery of the British Legation, and in the Greek Foreign Office, May 1873. Cf. p. 318.

intervention of the British Minister in this hypothetical case.

The result proved that his anxiety upon this point was unnecessary, as, the cost of his public funeral having been defrayed by the gratitude of the Greek nation, the sum realised by sale of his library and effects was found sufficient to meet the charges upon his estate.

"Privatus illi census erat brevis, commune magnum."

It is evident [says a contemporary letter from Athens] that in late years his expenses on himself and his house had been very small, but very large proportionately in assistance to others, especially to the families of any of the soldiers of the War of Independence who were in need; and all speak of the delicate way in which he was accustomed to give to those who needed, but were ashamed to ask. All this time he was living a life of great severity; his rooms in the Tower where he died were quite a soldier's barrack—the furniture the simplest and the barest—a life of stern self-denial, with gentle courtesy and loving-kindness and generosity towards all who came to him in need. His character fills me with admiration as really noble and heroic in action and in suffering, with little talk of Christianity but with very much of its spirit. He was a true crusader. His whole career in Greece seems to me an act of devotion and self-sacrifice to what he considered a holy cause, the rescue of a Christian people from slavery. There has run a solemn seriousness through his life, and strong sense of duty reaching far beyond the thought of self-glory or personal ambition, which distinguishes his life above all his contemporaries in the same cause. The deep reverence of some who speak of him, the respect of all, and affection of others, tell of a remarkable character. Lord Lyons writes to me from Paris—" His was the most chivalrous character I have known." And these are the words of Mr Finlay: "There could not be a nobler heart, and I think he was a perfect model of what he considered a perfect knight."

The king, the Greek Government and nation, paid him every honour in their power. He was laid in his grave in the Greek cemetery with every mark of the reverence and grief of a nation.

Two memorial inscriptions, written by two master-hands, attest the impression made by his character upon his own countrymen. On a tablet at the foot of a memorial window in the English church, put up by the British Government during the ministry of Mr Gladstone, are the words :—

"THIS WINDOW IS DEDICATED BY
THE BRITISH GOVERNMENT
TO
THE MEMORY OF
GENERAL SIR RICHARD CHURCH
WHO, AFTER DISTINGUISHED SERVICES IN THE BRITISH ARMY ON THE
SHORES OF THE MEDITERRANEAN,
DEVOTED HIMSELF TO
THE CAUSE OF GREECE AS A SOLDIER AND A CITIZEN,
AND WON, BY THE EXAMPLE OF A LONG AND NOBLE LIFE,
THE AFFECTION OF HER PEOPLE FOR HIMSELF
AND FOR ENGLAND."

The Greek monument at the grave in the cypress-grove bears upon it words in Greek and English :—

> "RICHARD CHURCH, GENERAL,
> WHO, HAVING GIVEN HIMSELF AND ALL THAT HE HAD
> TO RESCUE A CHRISTIAN RACE FROM OPPRESSION
> AND TO MAKE GREECE A NATION,
> LIVED FOR HER SERVICE AND DIED AMONGST HER PEOPLE,
> RESTS HERE IN PEACE AND FAITH.
> 1873."

THE END.

PRINTED BY WILLIAM BLACKWOOD AND SONS.

Catalogue

of

Messrs Blackwood & Sons' Publications

PHILOSOPHICAL CLASSICS FOR ENGLISH READERS.

EDITED BY WILLIAM KNIGHT, LL.D.,
Professor of Moral Philosophy in the University of St Andrews.

In crown 8vo Volumes, with Portraits, price 3s. 6d.

Contents of the Series.

DESCARTES, by Professor Mahaffy, Dublin.—BUTLER, by Rev. W. Lucas Collins, M.A.—BERKELEY, by Professor Campbell Fraser.—FICHTE, by Professor Adamson, Owens College, Manchester.—KANT, by Professor Wallace, Oxford.—HAMILTON, by Professor Veitch, Glasgow.—HEGEL, by the Master of Balliol.—LEIBNIZ, by J. Theodore Merz.—VICO, by Professor Flint, Edinburgh.—HOBBES, by Professor Croom Robertson.—HUME, by the Editor.—SPINOZA, by the Very Rev. Principal Caird, Glasgow.—BACON: Part I. The Life, by Professor Nichol.—BACON: Part II. Philosophy, by the same Author.—LOCKE, by Professor Campbell Fraser.

FOREIGN CLASSICS FOR ENGLISH READERS.

EDITED BY MRS OLIPHANT.

In crown 8vo, 2s. 6d.

Contents of the Series.

DANTE, by the Editor.—VOLTAIRE, by General Sir E. B. Hamley, K.C.B.—PASCAL, by Principal Tulloch.—PETRARCH, by Henry Reeve, C.B.—GOETHE, by A. Hayward, Q.C.—MOLIÈRE, by the Editor and F. Tarver, M.A.—MONTAIGNE, by Rev. W. L. Collins, M.A.—RABELAIS, by Walter Besant, M.A.—CALDERON, by E. J. Hasell.—SAINT SIMON, by Clifton W. Collins, M.A.—CERVANTES, by the Editor.—CORNEILLE AND RACINE, by Henry M. Trollope.—MADAME DE SÉVIGNÉ, by Miss Thackeray.—LA FONTAINE, AND OTHER FRENCH FABULISTS, by Rev. W. Lucas Collins, M.A.—SCHILLER, by James Sime, M.A., Author of 'Lessing, his Life and Writings.'—TASSO, by E. J. Hasell.—ROUSSEAU, by Henry Grey Graham.—ALFRED DE MUSSET, by C. F. Oliphant.

ANCIENT CLASSICS FOR ENGLISH READERS.

EDITED BY THE REV. W. LUCAS COLLINS, M.A.

Complete in 28 Vols. crown 8vo, cloth, price 2s. 6d. each. And may also be had in 14 Volumes, strongly and neatly bound, with calf or vellum back, £3, 10s.

Contents of the Series.

HOMER: THE ILIAD, by the Editor.—HOMER: THE ODYSSEY, by the Editor.—HERODOTUS, by George C. Swayne, M.A.—XENOPHON, by Sir Alexander Grant, Bart., LL.D.—EURIPIDES, by W. B. Donne.—ARISTOPHANES, by the Editor.—PLATO, by Clifton W. Collins, M.A.—LUCIAN, by the Editor.—ÆSCHYLUS, by the Right Rev. the Bishop of Colombo.—SOPHOCLES, by Clifton W. Collins, M.A.—HESIOD AND THEOGNIS, by the Rev. J. Davies, M.A.—GREEK ANTHOLOGY, by Lord Neaves.—VIRGIL, by the Editor.—HORACE, by Sir Theodore Martin, K.C.B.—JUVENAL, by Edward Walford, M.A.—PLAUTUS AND TERENCE, by the Editor—THE COMMENTARIES OF CÆSAR, by Anthony Trollope.—TACITUS, by W. B. Donne.—CICERO, by the Editor.—PLINY'S LETTERS, by the Rev. Alfred Church, M.A., and the Rev. W. J. Brodribb, M.A.—LIVY, by the Editor.—OVID, by the Rev. A. Church, M.A.—CATULLUS, TIBULLUS, AND PROPERTIUS, by the Rev. Jas. Davies, M.A.—DEMOSTHENES, by the Rev. W. J. Brodribb, M.A.—ARISTOTLE, by Sir Alexander Grant, Bart., LL.D.—THUCYDIDES, by the Editor.—LUCRETIUS, by W. H. Mallock, M.A.—PINDAR, by the Rev. F. D. Morice, M.A.

Saturday Review.—"It is difficult to estimate too highly the value of such a series as this in giving 'English readers' an insight, exact as far as it goes, into those olden times which are so remote, and yet to many of us so close."

CATALOGUE

OF

MESSRS BLACKWOOD & SONS'
PUBLICATIONS.

ALISON.
 History of Europe. By Sir ARCHIBALD ALISON, Bart., D.C.L.
  1. From the Commencement of the French Revolution to the Battle of Waterloo.
   LIBRARY EDITION, 14 vols., with Portraits. Demy 8vo, £10, 10s.
   ANOTHER EDITION, in 20 vols. crown 8vo, £6.
   PEOPLE'S EDITION, 13 vols. crown 8vo, £2, 11s.
  2. Continuation to the Accession of Louis Napoleon.
   LIBRARY EDITION, 8 vols. 8vo, £6, 7s. 6d.
   PEOPLE'S EDITION, 8 vols. crown 8vo, 34s.
 Epitome of Alison's History of Europe. Thirtieth Thousand, 7s. 6d.
 Atlas to Alison's History of Europe. By A. Keith Johnston.
  LIBRARY EDITION, demy 4to, £3, 3s.
  PEOPLE'S EDITION, 31s. 6d.
 Life of John Duke of Marlborough. With some Account of his Contemporaries, and of the War of the Succession. Third Edition. 2 vols. 8vo. Portraits and Maps, 30s.
 Essays: Historical, Political, and Miscellaneous. 3 vols. demy 8vo, 45s.

ACROSS FRANCE IN A CARAVAN: BEING SOME ACCOUNT OF A JOURNEY FROM BORDEAUX TO GENOA IN THE "ESCARGOT," taken in the Winter 1889-90. By the Author of 'A Day of my Life at Eton.' With fifty Illustrations by John Wallace, after Sketches by the Author, and a Map. Cheap Edition, demy 8vo, 7s. 6d.

ACTA SANCTORUM HIBERNIÆ; Ex Codice Salmanticensi. Nunc primum integre edita opera CAROLI DE SMEDT et JOSEPHI DE BACKER, e Soc. Jesu, Hagiographorum Bollandianorum; Auctore et Sumptus Largiente JOANNE PATRICIO MARCHIONE BOTHAE. In One handsome 4to Volume, bound in half roxburghe, £2, 2s.; in paper cover, 31s. 6d.

AGRICULTURAL HOLDINGS ACT, 1883. With Notes by a MEMBER OF THE HIGHLAND AND AGRICULTURAL SOCIETY. 8vo, 3s. 6d.

AIKMAN.
 Manures and the Principles of Manuring. By C. M. AIKMAN, D.Sc., F.R.S.E., &c., Professor of Chemistry, Glasgow Veterinary College; Examiner in Chemistry, University of Glasgow, &c. Crown 8vo, 6s. 6d.
 Farmyard Manure: Its Nature, Composition, and Treatment. Crown 8vo, 1s. 6d.

AIRD. Poetical Works of Thomas Aird. Fifth Edition, with Memoir of the Author by the Rev. JARDINE WALLACE, and Portrait. Crown 8vo, 7s. 6d.

ALLARDYCE.
The City of Sunshine. By ALEXANDER ALLARDYCE, Author of 'Earlscourt,' 'Balmoral: A Romance of the Queen's Country,' &c. New and Revised Edition. Crown 8vo, 6s.
Memoir of the Honourable George Keith Elphinstone, K.B., Viscount Keith of Stonehaven, Marischal, Admiral of the Red. 8vo, with Portrait, Illustrations, and Maps, 21s.

ALMOND. Sermons by a Lay Head-master. By HELY HUTCHINSON ALMOND, M.A. Oxon., Head-master of Loretto School. Crown 8vo, 5s.

ANCIENT CLASSICS FOR ENGLISH READERS. Edited by Rev. W. LUCAS COLLINS, M.A. Price 2s. 6d. each. For List of Vols., see p. 2.

AYTOUN.
Lays of the Scottish Cavaliers, and other Poems. By W. EDMONDSTOUNE AYTOUN, D.C.L., Professor of Rhetoric and Belles-Lettres in the University of Edinburgh. New Edition. Fcap. 8vo, 3s. 6d.
ANOTHER EDITION. Fcap. 8vo, 7s. 6d.
CHEAP EDITION. 1s. Cloth, 1s. 3d.
An Illustrated Edition of the Lays of the Scottish Cavaliers. From designs by Sir NOEL PATON. Small 4to, in gilt cloth, 21s.
Bothwell: a Poem. Third Edition. Fcap., 7s. 6d.
Poems and Ballads of Goethe. Translated by Professor AYTOUN and Sir THEODORE MARTIN, K.C.B. Third Edition. Fcap., 6s.
Bon Gaultier's Book of Ballads. By the SAME. Fifteenth Edition. With Illustrations by Doyle, Leech, and Crowquill. Fcap. 8vo, 5s.
The Ballads of Scotland. Edited by Professor AYTOUN. Fourth Edition. 2 vols. fcap. 8vo, 12s.
Memoir of William E. Aytoun, D.C.L. By Sir THEODORE MARTIN, K.C.B. With Portrait. Post 8vo, 12s.

BACH.
On Musical Education and Vocal Culture. By ALBERT B. BACH. Fourth Edition. 8vo, 7s. 6d.
The Principles of Singing. A Practical Guide for Vocalists and Teachers. With Course of Vocal Exercises. Second Edition. With Portrait of the Author. Crown 8vo, 6s.
The Art Ballad: Loewe and Schubert. With Musical Illustrations. With a Portrait of LOEWE. Third Edition. Small 4to, 5s.

BAIRD LECTURES.
Theism. By Rev. Professor FLINT, D.D., Edinburgh. Eighth Edition. Crown 8vo, 7s. 6d.
Anti-Theistic Theories. By the SAME. Fifth Edition. Crown 8vo, 10s. 6d.
The Inspiration of the Holy Scriptures. By Rev. ROBERT JAMIESON, D.D. Crown 8vo, 7s. 6d.
The Early Religion of Israel. As set forth by Biblical Writers and modern Critical Historians. By Rev. Professor ROBERTSON, D.D., Glasgow. Fourth Edition. Crown 8vo, 10s. 6d.
The Mysteries of Christianity. By Rev. Professor CRAWFORD, D.D. Crown 8vo, 7s. 6d.
Endowed Territorial Work: Its Supreme Importance to the Church and Country. By Rev. WILLIAM SMITH, D.D. Crown 8vo, 6s.

BALLADS AND POEMS. By MEMBERS OF THE GLASGOW BALLAD CLUB. Crown 8vo, 7s. 6d.

BELLAIRS.
  The Transvaal War, 1880-81. Edited by Lady BELLAIRS.
  With a Frontispiece and Map. 8vo, 15s.
  Gossips with Girls and Maidens, Betrothed and Free. New Edition. Crown 8vo, 3s. 6d. Cloth, extra gilt edges, 5s.

BELLESHEIM. History of the Catholic Church of Scotland. From the Introduction of Christianity to the Present Day. By ALPHONS BELLESHEIM, D.D., Canon of Aix-la-Chapelle. Translated, with Notes and Additions, by D. OSWALD HUNTER BLAIR, O.S.B., Monk of Fort Augustus. Cheap Edition. Complete in 4 vols. demy 8vo, with Maps. Price 21s. net.

BENTINCK. Racing Life of Lord George Cavendish Bentinck, M.P., and other Reminiscences. By JOHN KENT, Private Trainer to the Goodwood Stable. Edited by the Hon. FRANCIS LAWLEY. With Twenty-three full-page Plates, and Facsimile Letter. Third Edition. Demy 8vo, 25s.

BESANT.
  The Revolt of Man. By WALTER BESANT. Tenth Edition. Crown 8vo, 3s. 6d.
  Readings in Rabelais. Crown 8vo, 7s. 6d.

BEVERIDGE.
  Culross and Tulliallan; or Perthshire on Forth. Its History and Antiquities. With Elucidations of Scottish Life and Character from the Burgh and Kirk-Session Records of that District. By DAVID BEVERIDGE. 2 vols. 8vo, with Illustrations, 42s.
  Between the Ochils and the Forth; or, From Stirling Bridge to Aberdour. Crown 8vo, 6s.

BICKERDYKE. A Banished Beauty. By JOHN BICKERDYKE, Author of 'Days in Thule, with Rod, Gun, and Camera,' 'The Book of the All-Round Angler,' 'Curiosities of Ale and Beer,' &c. With Illustrations. Crown 8vo, 6s.

BIRCH.
  Examples of Stables, Hunting-Boxes, Kennels, Racing Establishments, &c. By JOHN BIRCH, Architect, Author of 'Country Architecture,' &c. With 30 Plates. Royal 8vo, 7s.
  Examples of Labourers' Cottages, &c. With Plans for Improving the Dwellings of the Poor in Large Towns. With 34 Plates. Royal 8vo, 7s.
  Picturesque Lodges. A Series of Designs for Gate Lodges, Park Entrances, Keepers', Gardeners', Bailiffs', Grooms', Upper and Under Servants' Lodges, and other Rural Residences. With 16 Plates. 4to, 12s. 6d.

BLACK. Heligoland and the Islands of the North Sea. By WILLIAM GEORGE BLACK. Crown 8vo, 4s.

BLACKIE.
  Lays and Legends of Ancient Greece. By JOHN STUART BLACKIE, Emeritus Professor of Greek in the University of Edinburgh. Second Edition. Fcap. 8vo, 5s.
  The Wisdom of Goethe. Fcap. 8vo. Cloth, extra gilt, 6s.
  Scottish Song: Its Wealth, Wisdom, and Social Significance. Crown 8vo. With Music. 7s. 6d.
  A Song of Heroes. Crown 8vo, 6s.

BLACKMORE. The Maid of Sker. By R. D. BLACKMORE, Author of 'Lorna Doone,' &c. New Edition. Crown 8vo, 6s.

BLACKWOOD.
  Blackwood's Magazine, from Commencement in 1817 to April 1895. Nos. 1 to 954, forming 157 Volumes.
  Index to Blackwood's Magazine. Vols. 1 to 50. 8vo, 15s.

List of Books Published by

BLACKWOOD.

Tales from Blackwood. First Series. Price One Shilling each, in Paper Cover. Sold separately at all Railway Bookstalls. They may also be had bound in 12 vols., cloth, 18s. Half calf, richly gilt, 30s. Or the 12 vols. in 6, roxburghe, 21s. Half red morocco, 28s.

Tales from Blackwood. Second Series. Complete in Twenty-four Shilling Parts. Handsomely bound in 12 vols., cloth, 30s. In leather back, roxburghe style, 37s. 6d. Half calf, gilt, 52s. 6d. Half morocco, 55s.

Tales from Blackwood. Third Series. Complete in Twelve Shilling Parts. Handsomely bound in 6 vols., cloth, 15s.; and in 12 vols., cloth, 18s. The 6 vols. in roxburghe, 21s. Half calf, 25s. Half morocco, 28s.

Travel, Adventure, and Sport. From 'Blackwood's Magazine.' Uniform with 'Tales from Blackwood.' In Twelve Parts, each price 1s. Handsomely bound in 6 vols., cloth, 15s. And in half calf, 25s.

New Educational Series. *See separate Catalogue.*

New Uniform Series of Novels (Copyright). Crown 8vo, cloth. Price 3s. 6d. each. Now ready:—

WENDERHOLME. By P. G. Hamerton.	BEGGAR MY NEIGHBOUR. By the Same.
THE STORY OF MARGRÉDEL. By D. Storrar Meldrum.	THE WATERS OF HERCULES. By the Same.
MISS MARJORIBANKS. By Mrs Oliphant.	FAIR TO SEE. By L. W. M. Lockhart.
THE PERPETUAL CURATE, and THE RECTOR. By the Same.	MINE IS THINE. By the Same.
SALEM CHAPEL, and THE DOCTOR'S FAMILY. By the Same.	DOUBLES AND QUITS. By the Same.
A SENSITIVE PLANT. By E. D. Gerard.	HURRISH. By the Hon. Emily Lawless.
LADY LEE'S WIDOWHOOD. By General Sir E. B. Hamley.	ALTIORA PETO. By Laurence Oliphant.
KATIE STEWART, and other Stories. By Mrs Oliphant.	PICCADILLY. By the Same. With Illustrations.
VALENTINE, AND HIS BROTHER. By the Same.	THE REVOLT OF MAN. By Walter Besant.
SONS AND DAUGHTERS. By the Same.	LADY BABY. By D. Gerard.
MARMORNE. By P. G. Hamerton.	THE BLACKSMITH OF VOE. By Paul Cushing.
REATA. By E. D. Gerard.	THE DILEMMA. By the Author of 'The Battle of Dorking.'
	MY TRIVIAL LIFE AND MISFORTUNE. By A Plain Woman.
	POOR NELLIE. By the Same.

Others in preparation.

Standard Novels. Uniform in size and binding. Each complete in one Volume.

FLORIN SERIES, Illustrated Boards. Bound in Cloth, 2s. 6d.

TOM CRINGLE'S LOG. By Michael Scott.	PEN OWEN. By Dean Hook.
THE CRUISE OF THE MIDGE. By the Same.	ADAM BLAIR. By J. G. Lockhart.
CYRIL THORNTON. By Captain Hamilton.	LADY LEE'S WIDOWHOOD. By General Sir E. B. Hamley.
ANNALS OF THE PARISH. By John Galt.	SALEM CHAPEL. By Mrs Oliphant.
THE PROVOST, &c. By the Same.	THE PERPETUAL CURATE. By the Same.
SIR ANDREW WYLIE. By the Same.	MISS MARJORIBANKS. By the Same.
THE ENTAIL. By the Same.	JOHN; A Love Story. By the Same.
MISS MOLLY. By Beatrice May Butt.	
REGINALD DALTON. By J. G. Lockhart.	

SHILLING SERIES, Illustrated Cover. Bound in Cloth, 1s. 6d.

THE RECTOR, and THE DOCTOR'S FAMILY. By Mrs Oliphant.	SIR FRIZZLE PUMPKIN, NIGHTS AT MESS, &c.
THE LIFE OF MANSIE WAUCH. By D. M. Moir.	THE SUBALTERN.
PENINSULAR SCENES AND SKETCHES. By F. Hardman.	LIFE IN THE FAR WEST. By G. F. Ruxton.
	VALERIUS: A Roman Story. By J. G. Lockhart.

BON GAULTIER'S BOOK OF BALLADS. Fifteenth Edition. With Illustrations by Doyle, Leech, and Crowquill. Fcap. 8vo, 5s.

BONNAR. Biographical Sketch of George Meikle Kemp, Architect of the Scott Monument, Edinburgh. By THOMAS BONNAR, F.S.A. Scot., Author of 'The Present Art Revival,' &c. With Three Portraits and numerous Illustrations. Post 8vo, 7s. 6d.

BRADDON. Thirty Years of Shikar. By Sir EDWARD BRADDON, K.C.M.G. With Illustrations by G. D. Giles, and Map of Oudh Forest Tracts and Nepal Terai Demy 8vo, 18s.

BROUGHAM. Memoirs of the Life and Times of Henry Lord Brougham. Written by HIMSELF. 3 vols. 8vo, £2, 8s. The Volumes are sold separately, price 16s. each.

BROWN. The Forester: A Practical Treatise on the Planting and Tending of Forest-trees and the General Management of Woodlands. By JAMES BROWN, LL.D. Sixth Edition, Enlarged. Edited by JOHN NISBET, D.Œc., Author of 'British Forest Trees,' &c. In 2 vols. royal 8vo, with 350 Illustrations, 42s. net.

BROWN. Stray Sport. By J. MORAY BROWN, Author of 'Shikar Sketches,' 'Powder, Spur, and Spear,' 'The Days when we went Hog-Hunting.' 2 vols. post 8vo, with Fifty Illustrations, 21s.

BROWN. A Manual of Botany, Anatomical and Physiological. For the Use of Students. By ROBERT BROWN, M.A., Ph.D. Crown 8vo, with numerous Illustrations, 12s. 6d.

BROWN. The Book of the Landed Estate. Containing Directions for the Management and Development of the Resources of Landed Property. By ROBERT E. BROWN, Factor and Estate Agent. Royal 8vo, with Illustrations, 21s.

BRUCE.
In Clover and Heather. Poems by WALLACE BRUCE. New and Enlarged Edition. Crown 8vo, 4s. 6d.
A limited number of Copies of the First Edition, on large hand-made paper, 12s. 6d.
Here's a Hand. Addresses and Poems. Crown 8vo, 5s. Large Paper Edition, limited to 100 copies, price 21s.

BRYDALL. Art in Scotland; its Origin and Progress. By ROBERT BRYDALL, Master of St George's Art School of Glasgow. 8vo, 12s. 6d.

BUCHAN. Introductory Text-Book of Meteorology. By ALEXANDER BUCHAN, LL.D., F.R.S.E., Secretary of the Scottish Meteorological Society, &c. New Edition. Crown 8vo, with Coloured Charts and Engravings.
[*In preparation.*

BUCHANAN. The Shirè Highlands (East Central Africa). By JOHN BUCHANAN, Planter at Zomba. Crown 8vo, 5s.

BURBIDGE.
Domestic Floriculture, Window Gardening, and Floral Decorations. Being practical directions for the Propagation, Culture, and Arrangement of Plants and Flowers as Domestic Ornaments. By F. W. BURBIDGE. Second Edition. Crown 8vo, with numerous Illustrations, 7s. 6d.
Cultivated Plants: Their Propagation and Improvement. Including Natural and Artificial Hybridisation, Raising from Seed, Cuttings, and Layers, Grafting and Budding, as applied to the Families and Genera in Cultivation. Crown 8vo, with numerous Illustrations, 12s. 6d.

BURGESS. The Viking Path. A Tale of the White Christ. By J. J. HALDANE BURGESS, Author of 'Rasmie's Büddie,' 'Shetland Sketches,' &c. Crown 8vo, 6s.

BURROWS. Commentaries on the History of England, from the Earliest Times to 1865. By MONTAGU BURROWS, Chichele Professor of Modern History in the University of Oxford; Captain R.N.; F.S.A., &c.; "Officier de l'Instruction Publique," France. Crown 8vo, 7s. 6d.

BURTON.
The History of Scotland: From Agricola's Invasion to the Extinction of the last Jacobite Insurrection. By JOHN HILL BURTON, D.C.L., Historiographer-Royal for Scotland. New and Enlarged Edition, 8 vols., and Index. Crown 8vo, £3, 3s.
History of the British Empire during the Reign of Queen Anne. In 3 vols. 8vo. 36s.
The Scot Abroad. Third Edition. Crown 8vo, 10s. 6d.

List of Books Published by

BURTON.
    The Book-Hunter. By JOHN HILL BURTON. New Edition. With Portrait. Crown 8vo, 7s. 6d.

BUTE.
    The Roman Breviary: Reformed by Order of the Holy Œcumenical Council of Trent; Published by Order of Pope St Pius V.; and Revised by Clement VIII. and Urban VIII.; together with the Offices since granted. Translated out of Latin into English by JOHN, Marquess of Bute, K.T. In 2 vols. crown 8vo, cloth boards, edges uncut. £2, 2s.

    The Altus of St Columba. With a Prose Paraphrase and Notes. In paper cover, 2s. 6d.

BUTT.
    Miss Molly. By BEATRICE MAY BUTT. Cheap Edition, 2s.
    Eugenie. Crown 8vo, 6s. 6d.
    Elizabeth, and other Sketches. Crown 8vo, 6s.
    Delicia. New Edition. Crown 8vo, 2s. 6d.

CAIRD.
    Sermons. By JOHN CAIRD, D.D., Principal of the University of Glasgow. Seventeenth Thousand. Fcap. 8vo, 5s.

    Religion in Common Life. A Sermon preached in Crathie Church, October 14, 1855, before Her Majesty the Queen and Prince Albert. Published by Her Majesty's Command. Cheap Edition, 3d.

CALDER. Chaucer's Canterbury Pilgrimage. Epitomised by WILLIAM CALDER. With Photogravure of the Pilgrimage Company, and other Illustrations, Glossary, &c. Crown 8vo, gilt edges, 4s. Cheaper Edition without Photogravure Plate. Crown 8vo, 2s. 6d.

CAMPBELL. Critical Studies in St Luke's Gospel: Its Demonology and Ebionitism. By COLIN CAMPBELL, D.D., Minister of the Parish of Dundee, formerly Scholar and Fellow of Glasgow University. Author of the 'Three First Gospels in Greek, arranged in parallel columns.' Post 8vo, 7s. 6d.

CAMPBELL. Sermons Preached before the Queen at Balmoral. By the Rev. A. A. CAMPBELL, Minister of Crathie. Published by Command of Her Majesty. Crown 8vo, 4s. 6d.

CAMPBELL. Records of Argyll. Legends, Traditions, and Recollections of Argyllshire Highlanders, collected chiefly from the Gaelic. With Notes on the Antiquity of the Dress, Clan Colours, or Tartans of the Highlanders. By Lord ARCHIBALD CAMPBELL. Illustrated with Nineteen full-page Etchings. 4to, printed on hand-made paper, £3, 3s.

CANTON. A Lost Epic, and other Poems. By WILLIAM CANTON. Crown 8vo, 5s.

CARRICK. Koumiss; or, Fermented Mare's Milk: and its uses in the Treatment and Cure of Pulmonary Consumption, and other Wasting Diseases. With an Appendix on the best Methods of Fermenting Cow's Milk. By GEORGE L. CARRICK, M.D., L.R.C.S.E. and L.R.C.P.E., Physician to the British Embassy, St Petersburg, &c. Crown 8vo, 10s. 6d.

CARSTAIRS.
    Human Nature in Rural India. By R. CARSTAIRS. Crown 8vo, 6s.
    British Work in India. Crown 8vo, 6s.

CAUVIN. A Treasury of the English and German Languages. Compiled from the best Authors and Lexicographers in both Languages. By JOSEPH CAUVIN, LL.D. and Ph.D., of the University of Göttingen, &c. Crown 8vo, 7s. 6d.

CHARTERIS. Canonicity; or, Early Testimonies to the Existence and Use of the Books of the New Testament. Based on Kirchhoffer's 'Quellensammlung.' Edited by A. H. CHARTERIS, D.D., Professor of Biblical Criticism in the University of Edinburgh. 8vo, 18s.

CHENNELLS. Recollections of an Egyptian Princess. By her English Governess (Miss E. CHENNELLS). Being a Record of Five Years' Residence at the Court of Ismael Pasha, Khédive. Second Edition. With Three Portraits. Post 8vo, 7s. 6d.

CHESNEY. The Dilemma. By General Sir GEORGE CHESNEY, K.C.B., M.P., Author of 'The Battle of Dorking,' &c. New Edition. Crown 8vo, 3s. 6d.

CHRISTISON. Life of Sir Robert Christison, Bart., M.D., D.C.L. Oxon., Professor of Medical Jurisprudence in the University of Edinburgh. Edited by his SONS. In 2 vols. 8vo. Vol. I.—Autobiography. 16s. Vol. II.—Memoirs. 16s.

CHURCH. Chapters in an Adventurous Life. Sir Richard Church in Italy and Greece. By E. M. CHURCH. With Illustrations. Demy 8vo. [In the press.

CHURCH SERVICE SOCIETY.
A Book of Common Order: being Forms of Worship issued by the Church Service Society. Sixth Edition. Crown 8vo, 6s. Also in 2 vols. crown 8vo, 6s. 6d.
Daily Offices for Morning and Evening Prayer throughout the Week. Crown 8vo, 3s. 6d.
Order of Divine Service for Children. Issued by the Church Service Society. With Scottish Hymnal. Cloth, 3d.

CLOUSTON. Popular Tales and Fictions: their Migrations and Transformations. By W. A. CLOUSTON, Editor of 'Arabian Poetry for English Readers,' &c. 2 vols. post 8vo, roxburghe binding, 25s.

COCHRAN. A Handy Text-Book of Military Law. Compiled chiefly to assist Officers preparing for Examination; also for all Officers of the Regular and Auxiliary Forces. Comprising also a Synopsis of part of the Army Act. By Major F. COCHRAN, Hampshire Regiment Garrison Instructor, North British District. Crown 8vo, 7s. 6d.

COLQUHOUN. The Moor and the Loch. Containing Minute Instructions in all Highland Sports, with Wanderings over Crag and Corrie, Flood and Fell. By JOHN COLQUHOUN. Cheap Edition. With Illustrations. Demy 8vo, 10s. 6d.

COLVILE. Round the Black Man's Garden. By ZÉLIE COLVILE, F.R.G.S. With 2 Maps and 50 Illustrations from Drawings by the Author and from Photographs. Demy 8vo, 16s.

CONSTITUTION AND LAW OF THE CHURCH OF SCOTLAND. With an Introductory Note by the late Principal Tulloch. New Edition, Revised and Enlarged. Crown 8vo, 3s. 6d.

COTTERILL. Suggested Reforms in Public Schools. By C. C. COTTERILL, M.A. Crown 8vo, 3s. 6d.

CRANSTOUN.
The Elegies of Albius Tibullus. Translated into English Verse, with Life of the Poet, and Illustrative Notes. By JAMES CRANSTOUN, LL.D., Author of a Translation of 'Catullus.' Crown 8vo, 6s. 6d.
The Elegies of Sextus Propertius. Translated into English Verse, with Life of the Poet, and Illustrative Notes. Crown 8vo, 7s. 6d.

CRAWFORD. An Atonement of East London, and other Poems. By HOWARD CRAWFORD, M.A. Crown 8vo, 5s.

CRAWFORD. Saracinesca. By F. MARION CRAWFORD, Author of 'Mr Isaacs,' &c., &c. Eighth Edition. Crown 8vo, 6s.

CRAWFORD.
The Doctrine of Holy Scripture respecting the Atonement. By the late THOMAS J. CRAWFORD, D.D., Professor of Divinity in the University of Edinburgh. Fifth Edition. 8vo, 12s.
The Fatherhood of God, Considered in its General and Special Aspects. Third Edition, Revised and Enlarged. 8vo, 9s.
The Preaching of the Cross, and other Sermons. 8vo, 7s. 6d.
The Mysteries of Christianity. Crown 8vo, 7s. 6d.

CROSS. Impressions of Dante, and of the New World; with a Few Words on Bimetallism. By J. W. CROSS, Editor of 'George Eliot's Life, as related in her Letters and Journals.' Post 8vo, 6s.

CUMBERLAND. Sport on the Pamir Steppes, in Chinese Turkistan, and the Himalayas. By Major C. S. CUMBERLAND. With Map and numerous Illustrations. In 1 vol. demy 8vo. [*In the press.*

CURSE OF INTELLECT. Fcap 8vo, 2s. 6d. net.

CUSHING.
The Blacksmith of Voe. By PAUL CUSHING, Author of 'The Bull i' th' Thorn,' 'Cut with his own Diamond.' Cheap Edition. Crown 8vo, 3s. 6d.

DAVIES.
Norfolk Broads and Rivers; or, The Waterways, Lagoons, and Decoys of East Anglia. By G. CHRISTOPHER DAVIES. Illustrated with Seven full-page Plates. New and Cheaper Edition. Crown 8vo, 6s.

Our Home in Aveyron. Sketches of Peasant Life in Aveyron and the Lot. By G. CHRISTOPHER DAVIES and Mrs BROUGHALL. Illustrated with full-page Illustrations. 8vo, 15s. Cheap Edition, 7s. 6d.

DE LA WARR. An Eastern Cruise in the 'Edeline.' By the Countess DE LA WARR. In Illustrated Cover. 2s.

DESCARTES. The Method, Meditations, and Principles of Philosophy of Descartes. Translated from the Original French and Latin. With a New Introductory Essay, Historical and Critical, on the Cartesian Philosophy. By Professor VEITCH, LL.D., Glasgow University. Tenth Edition. 6s. 6d.

DEWAR. Voyage of the "Nyanza," R.N.Y.C. Being the Record of a Three Years' Cruise in a Schooner Yacht in the Atlantic and Pacific, and her subsequent Shipwreck. By J. CUMMING DEWAR, late Captain King's Dragoon Guards and 11th Prince Albert's Hussars. With Two Autogravures, numerous Illustrations, and a Map. Demy 8vo, 21s.

DOGS, OUR DOMESTICATED: Their Treatment in reference to Food, Diseases, Habits, Punishment, Accomplishments. By 'MAGENTA.' Crown 8vo, 2s. 6d.

DOUGLAS. John Stuart Mill. A Study of his Philosophy. By CHARLES DOUGLAS, M.A., D.Sc., Lecturer in Moral Philosophy, and Assistant to the Professor of Moral Philosophy, in the University of Edinburgh. Crown 8vo, 4s. 6d. net.

DOUGLAS. Chinese Stories. By ROBERT K. DOUGLAS. With numerous Illustrations by Parkinson, Forestier, and others. New and Cheaper Edition. Small demy 8vo, 5s.

DU CANE. The Odyssey of Homer, Books I.-XII. Translated into English Verse. By Sir CHARLES DU CANE, K.C.M.G. 8vo, 10s. 6d.

DUDGEON. History of the Edinburgh or Queen's Regiment Light Infantry Militia, now 3rd Battalion The Royal Scots; with an Account of the Origin and Progress of the Militia, and a Brief Sketch of the Old Royal Scots. By Major R. C. DUDGEON, Adjutant 3rd Battalion the Royal Scots. Post 8vo, with Illustrations, 10s. 6d.

DUNCAN. Manual of the General Acts of Parliament relating to the Salmon Fisheries of Scotland from 1828 to 1882. By J. BARKER DUNCAN. Crown 8vo, 5s.

DUNSMORE. Manual of the Law of Scotland as to the Relations between Agricultural Tenants and the Landlords, Servants, Merchants, and Bowers. By W. DUNSMORE. 8vo, 7s. 6d.

ELIOT.
George Eliot's Life, Related in Her Letters and Journals. Arranged and Edited by her husband, J. W. CROSS. With Portrait and other Illustrations. Third Edition. 3 vols. post 8vo, 42s.

George Eliot's Life. (Cabinet Edition.) With Portrait and other Illustrations. 8 vols. crown 8vo, 15s.

George Eliot's Life. With Portrait and other Illustrations. New Edition, in one volume. Crown 8vo, 7s. 6d.

Works of George Eliot (Standard Edition). 21 volumes, crown 8vo. In buckram cloth, gilt top, 2s. 6d. per vol.; or in Roxburghe binding, 3s. 6d. per vol.

The following is the order of publication:—

ADAM BEDE. 2 vols. [*Vol. I. Ready.* | DANIEL DERONDA. 3 vols.
THE MILL ON THE FLOSS. 2 vols. | SILAS MARNER, and JUBAL. 2 vols.
FELIX HOLT, the Radical. 2 vols. | THE SPANISH GIPSY, and THEOPHRASTUS
ROMOLA. 2 vols. | SUCH. 2 vols.
SCENES OF CLERICAL LIFE. 2 vols. | ESSAYS. 1 vol.
MIDDLEMARCH. 3 vols.

Works of George Eliot (Cabinet Edition). 21 volumes, crown 8vo, price £5, 5s. Also to be had handsomely bound in half and full calf. The Volumes are sold separately, bound in cloth, price 5s. each.

Novels by George Eliot. Cheap Edition.
Adam Bede. Illustrated. 3s. 6d., cloth.—The Mill on the Floss. Illustrated. 3s. 6d., cloth.—Scenes of Clerical Life. Illustrated. 3s., cloth.—Silas Marner: the Weaver of Raveloe. Illustrated. 2s. 6d., cloth.—Felix Holt, the Radical. Illustrated. 3s. 6d., cloth.—Romola. With Vignette. 3s. 6d., cloth.

Middlemarch. Crown 8vo, 7s. 6d.

Daniel Deronda. Crown 8vo, 7s. 6d.

Essays. New Edition. Crown 8vo, 5s.

Impressions of Theophrastus Such. New Edition. Crown 8vo, 5s.

The Spanish Gypsy. New Edition. Crown 8vo, 5s.

The Legend of Jubal, and other Poems, Old and New. New Edition. Crown 8vo, 5s.

Wise, Witty, and Tender Sayings, in Prose and Verse. Selected from the Works of GEORGE ELIOT. New Edition. Fcap. 8vo, 3s. 6d.

The George Eliot Birthday Book. Printed on fine paper, with red border, and handsomely bound in cloth, gilt. Fcap. 8vo, 3s. 6d. And in French morocco or Russia, 5s.

ESSAYS ON SOCIAL SUBJECTS. Originally published in the 'Saturday Review.' New Edition. First and Second Series. 2 vols. crown 8vo, 6s. each.

FAITHS OF THE WORLD, The. A Concise History of the Great Religious Systems of the World. By various Authors. Crown 8vo, 5s.

FARRER. A Tour in Greece in 1880. By RICHARD RIDLEY FARRER. With Twenty-seven full-page Illustrations by Lord WINDSOR. Royal 8vo, with a Map, 21s.

FERRIER.
   Philosophical Works of the late James F. Ferrier, B.A. Oxon., Professor of Moral Philosophy and Political Economy, St Andrews. New Edition. Edited by Sir ALEXANDER GRANT, Bart., D.C.L., and Professor LUSHINGTON. 3 vols. crown 8vo, 34s. 6d.
   Institutes of Metaphysic. Third Edition. 10s. 6d.
   Lectures on the Early Greek Philosophy. 4th Edition. 10s. 6d.
   Philosophical Remains, including the Lectures on Early Greek Philosophy. New Edition. 2 vols. 24s.

FITZROY. Dogma and the Church of England. By A. I. FITZROY. Post 8vo, 7s. 6d.

FLINT.
   Historical Philosophy in France and French Belgium and Switzerland. By ROBERT FLINT, Corresponding Member of the Institute of France, Hon. Member of the Royal Society of Palermo, Professor in the University of Edinburgh, &c. 8vo, 21s.
   Agnosticism. Being the Croall Lecture for 1887-88. [*In the press.*
   Theism. Being the Baird Lecture for 1876. Eighth Edition, Revised. Crown 8vo, 7s. 6d.
   Anti-Theistic Theories. Being the Baird Lecture for 1877. Fifth Edition. Crown 8vo, 10s. 6d.

FOREIGN CLASSICS FOR ENGLISH READERS. Edited by Mrs OLIPHANT. Price 2s. 6d. *For List of Volumes, see page 2.*

FOSTER. The Fallen City, and other Poems. By WILL FOSTER. Crown 8vo, 6s.

FRANCILLON. Gods and Heroes; or, The Kingdom of Jupiter. By R. E. FRANCILLON. With 8 Illustrations. Crown 8vo, 5s.

FULLARTON.
   Merlin: A Dramatic Poem. By RALPH MACLEOD FULLARTON. Crown 8vo, 5s.
   Tanhäuser. Crown 8vo, 6s.
   Lallan Sangs and German Lyrics. Crown 8vo, 5s.

GALT.
   Novels by JOHN GALT. With General Introduction and Prefatory Notes by S. R. CROCKETT. The Text Revised and Edited by D. STORRAR MELDRUM, Author of 'The Story of Margrédel.' With Photogravure Illustrations from Drawings by John Wallace. Fcap. 8vo, 3s. net each vol.
   Annals of the Parish, and The Ayrshire Legatees. 2 vols.
   Sir Andrew Wylie. 2 vols. [*Immediately.*
   The Provost, and The Last of the Lairds. 2 vols. [*In the press.*
   The Entail. 2 vols. [*In the press.*
   See also STANDARD NOVELS, *p.* 6.

GENERAL ASSEMBLY OF THE CHURCH OF SCOTLAND.
   Scottish Hymnal, With Appendix Incorporated. Published for use in Churches by Authority of the General Assembly. 1. Large type, cloth, red edges, 2s. 6d.; French morocco, 4s. 2. Bourgeois type, limp cloth, 1s.; French morocco, 2s. 3. Nonpareil type, cloth, red edges, 6d.; French morocco, 1s. 4d. 4. Paper covers, 3d. 5. Sunday-School Edition, paper covers, 1d., cloth, 2d. No. 1, bound with the Psalms and Paraphrases, French morocco, 8s. No. 2, bound with the Psalms and Paraphrases, cloth, 2s.; French morocco, 3s.

GENERAL ASSEMBLY OF THE CHURCH OF SCOTLAND.
Prayers for Social and Family Worship. Prepared by a Special Committee of the General Assembly of the Church of Scotland. Entirely New Edition, Revised and Enlarged. Fcap. 8vo, red edges, 2s.
Prayers for Family Worship. A Selection of Four Weeks' Prayers. New Edition. Authorised by the General Assembly of the Church of Scotland Fcap. 8vo, red edges, 1s. 6d.
One Hundred Prayers. Prepared by a Committee of the General Assembly of the Church of Scotland. 16mo, cloth limp, 6d.

GERARD.
Reata: What's in a Name. By E. D. GERARD. Cheap Edition. Crown 8vo, 3s. 6d.
Beggar my Neighbour. Cheap Edition. Crown 8vo, 3s. 6d.
The Waters of Hercules. Cheap Edition. Crown 8vo, 3s. 6d.
A Sensitive Plant. Crown 8vo, 3s. 6d.

GERARD.
The Land beyond the Forest. Facts, Figures, and Fancies from Transylvania. By E. GERARD. With Maps and Illustrations. 2 vols. post 8vo, 25s.
Bis: Some Tales Retold. Crown 8vo, 6s.
A Secret Mission. 2 vols. crown 8vo, 17s.

GERARD.
Lady Baby. By DOROTHEA GERARD. Cheap Edition. Crown 8vo, 3s. 6d.
Recha. Second Edition. Crown 8vo, 6s.
The Rich Miss Riddell. Second Edition. Crown 8vo, 6s.

GERARD. Stonyhurst Latin Grammar. By Rev. JOHN GERARD. Second Edition. Fcap. 8vo, 3s.

GILL.
Free Trade: an Inquiry into the Nature of its Operation. By RICHARD GILL. Crown 8vo, 7s. 6d.
Free Trade under Protection. Crown 8vo, 7s. 6d.

GOETHE. Poems and Ballads of Goethe. Translated by Professor AYTOUN and Sir THEODORE MARTIN, K.C.B. Third Edition. Fcap. 8vo, 6s.

GOETHE'S FAUST. Translated into English Verse by Sir THEODORE MARTIN, K.C.B. Part I. Second Edition, crown 8vo, 6s. Ninth Edition, fcap., 3s. 6d. Part II. Second Edition, Revised. Fcap. 8vo, 6s.

GORDON CUMMING.
At Home in Fiji. By C. F. GORDON CUMMING. Fourth Edition, post 8vo. With Illustrations and Map. 7s. 6d.
A Lady's Cruise in a French Man-of-War. New and Cheaper Edition. 8vo. With Illustrations and Map. 12s. 6d.
Fire-Fountains. The Kingdom of Hawaii: Its Volcanoes, and the History of its Missions. With Map and Illustrations. 2 vols. 8vo, 25s.
Wanderings in China. New and Cheaper Edition. 8vo, with Illustrations, 10s.
Granite Crags: The Yô-semité Region of California. Illustrated with 8 Engravings. New and Cheaper Edition. 8vo, 8s. 6d.

GRAHAM. Manual of the Elections (Scot.) (Corrupt and Illegal Practices) Act, 1890. With Analysis, Relative Act of Sederunt, Appendix containing the Corrupt Practices Acts of 1883 and 1885, and Copious Index. By J. EDWARD GRAHAM, Advocate. 8vo, 4s. 6d.

GRAND.
A Domestic Experiment. By SARAH GRAND, Author of 'The Heavenly Twins,' 'Ideala: A Study from Life.' Crown 8vo, 6s.
Singularly Deluded. Crown 8vo, 6s.

GRANT. Bush-Life in Queensland. By A. C. GRANT. New Edition. Crown 8vo, 6s.

GRANT. Life of Sir Hope Grant. With Selections from his Correspondence. Edited by HENRY KNOLLYS, Colonel (H.P.) Royal Artillery, his former A.D.C., Editor of 'Incidents in the Sepoy War;' Author of 'Sketches of Life in Japan,' &c. With Portraits of Sir Hope Grant and other Illustrations. Maps and Plans. 2 vols. demy 8vo, 21s.

GRIER. In Furthest Ind. The Narrative of Mr EDWARD CARLYON of Ellswether, in the County of Northampton, and late of the Honourable East India Company's Service, Gentleman. Wrote by his own hand in the year of grace 1697. Edited, with a few Explanatory Notes, by SYDNEY C. GRIER. Post 8vo, 6s.

GUTHRIE-SMITH. Crispus: A Drama. By H. GUTHRIE-SMITH. Fcap. 4to, 5s.

HALDANE. Subtropical Cultivations and Climates. A Handy Book for Planters, Colonists, and Settlers. By R. C. HALDANE. Post 8vo, 9s.

HAMERTON.
 Wenderholme: A Story of Lancashire and Yorkshire Life. By P. G. HAMERTON, Author of 'A Painter's Camp.' New Edition. Crown 8vo, 3s. 6d.
 Marmorne. New Edition. Crown 8vo, 3s. 6d.

HAMILTON.
 Lectures on Metaphysics. By Sir WILLIAM HAMILTON, Bart., Professor of Logic and Metaphysics in the University of Edinburgh. Edited by the Rev. H. L. MANSEL, B.D., LL.D., Dean of St Paul's; and JOHN VEITCH, M.A., LL.D., Professor of Logic and Rhetoric, Glasgow. Seventh Edition. 2 vols. 8vo, 24s.
 Lectures on Logic. Edited by the SAME. Third Edition, Revised. 2 vols., 24s.
 Discussions on Philosophy and Literature, Education and University Reform. Third Edition. 8vo, 21s.
 Memoir of Sir William Hamilton, Bart., Professor of Logic and Metaphysics in the University of Edinburgh. By Professor VEITCH, of the University of Glasgow. 8vo, with Portrait, 18s.
 Sir William Hamilton: The Man and his Philosophy. Two Lectures delivered before the Edinburgh Philosophical Institution, January and February 1883. By Professor VEITCH. Crown 8vo, 2s.

HAMLEY.
 The Life of General Sir Edward Bruce Hamley, K.C.B., K.C.M.G. By ALEXANDER INNES SHAND. With two Photogravure Portraits and other Illustrations. 2 vols. demy 8vo, 21s.
 The Operations of War Explained and Illustrated. By General Sir EDWARD BRUCE HAMLEY, K.C.B., K.C.M.G. Fifth Edition, Revised throughout. 4to, with numerous Illustrations, 30s.
 National Defence; Articles and Speeches. Post 8vo, 6s.
 Shakespeare's Funeral, and other Papers. Post 8vo, 7s. 6d.
 Thomas Carlyle: An Essay. Second Edition. Crown 8vo, 2s. 6d.
 On Outposts. Second Edition. 8vo, 2s.
 Wellington's Career; A Military and Political Summary. Crown 8vo, 2s.
 Lady Lee's Widowhood. New Edition. Crown 8vo, 3s. 6d. Cheaper Edition, 2s. 6d.
 Our Poor Relations. A Philozoic Essay. With Illustrations, chiefly by Ernest Griset. Crown 8vo, cloth gilt, 3s. 6d.

HARRADEN. In Varying Moods : Short Stories. By BEATRICE HARRADEN, Author of 'Ships that Pass in the Night.' Eleventh Edition. Crown 8vo, 3s. 6d.

HARRIS.
Danovitch, and other Stories. By WALTER B. HARRIS, F.R.G.S., Author of 'The Land of an African Sultan; Travels in Morocco,' &c. Crown 8vo, 6s.

A Journey through the Yemen, and some General Remarks upon that Country. With 3 Maps and numerous Illustrations by Forestier and Wallace from Sketches and Photographs taken by the Author. Demy 8vo, 16s.

HAWKER. The Prose Works of Rev. R. S. HAWKER, Vicar of Morwenstow. Including 'Footprints of Former Men in Far Cornwall.' Re-edited, with Sketches never before published. With a Frontispiece. Crown 8vo, 3s. 6d.

HAY. The Works of the Right Rev. Dr George Hay, Bishop of Edinburgh. Edited under the Supervision of the Right Rev. Bishop STRAIN. With Memoir and Portrait of the Author. 5 vols. crown 8vo, bound in extra cloth, £1, 1s. The following Volumes may be had separately—viz.:
The Devout Christian Instructed in the Law of Christ from the Written Word. 2 vols., 8s.—The Pious Christian Instructed in the Nature and Practice of the Principal Exercises of Piety. 1 vol., 3s.

HEATLEY.
The Horse-Owner's Safeguard. A Handy Medical Guide for every Man who owns a Horse. By G. S. HEATLEY, M.R.C.V.S. Crown 8vo, 5s.

The Stock-Owner's Guide. A Handy Medical Treatise for every Man who owns an Ox or a Cow. Crown 8vo, 4s. 6d.

HEDDERWICK. Lays of Middle Age; and other Poems. By JAMES HEDDERWICK, LL.D., Author of 'Backward Glances.' Price 3s. 6d.

HEMANS.
The Poetical Works of Mrs Hemans. Copyright Editions. Royal 8vo, 5s. The Same with Engravings, cloth, gilt edges, 7s. 6d.

Select Poems of Mrs Hemans. Fcap., cloth, gilt edges, 3s.

HERKLESS. Cardinal Beaton : Priest and Politician. By JOHN HERKLESS, Professor of Church History, St Andrews. With a Portrait. Post 8vo, 7s. 6d.

HEWISON. The Isle of Bute in the Olden Time. With Illustrations, Maps, and Plans. By JAMES KING HEWISON, M.A., F.S.A. (Scot.), Minister of Rothesay. Vol. I., Celtic Saints and Heroes. Crown 4to, 15s. net. Vol. II., The Royal Stewards and the Brandanes. Crown 4to, 15s. net.

HOME PRAYERS. By Ministers of the Church of Scotland and Members of the Church Service Society. Second Edition. Fcap. 8vo, 3s.

HOMER.
The Odyssey. Translated into English Verse in the Spenserian Stanza. By PHILIP STANHOPE WORSLEY. New and Cheaper Edition. Post 8vo, 7s. 6d. net.

The Iliad. Translated by P. S. WORSLEY and Professor CONINGTON. 2 vols. crown 8vo, 21s.

HUTCHINSON. Hints on the Game of Golf. By HORACE G. HUTCHINSON. Eighth Edition, Enlarged. Fcap. 8vo, cloth, 1s.

HYSLOP. The Elements of Ethics. By JAMES H. HYSLOP, Ph.D., Instructor in Ethics, Columbia College, New York, Author of 'The Elements of Logic.' Post 8vo, 7s. 6d. net.

IDDESLEIGH.
Lectures and Essays. By the late EARL of IDDESLEIGH, G.C.B., D.C.L., &c. 8vo, 16s.

Life, Letters, and Diaries of Sir Stafford Northcote, First Earl of Iddesleigh. By ANDREW LANG. With Three Portraits and a View of Pynes. Third Edition. 2 vols. post 8vo, 31s. 6d.
POPULAR EDITION. With Portrait and View of Pynes. Post 8vo, 7s. 6d.

List of Books Published by

INDEX GEOGRAPHICUS: Being a List, alphabetically arranged, of the Principal Places on the Globe, with the Countries and Subdivisions of the Countries in which they are situated, and their Latitudes and Longitudes. Imperial 8vo, pp. 676, 21s.

JEAN JAMBON. Our Trip to Blunderland; or, Grand Excursion to Blundertown and Back. By JEAN JAMBON. With Sixty Illustrations designed by CHARLES DOYLE, engraved by DALZIEL. Fourth Thousand. Cloth, gilt edges, 6s. 6d. Cheap Edition, cloth, 3s. 6d. Boards, 2s. 6d.

JEBB. A Strange Career. The Life and Adventures of JOHN GLADWYN JEBB. By his Widow. With an Introduction by H. RIDER HAGGARD, and an Electrogravure Portrait of Mr Jebb. Third Edition. Small demy 8vo, 10s. 6d.

JENNINGS. Mr Gladstone: A Study. By LOUIS J. JENNINGS, M.P., Author of 'Republican Government in the United States,' 'The Croker Memoirs,' &c. Popular Edition. Crown 8vo, 1s.

JERNINGHAM.
Reminiscences of an Attaché. By HUBERT E. H. JERNINGHAM. Second Edition. Crown 8vo, 5s.
Diane de Breteuille. A Love Story. Crown 8vo, 2s. 6d.

JOHNSTON.
The Chemistry of Common Life. By Professor J. F. W. JOHNSTON. New Edition, Revised. By ARTHUR HERBERT CHURCH, M.A. Oxon.; Author of 'Food: its Sources, Constituents, and Uses,' &c. With Maps and 102 Engravings. Crown 8vo, 7s. 6d.
Elements of Agricultural Chemistry. An entirely New Edition from the Edition by Sir CHARLES A. CAMERON, M.D., F.R.C.S.I., &c. Revised and brought down to date by C. M. AIKMAN, M.A., B.Sc., F.R.S.E., Professor of Chemistry, Glasgow Veterinary College. Crown 8vo, 6s. 6d.
Catechism of Agricultural Chemistry. An entirely New Edition from the Edition by Sir CHARLES A. CAMERON. Revised and Enlarged by C. M. AIKMAN, M.A., &c. 92d Thousand. With numerous Illustrations. Crown 8vo, 1s.

JOHNSTON. Agricultural Holdings (Scotland) Acts, 1883 and 1889; and the Ground Game Act, 1880. With Notes, and Summary of Procedure, &c. By CHRISTOPHER N. JOHNSTON, M.A., Advocate. Demy 8vo, 5s.

JOKAI. Timar's Two Worlds. By MAURUS JOKAI. Authorised Translation by Mrs HEGAN KENNARD. Cheap Edition. Crown 8vo, 6s.

KEBBEL. The Old and the New: English Country Life. By T. E. KEBBEL, M.A., Author of 'The Agricultural Labourers,' 'Essays in History and Politics,' 'Life of Lord Beaconsfield.' Crown 8vo, 5s.

KING. The Metamorphoses of Ovid. Translated in English Blank Verse. By HENRY KING, M.A., Fellow of Wadham College, Oxford, and of the Inner Temple, Barrister-at-Law. Crown 8vo, 10s. 6d.

KINGLAKE.
History of the Invasion of the Crimea. By A. W. KINGLAKE. Cabinet Edition, Revised. With an Index to the Complete Work. Illustrated with Maps and Plans. Complete in 9 vols., crown 8vo, at 6s. each.
History of the Invasion of the Crimea. Demy 8vo. Vol. VI. Winter Troubles. With a Map, 16s. Vols. VII. and VIII. From the Morrow of Inkerman to the Death of Lord Raglan. With an Index to the Whole Work. With Maps and Plans. 28s.
Eothen. A New Edition, uniform with the Cabinet Edition of the 'History of the Invasion of the Crimea.' 6s.

KLEIN. Among the Gods. Scenes of India, with Legends by the Way. By AUGUSTA KLEIN. With 22 Full-page Illustrations. Demy 8vo, 15s.

KNEIPP. My Water-Cure. As Tested through more than Thirty Years, and Described for the Healing of Diseases and the Preservation of Health. By SEBASTIAN KNEIPP, Parish Priest of Wörishofen (Bavaria). With a Portrait and other Illustrations. Authorised English Translation from the Thirtieth German Edition, by A. de F. Cheap Edition. With an Appendix, containing the Latest Developments of Pfarrer Kneipp's System, and a Preface by E. Gerard. Crown 8vo, 3s. 6d.

KNOLLYS. The Elements of Field-Artillery. Designed for the Use of Infantry and Cavalry Officers. By HENRY KNOLLYS, Colonel Royal Artillery; Author of 'From Sedan to Saarbrück,' Editor of 'Incidents in the Sepoy War,' &c. With Engravings. Crown 8vo, 7s. 6d.

LAMINGTON. In the Days of the Dandies. By the late Lord LAMINGTON. Crown 8vo. Illustrated cover, 1s.; cloth, 1s. 6d.

LANG. Life, Letters, and Diaries of Sir Stafford Northcote, First Earl of Iddesleigh. By ANDREW LANG. With Three Portraits and a View of Pynes. Third Edition. 2 vols. post 8vo, 31s. 6d.
POPULAR EDITION. With Portrait and View of Pynes. Post 8vo, 7s. 6d.

LAWLESS. Hurrish: A Study. By the Hon. EMILY LAWLESS, Author of 'A Chelsea Householder,' &c. Fourth Edition. Crown 8vo, 3s. 6d.

LEES. A Handbook of the Sheriff and Justice of Peace Small Debt Courts. With Notes, References, and Forms. By J. M. LEES, Advocate, Sheriff of Stirling, Dumbarton, and Clackmannan. 8vo, 7s. 6d.

LINDSAY. The Progressiveness of Modern Christian Thought. By the Rev. JAMES LINDSAY, M.A., B.D., B.Sc., F.R.S.E., F.G.S., Minister of the Parish of St Andrew's, Kilmarnock. Crown 8vo, 6s.

LOCKHART.
Doubles and Quits. By LAURENCE W. M. LOCKHART. New Edition. Crown 8vo, 3s. 6d.
Fair to See. New Edition. Crown 8vo, 3s. 6d.
Mine is Thine. New Edition. Crown 8vo, 3s. 6d.

LOCKHART.
The Church of Scotland in the Thirteenth Century. The Life and Times of David de Bernham of St Andrews (Bishop), A.D. 1239 to 1253. With List of Churches dedicated by him, and Dates. By WILLIAM LOCKHART, A.M., D.D., F.S.A. Scot., Minister of Colinton Parish. 2d Edition. 8vo, 6s.
Dies Tristes: Sermons for Seasons of Sorrow. Crown 8vo, 6s.

LORIMER.
The Institutes of Law: A Treatise of the Principles of Jurisprudence as determined by Nature. By the late JAMES LORIMER, Professor of Public Law and of the Law of Nature and Nations in the University of Edinburgh. New Edition, Revised and much Enlarged. 8vo, 18s.
The Institutes of the Law of Nations. A Treatise of the Jural Relation of Separate Political Communities. In 2 vols. 8vo. Volume I., price 16s. Volume II., price 20s.

LOVE. Scottish Church Music. Its Composers and Sources. With Musical Illustrations. By JAMES LOVE. Post 8vo, 7s. 6d.

LUGARD. The Rise of our East African Empire: Early Efforts in Uganda and Nyasaland. By F. D. LUGARD, Captain Norfolk Regiment. With 130 Illustrations from Drawings and Photographs under the personal superintendence of the Author, and 14 specially prepared Maps. In 2 vols. large demy 8vo, 42s.

M'CHESNEY. Kathleen Clare: Her Book, 1637-41. Edited by DORA GREENWELL M'CHESNEY. With Frontispiece. In 1 vol. crown 8vo.
[*In the Press.*

M'COMBIE. Cattle and Cattle-Breeders. By WILLIAM M'COMBIE, Tillyfour. New Edition, Enlarged, with Memoir of the Author by JAMES MACDONALD, F.R.S.E., Secretary Highland and Agricultural Society of Scotland. Crown 8vo, 3s. 6d.

M'CRIE.
Works of the Rev. Thomas M'Crie, D.D. Uniform Edition.
4 vols. crown 8vo, 24s.
Life of John Knox. Crown 8vo, 6s. Another Edition, 3s. 6d.
Life of Andrew Melville. Crown 8vo, 6s.
History of the Progress and Suppression of the Reformation in Italy in the Sixteenth Century. Crown 8vo, 4s.
History of the Progress and Suppression of the Reformation in Spain in the Sixteenth Century. Crown 8vo, 3s. 6d.

M'CRIE. The Public Worship of Presbyterian Scotland. Historically treated. With copious Notes, Appendices, and Index. The Fourteenth Series of the Cunningham Lectures. By the Rev. CHARLES G. M'CRIE, D.D. Demy 8vo, 10s. 6d.

MACDONALD. A Manual of the Criminal Law (Scotland) Procedure Act, 1887. By NORMAN DORAN MACDONALD. Revised by the LORD JUSTICE-CLERK. 8vo, 10s. 6d.

MACDONALD.
Stephens' Book of the Farm. Fourth Edition. Revised and in great part Rewritten by JAMES MACDONALD, F.R.S.E., Secretary, Highland and Agricultural Society of Scotland. Complete in 3 vols., bound with leather back, gilt top, £3, 3s. In Six Divisional Vols., bound in cloth, each 10s. 6d.
Stephens' Catechism of Practical Agriculture. New Edition. Revised by JAMES MACDONALD. With numerous Illustrations. Crown 8vo, 1s.
Pringle's Live Stock of the Farm. Third Edition. Revised and Edited by JAMES MACDONALD. Crown 8vo, 7s. 6d.
M'Combie's Cattle and Cattle-Breeders. New Edition, Enlarged, with Memoir of the Author by JAMES MACDONALD. Crown 8vo, 3s. 6d.
History of Polled Aberdeen and Angus Cattle. Giving an Account of the Origin, Improvement, and Characteristics of the Breed. By JAMES MACDONALD and JAMES SINCLAIR. Illustrated with numerous Animal Portraits. Post 8vo, 12s. 6d.

MACDOUGALL AND DODDS. A Manual of the Local Government (Scotland) Act, 1894. With Introduction, Explanatory Notes, and Copious Index. By J. PATTEN MACDOUGALL, Legal Secretary to the Lord Advocate, and J. M. DODDS. Tenth Thousand, Revised. Crown 8vo, 2s. 6d. net.

MACINTYRE. Hindu-Koh: Wanderings and Wild Sports on and beyond the Himalayas. By Major-General DONALD MACINTYRE, V.C., late Prince of Wales' Own Goorkhas, F.R.G.S. *Dedicated to H.R.H. The Prince of Wales.* New and Cheaper Edition, Revised, with numerous Illustrations. Post 8vo, 3s. 6d.

MACKAY. A Sketch of the History of Fife and Kinross. A Study of Scottish History and Character. By Æ. J. G. MACKAY, Sheriff of these Counties. Crown 8vo, 6s.

MACKAY.
A Manual of Modern Geography; Mathematical, Physical, and Political. By the Rev. ALEXANDER MACKAY, LL.D., F.R.G.S. 11th Thousand, Revised to the present time. Crown 8vo, pp. 688, 7s. 6d.
Elements of Modern Geography. 55th Thousand, Revised to the present time. Crown 8vo, pp. 300, 3s.
The Intermediate Geography. Intended as an Intermediate Book between the Author's 'Outlines of Geography' and 'Elements of Geography.' Seventeenth Edition, Revised. Crown 8vo, pp. 238, 2s.
Outlines of Modern Geography. 191st Thousand, Revised to the present time. 18mo, pp. 128, 1s.
First Steps in Geography. 105th Thousand. 18mo, pp. 56. Sewed, 4d.; cloth, 6d.
Elements of Physiography and Physical Geography. New Edition. Rewritten and Enlarged. With numerous Illustrations. Crown 8vo.
[*In the press.*

MACKENZIE. Studies in Roman Law. With Comparative Views of the Laws of France, England, and Scotland. By Lord MACKENZIE, one of the Judges of the Court of Session in Scotland. Sixth Edition, Edited by JOHN KIRKPATRICK, M.A., LL.B., Advocate, Professor of History in the University of Edinburgh. 8vo, 12s.

MACPHERSON. Glimpses of Church and Social Life in the Highlands in Olden Times. By ALEXANDER MACPHERSON, F.S.A. Scot. With 6 Photogravure Portraits and other full-page Illustrations. Small 4to, 25s.

M'PHERSON.
Summer Sundays in a Strathmore Parish. By J. GORDON M'PHERSON, Ph.D., F.R.S.E., Minister of Ruthven. Crown 8vo, 5s.
Golf and Golfers. Past and Present. With an Introduction by the Right Hon. A. J. BALFOUR, and a Portrait of the Author. Fcap. 8vo, 1s. 6d.

MACRAE. A Handbook of Deer-Stalking. By ALEXANDER MACRAE, late Forester to Lord Henry Bentinck. With Introduction by Horatio Ross, Esq. Fcap. 8vo, with 2 Photographs from Life. 3s. 6d.

MAIN. Three Hundred English Sonnets. Chosen and Edited by DAVID M. MAIN. Fcap. 8vo, 6s.

MAIR. A Digest of Laws and Decisions, Ecclesiastical and Civil, relating to the Constitution, Practice, and Affairs of the Church of Scotland. With Notes and Forms of Procedure. By the Rev. WILLIAM MAIR, D.D., Minister of the Parish of Earlston. Crown 8vo. [*New Edition in preparation.*

MARCHMONT AND THE HUMES OF POLWARTH. By One of their Descendants. With numerous Portraits and other Illustrations. Crown 4to, 21s. net.

MARSHALL. It Happened Yesterday. A Novel. By FREDERICK MARSHALL, Author of 'Claire Brandon,' 'French Home Life.' Crown 8vo, 6s.

MARSHMAN. History of India. From the Earliest Period to the present time. By JOHN CLARK MARSHMAN, C.S.I. Third and Cheaper Edition. Post 8vo, with Map, 6s.

MARTIN.
Goethe's Faust. Part I. Translated by Sir THEODORE MARTIN, K.C.B. Second Edition, crown 8vo, 6s. Ninth Edition, fcap. 8vo, 3s. 6d.
Goethe's Faust. Part II. Translated into English Verse. Second Edition, Revised. Fcap. 8vo, 6s.
The Works of Horace. Translated into English Verse, with Life and Notes. 2 vols. New Edition. Crown 8vo, 21s.
Poems and Ballads of Heinrich Heine. Done into English Verse. Third Edition. Small crown 8vo, 5s.
The Song of the Bell, and other Translations from Schiller, Goethe, Uhland, and Others. Crown 8vo, 7s. 6d.
Madonna Pia: A Tragedy; and Three Other Dramas. Crown 8vo, 7s. 6d.
Catullus. With Life and Notes. Second Edition, Revised and Corrected. Post 8vo, 7s. 6d.
The 'Vita Nuova' of Dante. Translated, with an Introduction and Notes. Third Edition. Small crown 8vo, 5s.
Aladdin: A Dramatic Poem. By ADAM OEHLENSCHLAEGER. Fcap. 8vo, 5s.
Correggio: A Tragedy. By OEHLENSCHLAEGER. With Notes. Fcap. 8vo, 3s.

MARTIN. On some of Shakespeare's Female Characters. By HELENA FAUCIT, Lady MARTIN. Dedicated by permission to Her Most Gracious Majesty the Queen. Fifth Edition. With a Portrait by Lehmann. Demy 8vo, 7s. 6d.

MARWICK. Observations on the Law and Practice in regard to Municipal Elections and the Conduct of the Business of Town Councils and Commissioners of Police in Scotland. By Sir JAMES D. MARWICK, LL.D., Town-Clerk of Glasgow. Royal 8vo, 30s.

MATHESON.
Can the Old Faith Live with the New? or, The Problem of Evolution and Revelation. By the Rev. GEORGE MATHESON, D.D. Third Edition. Crown 8vo, 7s. 6d.
The Psalmist and the Scientist; or, Modern Value of the Religious Sentiment. Third Edition. Crown 8vo, 5s.
Spiritual Development of St Paul. Third Edition. Cr. 8vo, 5s.
The Distinctive Messages of the Old Religions. Second Edition. Crown 8vo, 5s.
Sacred Songs. New and Cheaper Edition. Crown 8vo, 2s. 6d.

MAURICE. The Balance of Military Power in Europe. An Examination of the War Resources of Great Britain and the Continental States. By Colonel MAURICE, R.A., Professor of Military Art and History at the Royal Staff College. Crown 8vo, with a Map, 6s.

MAXWELL.
A Duke of Britain. A Romance of the Fourth Century. By Sir HERBERT MAXWELL, Bart., M.P., F.S.A., &c., Author of 'Passages in the Life of Sir Lucian Elphin.' Crown 8vo, 6s.
Life and Times of the Rt. Hon. William Henry Smith, M.P. With Portraits and numerous Illustrations by Herbert Railton, G. L. Seymour, and Others. 2 vols. demy 8vo, 25s.
POPULAR EDITION. With a Portrait and other Illustrations. Crown 8vo, 3s. 6d.
Scottish Land Names: Their Origin and Meaning. Being the Rhind Lectures in Archæology for 1893. Post 8vo, 6s.
Meridiana: Noontide Essays. Post 8vo, 7s. 6d.

MELDRUM. The Story of Margrédel: Being a Fireside History of a Fifeshire Family. By D. STORRAR MELDRUM. Cheap Edition. Crown 8vo, 3s. 6d.

MICHEL. A Critical Inquiry into the Scottish Language. With the view of Illustrating the Rise and Progress of Civilisation in Scotland. By FRANCISQUE-MICHEL, F.S.A. Lond. and Scot., Correspondant de l'Institut de France, &c. 4to, printed on hand-made paper, and bound in roxburghe, 66s.

MICHIE.
The Larch: Being a Practical Treatise on its Culture and General Management. By CHRISTOPHER Y. MICHIE, Forester, Cullen House. Crown 8vo, with Illustrations. New and Cheaper Edition, Enlarged, 5s.
The Practice of Forestry. Crown 8vo, with Illustrations. 6s.

MIDDLETON. The Story of Alastair Bhan Comyn; or, The Tragedy of Dunphail. A Tale of Tradition and Romance. By the Lady MIDDLETON. Square 8vo, 10s. Cheaper Edition, 5s.

MILLER. Landscape Geology. A Plea for the Study of Geology by Landscape Painters. By HUGH MILLER, of H.M. Geological Survey. Crown 8vo, 3s. Cheap Edition, paper cover, 1s.

MINTO.
A Manual of English Prose Literature, Biographical and Critical: designed mainly to show Characteristics of Style. By W. MINTO, M.A., Hon. LL.D. of St Andrews; Professor of Logic in the University of Aberdeen. Third Edition, Revised. Crown 8vo, 7s. 6d.
Characteristics of English Poets, from Chaucer to Shirley. New Edition, Revised. Crown 8vo, 7s. 6d.
Plain Principles of Prose Composition. Crown 8vo, 1s. 6d.
The Literature of the Georgian Era. Edited, with a Biographical Introduction, by Professor KNIGHT, St Andrews. Post 8vo, 6s.

MOIR. Life of Mansie Wauch, Tailor in Dalkeith. By D. M.
MOIR. With 8 Illustrations on Steel, by the late GEORGE CRUIKSHANK. Crown 8vo, 3s. 6d. Another Edition, fcap. 8vo, 1s. 6d.

MOLE. For the Sake of a Slandered Woman. By MARION MOLE. Fcap. 8vo, 2s. 6d. net.

MOMERIE.
Defects of Modern Christianity, and other Sermons. By ALFRED WILLIAMS MOMERIE, M.A., D.Sc., LL.D. Fifth Edition. Crown 8vo, 5s.
The Basis of Religion. Being an Examination of Natural Religion. Third Edition. Crown 8vo, 2s. 6d.
The Origin of Evil, and other Sermons. Eighth Edition, Enlarged. Crown 8vo, 5s.
Personality. The Beginning and End of Metaphysics, and a Necessary Assumption in all Positive Philosophy. Fifth Edition, Revised. Crown 8vo, 3s.
Agnosticism. Fourth Edition, Revised. Crown 8vo, 5s.
Preaching and Hearing; and other Sermons. Fourth Edition, Enlarged. Crown 8vo, 5s.
Belief in God. Third Edition. Crown 8vo, 3s.
Inspiration; and other Sermons. Second Edition, Enlarged. Crown 8vo, 5s.
Church and Creed. Third Edition. Crown 8vo, 4s. 6d.
The Future of Religion, and other Essays. Second Edition. Crown 8vo, 3s. 6d.

MONTAGUE. Military Topography. Illustrated by Practical Examples of a Practical Subject. By Major-General W. E. MONTAGUE, C.B., P.S.C., late Garrison Instructor Intelligence Department, Author of 'Campaigning in South Africa.' With Forty-one Diagrams. Crown 8vo, 5s.

MONTALEMBERT. Memoir of Count de Montalembert. A Chapter of Recent French History. By Mrs OLIPHANT, Author of the 'Life of Edward Irving,' &c. 2 vols. crown 8vo, £1, 4s.

MORISON.
Doorside Ditties. By JEANIE MORISON. With a Frontispiece. Crown 8vo, 3s. 6d.
Æolus. A Romance in Lyrics. Crown 8vo, 3s.
There as Here. Crown 8vo, 3s.
⁎ A limited impression on hand-made paper, bound in vellum, 7s. 6d.
Selections from Poems. Crown 8vo, 4s. 6d.
Sordello. An Outline Analysis of Mr Browning's Poem. Crown 8vo, 3s.
Of "Fifine at the Fair," "Christmas Eve and Easter Day," and other of Mr Browning's Poems. Crown 8vo, 3s.
The Purpose of the Ages. Crown 8vo, 9s.
Gordon: An Our-day Idyll. Crown 8vo, 3s.
Saint Isadora, and other Poems. Crown 8vo, 1s. 6d.
Snatches of Song. Paper, 1s. 6d.; Cloth, 3s.
Pontius Pilate. Paper, 1s. 6d.; Cloth, 3s.
Mill o' Forres. Crown 8vo, 1s.
Ane Booke of Ballades. Fcap. 4to, 1s.

MOZLEY. Essays from 'Blackwood.' By the late ANNE MOZLEY, Author of 'Essays on Social Subjects'; Editor of 'The Letters and Correspondence of Cardinal Newman,' 'Letters of the Rev. J. B. Mozley,' &c. With a Memoir by her Sister, FANNY MOZLEY. Post 8vo, 7s. 6d.

MUNRO. On Valuation of Property. By WILLIAM MUNRO, M.A., Her Majesty's Assessor of Railways and Canals for Scotland. Second Edition, Revised and Enlarged. 8vo, 3s. 6d.

MURDOCH. Manual of the Law of Insolvency and Bankruptcy: Comprehending a Summary of the Law of Insolvency, Notour Bankruptcy, Composition-contracts, Trust-deeds, Cessios, and Sequestrations; and the Winding-up of Joint-Stock Companies in Scotland; with Annotations on the various Insolvency and Bankruptcy Statutes; and with Forms of Procedure applicable to these Subjects. By JAMES MURDOCH, Member of the Faculty of Procurators in Glasgow. Fifth Edition, Revised and Enlarged. 8vo, 12s. net.

MY TRIVIAL LIFE AND MISFORTUNE: A Gossip with no Plot in Particular. By A PLAIN WOMAN. Cheap Edition. Crown 8vo, 3s. 6d.

By the SAME AUTHOR.

POOR NELLIE. Cheap Edition. Crown 8vo, 3s. 6d.

MY WEATHER-WISE COMPANION. Presented by B. T. Fcap. 8vo, 1s. net.

NAPIER. The Construction of the Wonderful Canon of Logarithms. By JOHN NAPIER of Merchiston. Translated, with Notes, and a Catalogue of Napier's Works, by WILLIAM RAE MACDONALD. Small 4to, 15s. *A few large-paper copies on Whatman paper*, 30s.

NEAVES.
Songs and Verses, Social and Scientific. By An Old Contributor to 'Maga.' By the Hon. Lord NEAVES. Fifth Edition. Fcap. 8vo, 4s.
The Greek Anthology. Being Vol. XX. of 'Ancient Classics for English Readers.' Crown 8vo, 2s. 6d.

NICHOLSON.
A Manual of Zoology, for the use of Students. With a General Introduction on the Principles of Zoology. By HENRY ALLEYNE NICHOLSON, M.D. D.Sc., F.L.S., F.G.S., Regius Professor of Natural History in the University of Aberdeen. Seventh Edition, Rewritten and Enlarged. Post 8vo, pp. 956, with 555 Engravings on Wood, 18s.
Text-Book of Zoology, for Junior Students. Fifth Edition, Rewritten and Enlarged. Crown 8vo, with 358 Engravings on Wood, 10s. 6d.
Introductory Text-Book of Zoology, for the use of Junior Classes. Sixth Edition, Revised and Enlarged, with 166 Engravings, 3s.
Outlines of Natural History, for Beginners: being Descriptions of a Progressive Series of Zoological Types. Third Edition, with Engravings, 1s. 6d.
A Manual of Palæontology, for the use of Students. With a General Introduction on the Principles of Palæontology. By Professor H. ALLEYNE NICHOLSON and RICHARD LYDEKKER, B.A. Third Edition, entirely Rewritten and greatly Enlarged. 2 vols. 8vo, £3, 3s.
The Ancient Life-History of the Earth. An Outline of the Principles and Leading Facts of Palæontological Science. Crown 8vo, with 276 Engravings, 10s. 6d.
On the "Tabulate Corals" of the Palæozoic Period, with Critical Descriptions of Illustrative Species. Illustrated with 15 Lithographed Plates and numerous Engravings. Super-royal 8vo, 21s.
Synopsis of the Classification of the Animal Kingdom. 8vo, with 106 Illustrations, 6s.

NICHOLSON.
On the Structure and Affinities of the Genus Monticulipora and its Sub-Genera, with Critical Descriptions of Illustrative Species. Illustrated with numerous Engravings on Wood and Lithographed Plates. Super-royal 8vo, 18s.

NICHOLSON.
Thoth. A Romance. By JOSEPH SHIELD NICHOLSON, M.A., D.Sc., Professor of Commercial and Political Economy and Mercantile Law in the University of Edinburgh. Third Edition. Crown 8vo, 4s. 6d.

A Dreamer of Dreams. A Modern Romance. Second Edition. Crown 8vo, 6s.

NICOLSON AND MURE.
A Handbook to the Local Government (Scotland) Act, 1889. With Introduction, Explanatory Notes, and Index. By J. BADENACH NICOLSON, Advocate, Counsel to the Scotch Education Department, and W. J. MURE, Advocate, Legal Secretary to the Lord Advocate for Scotland. Ninth Reprint. 8vo, 5s.

OLIPHANT.
Masollam: A Problem of the Period. A Novel. By LAURENCE OLIPHANT. 3 vols. post 8vo, 25s. 6d.

Scientific Religion; or, Higher Possibilities of Life and Practice through the Operation of Natural Forces. Second Edition. 8vo, 16s.

Altiora Peto. Cheap Edition. Crown 8vo, boards, 2s. 6d.; cloth, 3s. 6d. Illustrated Edition. Crown 8vo, cloth, 6s.

Piccadilly. With Illustrations by Richard Doyle. New Edition, 3s. 6d. Cheap Edition, boards, 2s. 6d.

Traits and Travesties; Social and Political. Post 8vo, 10s. 6d.

Episodes in a Life of Adventure; or, Moss from a Rolling Stone. Fifth Edition. Post 8vo, 6s.

Haifa: Life in Modern Palestine. Second Edition. 8vo, 7s. 6d.

The Land of Gilead. With Excursions in the Lebanon. With Illustrations and Maps. Demy 8vo, 21s.

Memoir of the Life of Laurence Oliphant, and of Alice Oliphant, his Wife. By Mrs M. O. W. OLIPHANT. Seventh Edition. 2 vols. post 8vo, with Portraits. 21s.

POPULAR EDITION. With a New Preface. Post 8vo, with Portraits. 7s. 6d.

OLIPHANT.
Who was Lost and is Found. By Mrs OLIPHANT. Second Edition. Crown 8vo, 6s.

Miss Marjoribanks. New Edition. Crown 8vo, 3s. 6d.

The Perpetual Curate, and The Rector. New Edition. Crown 8vo, 3s 6d.

Salem Chapel, and The Doctor's Family. New Edition. Crown 8vo, 3s. 6d.

Katie Stewart, and other Stories. New Edition. Crown 8vo, cloth, 3s. 6d.

Valentine and his Brother. New Edition. Crown 8vo, 3s. 6d.

Sons and Daughters. Crown 8vo, 3s. 6d.

Katie Stewart. Illustrated boards, 2s. 6d.

Two Stories of the Seen and the Unseen. The Open Door —Old Lady Mary. Paper covers, 1s.

OLIPHANT.
Notes of a Pilgrimage to Jerusalem and the Holy Land. By F. R. OLIPHANT. Crown 8vo, 3s. 6d.

OSWALD.
By Fell and Fjord; or, Scenes and Studies in Iceland. By E. J. OSWALD. Post 8vo, with Illustrations. 7s. 6d.

PAGE.
  Introductory Text-Book of Geology. By DAVID PAGE, LL.D., Professor of Geology in the Durham University of Physical Science, Newcastle, and Professor LAPWORTH of Mason Science College, Birmingham. With Engravings and Glossarial Index. Twelfth Edition, Revised and Enlarged. 3s. 6d.
  Advanced Text-Book of Geology, Descriptive and Industrial. With Engravings, and Glossary of Scientific Terms. New Edition, by Professor LAPWORTH. [*In preparation.*
  Introductory Text-Book of Physical Geography. With Sketch-Maps and Illustrations. Edited by Professor LAPWORTH, LL.D., F.G.S., &c., Mason Science College, Birmingham. Thirteenth Edition, Revised and Enlarged. 2s. 6d.
  Advanced Text-Book of Physical Geography. Third Edition. Revised and Enlarged by Professor LAPWORTH. With Engravings. 5s.

PATON.
  Spindrift. By Sir J. NOEL PATON. Fcap., cloth, 5s.
  Poems by a Painter. Fcap., cloth, 5s.

PATON. Body and Soul. A Romance in Transcendental Pathology. By FREDERICK NOEL PATON. Third Edition. Crown 8vo, 1s.

PATRICK. The Apology of Origen in Reply to Celsus. A Chapter in the History of Apologetics. By the Rev. J. PATRICK, B.D. Post 8vo, 7s. 6d.

PAUL. History of the Royal Company of Archers, the Queen's Body-Guard for Scotland. By JAMES BALFOUR PAUL, Advocate of the Scottish Bar. Crown 4to, with Portraits and other Illustrations. £2, 2s.

PEILE. Lawn Tennis as a Game of Skill. With latest revised Laws as played by the Best Clubs. By Captain S. C. F. PEILE, B.S.C. Cheaper Edition. Fcap., cloth, 1s.

PETTIGREW. The Handy Book of Bees, and their Profitable Management. By A. PETTIGREW. Fifth Edition, Enlarged, with Engravings. Crown 8vo, 3s. 6d.

PFLEIDERER. Philosophy and Development of Religion. Being the Edinburgh Gifford Lectures for 1894. By OTTO PFLEIDERER, D.D., Professor of Theology at Berlin University. In 2 vols. post 8vo, 15s. net.

PHILOSOPHICAL CLASSICS FOR ENGLISH READERS. Edited by WILLIAM KNIGHT, LL.D., Professor of Moral Philosophy, University of St Andrews. In crown 8vo volumes, with Portraits, price 3s. 6d.
[*For List of Volumes, see page 2.*

POLLARD. A Study in Municipal Government: The Corporation of Berlin. By JAMES POLLARD, C.A., Chairman of the Edinburgh Public Health Committee, and Secretary of the Edinburgh Chamber of Commerce. Second Edition, Revised. Crown 8vo, 3s. 6d.

POLLOK. The Course of Time: A Poem. By ROBERT POLLOK, A.M. Cottage Edition, 32mo, 8d. The Same, cloth, gilt edges, 1s. 6d. Another Edition, with Illustrations by Birket Foster and others, fcap., cloth, 3s. 6d., or with edges gilt, 4s.

PORT ROYAL LOGIC. Translated from the French; with Introduction, Notes, and Appendix. By THOMAS SPENCER BAYNES, LL.D., Professor in the University of St Andrews. Tenth Edition, 12mo, 4s.

POTTS AND DARNELL.
  Aditus Faciliores: An Easy Latin Construing Book, with Complete Vocabulary. By A. W. POTTS, M.A., LL.D., and the Rev. C. DARNELL, M.A., Head-Master of Cargilfield Preparatory School, Edinburgh. Tenth Edition, fcap. 8vo, 3s. 6d.

POTTS AND DARNELL.
  Aditus Faciliores Graeci. An Easy Greek Construing Book,
  with Complete Vocabulary. Fifth Edition, Revised. Fcap. 8vo, 3s.

POTTS. School Sermons. By the late ALEXANDER WM. POTTS,
  LL.D., First Head-Master of Fettes College. With a Memoir and Portrait.
  Crown 8vo, 7s. 6d.

PRINGLE. The Live - Stock of the Farm. By ROBERT O.
  PRINGLE. Third Edition. Revised and Edited by JAMES MACDONALD. Crown
  8vo, 7s. 6d.

PRYDE. Pleasant Memories of a Busy Life. By DAVID PRYDE,
  M.A., LL.D., Author of 'Highways of Literature,' 'Great Men in European History,' 'Biographical Outlines of English Literature,' &c. With a Mezzotint Portrait. Post 8vo, 6s.

PUBLIC GENERAL STATUTES AFFECTING SCOTLAND
  from 1707 to 1847, with Chronological Table and Index. 3 vols. large 8vo, £3, 3s.

PUBLIC GENERAL STATUTES AFFECTING SCOTLAND,
  COLLECTION OF. Published Annually, with General Index.

RAE. The Syrian Church in India. By GEORGE MILNE RAE,
  M.A., D.D., Fellow of the University of Madras; late Professor in the Madras
  Christian College. With 6 full-page Illustrations. Post 8vo, 10s. 6d.

RAMSAY. Scotland and Scotsmen in the Eighteenth Century.
  Edited from the MSS. of JOHN RAMSAY, Esq. of Ochtertyre, by ALEXANDER
  ALLARDYCE, Author of 'Memoir of Admiral Lord Keith, K.B.,' &c. 2 vols.
  8vo, 31s. 6d.

RANKIN. The Zambesi Basin and Nyassaland. By DANIEL J.
  RANKIN, F.R.S.G.S., M.R.A.S. With 3 Maps and 10 full-page Illustrations.
  Post 8vo, 10s. 6d.

RANKIN.
  A Handbook of the Church of Scotland. By JAMES RANKIN,
  D.D., Minister of Muthill; Author of 'Character Studies in the Old Testament,
  &c. An entirely New and much Enlarged Edition. Crown 8vo, with 2 Maps,
  7s. 6d.
  The First Saints. Post 8vo, 7s. 6d.
  The Creed in Scotland. An Exposition of the Apostles
  Creed. With Extracts from Archbishop Hamilton's Catechism of 1552, John
  Calvin's Catechism of 1556, and a Catena of Ancient Latin and other Hymns.
  Post 8vo, 7s. 6d.
  The Worthy Communicant. A Guide to the Devout Observance of the Lord's Supper. Limp cloth, 1s. 3d.
  The Young Churchman. Lessons on the Creed, the Commandments, the Means of Grace, and the Church. Limp cloth, 1s. 3d.
  First Communion Lessons. 25th Edition. Paper Cover, 2d.

RECORDS OF THE TERCENTENARY FESTIVAL OF THE
  UNIVERSITY OF EDINBURGH. Celebrated in April 1884. Published under
  the Sanction of the Senatus Academicus. Large 4to, £2, 12s. 6d.

ROBERTSON. The Early Religion of Israel. As set forth by
  Biblical Writers and Modern Critical Historians. Being the Baird Lecture for
  1888-89. By JAMES ROBERTSON, D.D., Professor of Oriental Languages in the
  University of Glasgow. Fourth Edition. Crown 8vo, 10s. 6d.

ROBERTSON.
  Orellana, and other Poems. By J. LOGIE ROBERTSON,
  M.A. Fcap. 8vo. Printed on hand-made paper. 6s.
  A History of English Literature. For Secondary Schools.
  With an Introduction by Professor MASSON, Edinburgh University. Cr. 8vo, 3s.

ROBERTSON. Our Holiday among the Hills. By JAMES and JANET LOGIE ROBERTSON. Fcap. 8vo, 3s. 6d.

ROBERTSON. Essays and Sermons. By the late W. ROBERTSON, B.D., Minister of the Parish of Sprouston. With a Memoir and Portrait. Crown 8vo, 5s. 6d.

RODGER. Aberdeen Doctors at Home and Abroad. The Story of a Medical School. By ELLA HILL BURTON RODGER. Demy 8vo, 10s. 6d.

ROSCOE. Rambles with a Fishing-Rod. By E. S. ROSCOE. Crown 8vo, 4s. 6d.

ROSS. Old Scottish Regimental Colours. By ANDREW ROSS, S.S.C., Hon. Secretary Old Scottish Regimental Colours Committee. Dedicated by Special Permission to Her Majesty the Queen. Folio. £2, 12s. 6d.

RUTLAND.
Notes of an Irish Tour in 1846. By the DUKE OF RUTLAND, G.C.B. (Lord JOHN MANNERS). New Edition. Crown 8vo, 2s. 6d.

Correspondence between the Right Honble. William Pitt and Charles Duke of Rutland, Lord-Lieutenant of Ireland, 1781-1787. With Introductory Note by JOHN DUKE OF RUTLAND. 8vo, 7s. 6d.

RUTLAND.
Gems of German Poetry. Translated by the DUCHESS OF RUTLAND (Lady JOHN MANNERS). [*New Edition in preparation.*

Impressions of Bad-Homburg. Comprising a Short Account of the Women's Associations of Germany under the Red Cross. Crown 8vo, 1s. 6d.

Some Personal Recollections of the Later Years of the Earl of Beaconsfield, K.G. Sixth Edition. 6d.

Employment of Women in the Public Service. 6d.

Some of the Advantages of Easily Accessible Reading and Recreation Rooms and Free Libraries. With Remarks on Starting and Maintaining them. Second Edition. Crown 8vo, 1s.

A Sequel to Rich Men's Dwellings, and other Occasional Papers. Crown 8vo, 2s. 6d.

Encouraging Experiences of Reading and Recreation Rooms, Aims of Guilds, Nottingham Social Guide, Existing Institutions, &c., &c. Crown 8vo, 1s.

SCHEFFEL. The Trumpeter. A Romance of the Rhine. By JOSEPH VICTOR VON SCHEFFEL. Translated from the Two Hundredth German Edition by JESSIE BECK and LOUISA LORIMER. With an Introduction by Sir THEODORE MARTIN, K.C.B. Long 8vo, 3s. 6d.

SCHILLER. Wallenstein. A Dramatic Poem. By FRIEDRICH VON SCHILLER. Translated by C. G. N. LOCKHART. Fcap. 8vo, 7s. 6d.

SCOTCH LOCH FISHING. By "BLACK PALMER." Crown 8vo, interleaved with blank pages, 4s.

SCOTT. Tom Cringle's Log. By MICHAEL SCOTT. New Edition. With 19 Full-page Illustrations. Crown 8vo, 3s. 6d.

SCOUGAL. Prisons and their Inmates; or, Scenes from a Silent World. By FRANCIS SCOUGAL. Crown 8vo, boards, 2s.

SELLAR'S Manual of the Acts relating to Education in Scotland. By J. EDWARD GRAHAM, B.A. Oxon., Advocate. Ninth Edition. Demy 8vo, 12s. 6d.

SETH.
   Scottish Philosophy. A Comparison of the Scottish and German Answers to Hume. Balfour Philosophical Lectures, University of Edinburgh. By ANDREW SETH, LL.D., Professor of Logic and Metaphysics in Edinburgh University. Second Edition. Crown 8vo, 5s.
   Hegelianism and Personality. Balfour Philosophical Lectures. Second Series. Second Edition. Crown 8vo, 5s.

SETH. A Study of Ethical Principles. By JAMES SETH, M.A., Professor of Philosophy in Brown University, U.S.A. Post 8vo, 10s. 6d. net.

SHADWELL. The Life of Colin Campbell, Lord Clyde. Illustrated by Extracts from his Diary and Correspondence. By Lieutenant-General SHADWELL, C.B. With Portrait, Maps, and Plans. 2 vols. 8vo, 36s.

SHAND.
   The Life of General Sir Edward Bruce Hamley, K.C.B., K.C.M.G. By ALEX. INNES SHAND, Author of 'Kilcarra,' 'Against Time,' &c. With two Photogravure Portraits and other Illustrations. 2 vols. demy 8vo, 21s.
   Half a Century; or, Changes in Men and Manners. Second Edition. 8vo, 12s. 6d.
   Letters from the West of Ireland. Reprinted from the 'Times.' Crown 8vo, 5s.

SHARPE. Letters from and to Charles Kirkpatrick Sharpe. Edited by ALEXANDER ALLARDYCE, Author of 'Memoir of Admiral Lord Keith, K.B.,' &c. With a Memoir by the Rev. W. K. R. BEDFORD. In 2 vols. 8vo. Illustrated with Etchings and other Engravings. £2, 12s. 6d.

SIM. Margaret Sim's Cookery. With an Introduction by L. B. WALFORD, Author of 'Mr Smith: A Part of his Life,' &c. Crown 8vo, 5s.

SIMPSON. The Wild Rabbit in a New Aspect; or, Rabbit-Warrens that Pay. A book for Landowners, Sportsmen, Land Agents, Farmers, Gamekeepers, and Allotment Holders. A Record of Recent Experiments conducted on the Estate of the Right Hon. the Earl of Wharncliffe at Wortley Hall. By J. SIMPSON. Second Edition, Enlarged. Small crown 8vo, 5s.

SKELTON.
   Maitland of Lethington; and the Scotland of Mary Stuart. A History. By JOHN SKELTON, Advocate, C.B., LL.D., Author of 'The Essays of Shirley.' Limited Edition, with Portraits. Demy 8vo, 2 vols., 28s. net.
   The Handbook of Public Health. A Complete Edition of the Public Health and other Sanitary Acts relating to Scotland. Annotated, and with the Rules, Instructions, and Decisions of the Board of Supervision brought up to date with relative forms. Second Edition. With Introduction, containing the Administration of the Public Health Act in Counties. 8vo, 8s. 6d.
   The Local Government (Scotland) Act in Relation to Public Health. A Handy Guide for County and District Councillors, Medical Officers, Sanitary Inspectors, and Members of Parochial Boards. Second Edition. With a new Preface on appointment of Sanitary Officers. Crown 8vo, 2s.

SKRINE. Columba: A Drama. By JOHN HUNTLEY SKRINE, Warden of Glenalmond; Author of 'A Memory of Edward Thring.' Fcap. 4to, 6s.

SMITH. For God and Humanity. A Romance of Mount Carmel. By HASKETT SMITH, Author of 'The Divine Epiphany,' &c. 3 vols. post 8vo, 25s. 6d.

SMITH.
   Thorndale; or, The Conflict of Opinions. By WILLIAM SMITH, Author of 'A Discourse on Ethics,' &c. New Edition. Crown 8vo, 10s. 6d.
   Gravenhurst; or, Thoughts on Good and Evil. Second Edition. With Memoir and Portrait of the Author. Crown 8vo, 8s.

SMITH. The Story of William and Lucy Smith. Edited by GEORGE MERRIAM. Large post 8vo, 12s. 6d.

SMITH. Memoir of the Families of M'Combie and Thoms, originally M'Intosh and M'Thomas. Compiled from History and Tradition. By WILLIAM M'COMBIE SMITH. With Illustrations. 8vo, 7s. 6d.

SMITH. Greek Testament Lessons for Colleges, Schools, and Private Students, consisting chiefly of the Sermon on the Mount and the Parables of our Lord. With Notes and Essays. By the Rev. J. HUNTER SMITH, M.A., King Edward's School, Birmingham. Crown 8vo, 6s.

SMITH. The Secretary for Scotland. Being a Statement of the Powers and Duties of the new Scottish Office. With a Short Historical Introduction, and numerous references to important Administrative Documents. By W. C. SMITH, LL.B., Advocate. 8vo, 6s.

"SON OF THE MARSHES, A."
From Spring to Fall; or, When Life Stirs. By "A SON OF THE MARSHES." Crown 8vo, 3s. 6d.
Within an Hour of London Town: Among Wild Birds and their Haunts. Edited by J. A. OWEN. Cheap Uniform Edition. Crown 8vo, 3s. 6d.
With the Woodlanders, and By the Tide. Cheap Uniform Edition. Crown 8vo, 3s. 6d.
On Surrey Hills. Cheap Uniform Edition. Crown 8vo, 3s. 6d.
Annals of a Fishing Village. Cheap Uniform Edition. Crown 8vo, 3s. 6d.

SORLEY. The Ethics of Naturalism. Being the Shaw Fellowship Lectures, 1884. By W. R. SORLEY, M.A., Fellow of Trinity College, Cambridge, Professor of Moral Philosophy in the University of Aberdeen. Crown 8vo, 6s.

SPEEDY. Sport in the Highlands and Lowlands of Scotland with Rod and Gun. By TOM SPEEDY. Second Edition, Revised and Enlarged. With Illustrations by Lieut.-General Hope Crealocke, C.B., C.M.G., and others. 8vo, 15s.

SPROTT. The Worship and Offices of the Church of Scotland. By GEORGE W. SPROTT, D.D., Minister of North Berwick. Crown 8vo, 6s.

STATISTICAL ACCOUNT OF SCOTLAND. Complete, with Index. 15 vols. 8vo, £16, 16s.

STEPHENS.
The Book of the Farm; detailing the Labours of the Farmer, Farm-Steward, Ploughman, Shepherd, Hedger, Farm-Labourer, Field-Worker, and Cattle-man. Illustrated with numerous Portraits of Animals and Engravings of Implements, and Plans of Farm Buildings. Fourth Edition. Revised, and in great part Rewritten by JAMES MACDONALD, F.R.S.E., Secretary, Highland and Agricultural Society of Scotland. Complete in Six Divisional Volumes, bound in cloth, each 10s. 6d., or handsomely bound, in 3 volumes, with leather back and gilt top, £3, 3s.
Catechism of Practical Agriculture. New Edition. Revised by JAMES MACDONALD, F.R.S.E. With numerous Illustrations. Crown 8vo, 1s.
The Book of Farm Implements and Machines. By J. SLIGHT and R. SCOTT BURN, Engineers. Edited by HENRY STEPHENS. Large 8vo, £2, 2s.

STEVENSON. British Fungi. (Hymenomycetes.) By Rev. JOHN STEVENSON, Author of 'Mycologia Scotica,' Hon. Sec. Cryptogamic Society of Scotland. Vols. I. and II., post 8vo, with Illustrations, price 12s. 6d. net each.

STEWART.
Advice to Purchasers of Horses. By JOHN STEWART, V.S. New Edition. 2s. 6d.
Stable Economy. A Treatise on the Management of Horses in relation to Stabling, Grooming, Feeding, Watering, and Working. Seventh Edition. Fcap. 8vo, 6s. 6d.

STEWART. A Hebrew Grammar, with the Pronunciation, Syllabic Division and Tone of the Words, and Quantity of the Vowels. By Rev. DUNCAN STEWART, D.D. Fourth Edition. 8vo, 3s. 6d.

STEWART. Boethius: An Essay. By HUGH FRASER STEWART, M.A., Trinity College, Cambridge. Crown 8vo, 7s. 6d.

STODDART. Sir Philip Sidney: Servant of God. By ANNA M. STODDART. Illustrated by MARGARET L. HUGGINS. With a New Portrait of Sir Philip Sidney. Small 4to, with a specially designed Cover. 5s.

STODDART. Angling Songs. By THOMAS TOD STODDART. New Edition, with a Memoir by ANNA M. STODDART. Crown 8vo, 7s. 6d.

STORMONTH.
Etymological and Pronouncing Dictionary of the English Language. Including a very Copious Selection of Scientific Terms. For use in Schools and Colleges, and as a Book of General Reference. By the Rev. JAMES STORMONTH. The Pronunciation carefully revised by the Rev. P. H. PHELP, M.A. Cantab. Eleventh Edition, with Supplement. Crown 8vo, pp. 800. 7s. 6d.
Dictionary of the English Language, Pronouncing, Etymological, and Explanatory. Revised by the Rev. P. H. PHELP. Library Edition. New and Cheaper Edition, with Supplement. Imperial 8vo, handsomely bound in half morocco, 18s. net.
The School Etymological Dictionary and Word-Book. Fourth Edition. Fcap. 8vo, pp. 254. 2s.

STORY.
Nero; A Historical Play. By W. W. STORY, Author of 'Roba di Roma.' Fcap. 8vo, 6s.
Vallombrosa. Post 8vo, 5s.
Poems. 2 vols., 7s. 6d.
Fiammetta. A Summer Idyl. Crown 8vo, 7s. 6d.
Conversations in a Studio. 2 vols. crown 8vo, 12s. 6d.
Excursions in Art and Letters. Crown 8vo, 7s. 6d.
A Poet's Portfolio: Later Readings. 18mo, 3s. 6d.

STRACHEY. Talk at a Country House. Fact and Fiction. By Sir EDWARD STRACHEY, Bart. With a Portrait of the Author. Crown 8vo, 4s. 6d. net.

STURGIS.
John-a-Dreams. A Tale. By JULIAN STURGIS. New Edition. Crown 8vo, 3s. 6d.
Little Comedies, Old and New. Crown 8vo, 7s. 6d.

SUTHERLAND (DUCHESS OF). How I Spent my Twentieth Year. Being a Record of a Tour Round the World, 1886-87. By the DUCHESS OF SUTHERLAND (MARCHIONESS OF STAFFORD). With Illustrations. Crown 8vo, 7s. 6d.

SUTHERLAND. Handbook of Hardy Herbaceous and Alpine Flowers, for General Garden Decoration. Containing Descriptions of upwards of 1000 Species of Ornamental Hardy Perennial and Alpine Plants; along with Concise and Plain Instructions for their Propagation and Culture. By WILLIAM SUTHERLAND, Landscape Gardener; formerly Manager of the Herbaceous Department at Kew. Crown 8vo, 7s. 6d.

TAYLOR. The Story of my Life. By the late Colonel
MEADOWS TAYLOR, Author of 'The Confessions of a Thug,' &c., &c. Edited by his Daughter. New and Cheaper Edition, being the Fourth. Crown 8vo, 6s.

THOMSON.
The Diversions of a Prime Minister. By Basil Thomson.
With a Map, numerous Illustrations by J. W. CAWSTON and others, and Reproductions of Rare Plates from Early Voyages of Sixteenth and Seventeenth Centuries. Small demy 8vo, 15s.

South Sea Yarns. With 10 Full-page Illustrations. Crown 8vo, 6s.

THOMSON.
Handy Book of the Flower-Garden: being Practical Directions for the Propagation, Culture, and Arrangement of Plants in Flower-Gardens all the year round. With Engraved Plans. By DAVID THOMSON, Gardener to his Grace the Duke of Buccleuch, K.T., at Drumlanrig. Fourth and Cheaper Edition. Crown 8vo, 5s.

The Handy Book of Fruit-Culture under Glass: being a series of Elaborate Practical Treatises on the Cultivation and Forcing of Pines, Vines, Peaches, Figs, Melons, Strawberries, and Cucumbers. With Engravings of Hothouses, &c. Second Edition, Revised and Enlarged. Crown 8vo, 7s. 6d.

THOMSON. A Practical Treatise on the Cultivation of the Grape Vine. By WILLIAM THOMSON, Tweed Vineyards. Tenth Edition. 8vo, 5s.

THOMSON. Cookery for the Sick and Convalescent. With Directions for the Preparation of Poultices, Fomentations, &c. By BARBARA THOMSON. Fcap. 8vo, 1s. 6d.

THORBURN. Asiatic Neighbours. By S. S. THORBURN, Bengal Civil Service, Author of 'Bannú; or, Our Afghan Frontier,' 'David Leslie: A Story of the Afghan Frontier,' 'Musalmans and Money-Lenders in the Panjab.' With Two Maps. Demy 8vo, 10s. 6d. net.

THORNTON. Opposites. A Series of Essays on the Unpopular Sides of Popular Questions. By LEWIS THORNTON. 8vo, 12s. 6d.

TRANSACTIONS OF THE HIGHLAND AND AGRICULTURAL SOCIETY OF SCOTLAND. Published annually, price 5s.

TRAVEL, ADVENTURE, AND SPORT. From 'Blackwood's Magazine.' Uniform with 'Tales from Blackwood.' In 12 Parts, each price 1s. Handsomely bound in 6 vols., cloth, 15s.; half calf, 25s.

TRAVERS. Mona Maclean, Medical Student. A Novel. By GRAHAM TRAVERS. Tenth Edition. Crown 8vo, 6s.

TULLOCH.
Rational Theology and Christian Philosophy in England in the Seventeenth Century. By JOHN TULLOCH, D.D., Principal of St Mary's College in the University of St Andrews; and one of her Majesty's Chaplains in Ordinary in Scotland. Second Edition. 2 vols. 8vo, 16s.

Modern Theories in Philosophy and Religion. 8vo, 15s.

Luther, and other Leaders of the Reformation. Third Edition, Enlarged. Crown 8vo, 3s. 6d.

Memoir of Principal Tulloch, D.D., LL.D. By Mrs OLIPHANT, Author of 'Life of Edward Irving.' Third and Cheaper Edition. 8vo, with Portrait, 7s. 6d.

TWEEDIE. The Arabian Horse: His Country and People.
By Major-General W. TWEEDIE, C.S.I., Bengal Staff Corps; for many years H.B.M.'s Consul-General, Baghdad, and Political Resident for the Government of India in Turkish Arabia. In one vol. royal 4to, with Seven Coloured Plates and other Illustrations, and a Map of the Country. Price £3, 3s. net.

VEITCH.
The History and Poetry of the Scottish Border: their Main Features and Relations. By JOHN VEITCH, LL.D., Professor of Logic and Rhetoric in the University of Glasgow. New and Enlarged Edition. 2 vols. demy 8vo, 16s.
Institutes of Logic. Post 8vo, 12s. 6d.
The Feeling for Nature in Scottish Poetry. From the Earliest Times to the Present Day. 2 vols. fcap. 8vo, in roxburghe binding, 15s.
Merlin and other Poems. Fcap. 8vo, 4s. 6d.
Knowing and Being. Essays in Philosophy. First Series. Crown 8vo, 5s.
Dualism and Monism; Or, Relation and Reality: A Criticism. Essays in Philosophy. Second Series. In 1 vol. crown 8vo. [*In the press.*

VIRGIL. The Æneid of Virgil. Translated in English Blank Verse by G. K. RICKARDS M.A., and Lord RAVENSWORTH. 2 vols. fcap. 8vo, 10s.

WACE. Christianity and Agnosticism. Reviews of some Recent Attacks on the Christian Faith. By HENRY WACE, D.D., Principal of King's College, London; Preacher of Lincoln's Inn; Chaplain to the Queen. Post 8vo, 10s. 6d. net.

WADDELL. An Old Kirk Chronicle: Being a History of Auldhame, Tyninghame, and Whitekirk, in East Lothian. From Session Records, 1615 to 1850. By Rev. P. HATELY WADDELL, B.D., Minister of the United Parish. Small Paper Edition, 200 Copies. Price £1. Large Paper Edition, 50 Copies. Price £1, 10s.

WALFORD. Four Biographies from 'Blackwood': Jane Taylor, Hannah More, Elizabeth Fry, Mary Somerville. By L. B. WALFORD. Crown 8vo, 5s.

WARREN'S (SAMUEL) WORKS:—
Diary of a Late Physician. Cloth, 2s. 6d.; boards, 2s.
Ten Thousand A-Year. Cloth, 3s. 6d.; boards, 2s. 6d.
Now and Then. The Lily and the Bee. Intellectual and Moral Development of the Present Age. 4s. 6d.
Essays: Critical, Imaginative, and Juridical. 5s.

WEBSTER. The Angler and the Loop-Rod. By DAVID WEBSTER. Crown 8vo, with Illustrations, 7s. 6d.

WENLEY.
Socrates and Christ: A Study in the Philosophy of Religion. By R. M. WENLEY, M.A., D.Sc., Lecturer on Mental and Moral Philosophy in Queen Margaret College, Glasgow; formerly Examiner in Philosophy in the University of Glasgow. Crown 8vo, 6s.
Aspects of Pessimism. Crown 8vo, 6s.

WERNER. A Visit to Stanley's Rear-Guard at Major Barttelot's Camp on the Aruhwimi. With an Account of River-Life on the Congo. By J. R. WERNER, F.R.G.S., Engineer, late in the Service of the Etat Independant du Congo. With Maps, Portraits, and other Illustrations. 8vo, 16s.

WESTMINSTER ASSEMBLY. Minutes of the Westminster Assembly, while engaged in preparing their Directory for Church Government, Confession of Faith, and Catechisms (November 1644 to March 1649). Edited by the Rev. Professor ALEX. T. MITCHELL, of St Andrews, and the Rev. JOHN STRUTHERS, LL.D. With a Historical and Critical Introduction by Professor Mitchell. 8vo, 15s.

WHITE.
The Eighteen Christian Centuries. By the Rev. JAMES WHITE. Seventh Edition. Post 8vo, with Index, 6s.
History of France, from the Earliest Times. Sixth Thousand. Post 8vo, with Index, 6s.

WHITE.
   Archæological Sketches in Scotland—Kintyre and Knapdale. By Colonel T. P. WHITE, R.E., of the Ordnance Survey. With numerous Illustrations. 2 vols. folio, £4, 4s. Vol. I., Kintyre, sold separately, £2, 2s.
   The Ordnance Survey of the United Kingdom. A Popular Account. Crown 8vo, 5s.

WILLIAMSON. The Horticultural Handbook and Exhibitor's Guide. A Treatise on Cultivating, Exhibiting, and Judging Plants, Flowers, Fruits, and Vegetables. By W. WILLIAMSON, Gardener. Revised by MALCOLM DUNN, Gardener to his Grace the Duke of Buccleuch and Queensberry, Dalkeith Park. New and Cheaper Edition, enlarged. Crown 8vo, paper cover, 2s.; cloth, 2s. 6d.

WILLIAMSON. Poems of Nature and Life. By DAVID R. WILLIAMSON, Minister of Kirkmaiden. Fcap. 8vo, 3s.

WILLIAMSON. Light from Eastern Lands on the Lives of Abraham, Joseph, and Moses. By the Rev. ALEX. WILLIAMSON, Author of 'The Missionary Heroes of the Pacific,' 'Sure and Comfortable Words,' 'Ask and Receive,' &c. Crown 8vo, 3s. 6d.

WILLS. Behind an Eastern Veil. A Plain Tale of Events occurring in the Experience of a Lady who had a unique opportunity of observing the Inner Life of Ladies of the Upper Class in Persia. By C. J. WILLS, Author of 'In the Land of the Lion and Sun,' 'Persia as it is,' &c., &c. Demy 8vo, 9s.

WILLS AND GREENE. Drawing-Room Dramas for Children. By W. G. WILLS and the Hon. Mrs GREENE. Crown 8vo, 6s.

WILSON.
   Works of Professor Wilson. Edited by his Son-in-Law, Professor FERRIER. 12 vols. crown 8vo, £2, 8s.
   Christopher in his Sporting-Jacket. 2 vols., 8s.
   Isle of Palms, City of the Plague, and other Poems. 4s.
   Lights and Shadows of Scottish Life, and other Tales. 4s.
   Essays, Critical and Imaginative. 4 vols., 16s.
   The Noctes Ambrosianæ. 4 vols., 16s.
   Homer and his Translators, and the Greek Drama. Crown 8vo, 4s.

WORSLEY.
   Poems and Translations. By PHILIP STANHOPE WORSLEY, M.A. Edited by EDWARD WORSLEY. Second Edition, Enlarged. Fcap. 8vo, 6s.
   Homer's Odyssey. Translated into English Verse in the Spenserian Stanza. By P. S. WORSLEY. New and Cheaper Edition. Post 8vo, 7s. 6d. net.
   Homer's Iliad. Translated by P. S. Worsley and Prof. Conington. 2 vols. crown 8vo, 21s.

YATE. England and Russia Face to Face in Asia. A Record of Travel with the Afghan Boundary Commission. By Captain A. C. YATE, Bombay Staff Corps. 8vo, with Maps and Illustrations, 21s.

YATE. Northern Afghanistan; or, Letters from the Afghan Boundary Commission. By Major C. E. YATE, C.S.I., C.M.G. Bombay Staff Corps, F.R.G.S. 8vo, with Maps, 18s.

YULE. Fortification: For the use of Officers in the Army, and Readers of Military History. By Colonel YULE, Bengal Engineers. 8vo, with Numerous Illustrations, 10s.

4/95.

www.ingramcontent.com/pod-product-compliance
Lightning Source LLC
Chambersburg PA
CBHW032009220426
43664CB00006B/188